AN INTRODUCTION TO ZOOLOGY

BY

HARRY LISTER, M.Sc

DISCOVERY PUBLISHING HOUSE
NEW DELHI- 1100 02

Published by:
Namit Wasan
DISCOVERY PUBLISHING HOUSE PVT. LTD.
4383/4B, Ansari Road, Darya Ganj
New Delhi-110 002 (India)
Phone : +91-11-23279245; 23253475; 43596065
E-mail : discoverybooksindia@gmail.com
discoverypublishinghouse@gmail.com
namitwasan9@gmail.com
web : www.discoverypublishinggroup.com

Reprinted: **2020**

ISBN: 978-81-7141-512-0

An Introduction to Zoology

Printed at:
Infinity Imaging Systems
Delhi

PREFACE TO THE SECOND EDITION

This book makes no pretence to be a complete textbook of Zoology. It has been written primarily for the student revising for a First Year Examination in Zoology. Therefore it aims at giving in a small compass the essential knowledge required for the First M.B., Intermediate Science, Agriculture and Horticulture Examinations. It also covers the syllabus for the Higher School Certificate Examinations.

The need of a cheaper book covering the systematic Zoology of the above curricula has long been felt, and this book is an attempt to satisfy that need. Hence, the student must remember that reference should be made to larger textbooks which treat the subject more fully and yet may be too expensive to buy for a First Examination. Teachers and others interested in Zoology should find it an interesting and useful introduction to the subject.

In this revised edition certain corrections, alterations and additions have been made to render the book even more suitable for schools and other students starting the study of Zoology. A chapter on the Molluscs is added and also an important one on General Physiology and Histology, which replaces the Histology chapter in the first edition. The tabulative method of setting down the work has resulted in a great saving of space and so enabled more material to go into a small compass.

My thanks are due to Mr. R. E. Lister, B.Sc., for help in reading the proofs and preparing the index.

HARRY LISTER.

CONTENTS

CHAPTER		PAGE
I.	**Introduction** - - - - GAMETOGENESIS AND CLASSIFICATION.	1
II.	**Protozoa** - - - - SARCODINA—FLAGELLATA.	13
III.	**Protozoa** (*continued*) - - - CILIATA — SPOROZOA — CONCLUSION TO PROTOZOA.	29
IV.	**Metazoa** - - - - INTRODUCTION — CŒLENTERATA — HYDROZOA—SCYPHOZOA—ANTHOZOA.	51
V.	**Platyhelminthes** - - - TURBELLARIA—TREMATODA—CESTODA.	66
	Nemathelminthes - - - ASCARIS.	81
VI.	**Chætopoda** - - - - POLYCHÆTA—OLIGOCHÆTA.	86
VII.	**Arthropoda** - - - - CRUSTACEA—INSECTA—ARACHNIDA	98
VIII.	**Mollusca** - - - -	116
IX.	**Chordata** - - - - AMPHIOXUS.	119
X.	**Craniata** - - - - SCYLLIUM.	127

CHAPTER		PAGE
XI.	**Amphibia** - - - -	145
	RANA.	
XII.	**Reptilia and Aves** - - -	162
XIII.	**Mammalia** - - - -	165
	LEPUS—ORDERS.	
XIV.	**General Physiology and Histology** -	189
XV.	**Embryology** - - - -	231
	SEGMENTATION — DEVELOPMENT OF (i.) AMPHIOXUS; (ii.) RANA; (iii.) GALLUS—FŒTAL MEMBRANES IN BIRD AND MAMMAL.	
XVI.	**Variation — Heredity and Mendelism —Evolution** - - -	249
	Appendix - - - -	270
	ROOTS OF TECHNICAL WORDS.	
	Index - - - - -	273

CHAPTER I

INTRODUCTION—GAMETOGENESIS AND CLASSIFICATION

THE animate world and the physical or inanimate world both possess certain chemical and physical features in common. Living organisms, however, are capable of transforming substances unlike themselves into material which is finally incorporated into the living material—**protoplasm.** The capacity to do this enables living things to add new protoplasm throughout the whole of their body (not on the outside only, as in crystals), and so enables them to grow by the **assimilation** of their food material. The result of this ability to grow enables living organisms to **reproduce** new organisms like themselves. Thus, the fundamental difference between living and non-living things is that the former alone show **growth by assimilation,** and **reproduction.**

All living things are made of the substance known as **protoplasm,** and, in addition, in most cases a supporting ground substance made by the protoplasm. In the lowest animals the whole organism consists of a very small piece of protoplasm only. It contains, however, a smaller portion of denser and more specialized protoplasm which controls the activities of the protoplasmic mass. Thus, a very small organism might consist of a mass of general protoplasm, or **cytoplasm,** with a controlling centre—the

nucleus—made of specialized protoplasm—**nucleoplasm.**

This scheme of construction obtains in the lower animals (Protozoa), each organism being just a " blob " of cytoplasm with a nucleus. Such a unit— " a little mass of protoplasm containing a nucleus " —is termed a cell. (N.B.—Cell, therefore, refers to the living mass, and not to anything which that mass may secrete outside of itself.) Thus each protozoön consists of a single cell.

Animals other than the Protozoa have their bodies made of a number of cells which work together for their mutual benefit. In the case of organisms which are cell aggregates each cell is not constructed upon exactly similar lines, but is specialized for particular work. Thus, nerve cells, bone cells, muscle cells, etc., are formed. Sets of similar cells are technically known as **tissues**—*e.g.*, muscle tissue. Usually a number of tissues may be associated together for the performance of one type of work. Such associations are known as **organs**—*e.g.*, stomach, of glandular, muscular, and connective tissue. Many organs may collaborate to perform a series of reactions, and so **systems** are formed—*e.g.*, digestive system of teeth, tongue, salivary glands, stomach, intestine, etc., all reacting upon food material. The body of the higher animals therefore consists of a number of systems all working towards the common good of the organism as a whole.

The essential components of living protoplasm cannot be stated, because as soon as a minute analysis of the living compound is attempted, protoplasm is killed. The dead material is, of course, very closely related to protoplasm, but is not actually that substance. Protoplasm consists of small quantities of mineral salts in water together with certain colloidal organic compounds. The protoplasm may contain large spaces filled with fluid, which are called **vacuoles.** The finer structure of protoplasm is probably like that of an emulsion, with a continuous phase of water containing dissolved organic and inorganic substances and a discontinuous or disperse phase of extremely minute droplets of protein material.

Cell Division (Mitosis).

The nucleus consists of a **nuclear membrane** containing nuclear fluid or sap and certain more solid bodies known as **chromosomes** and which stain deeply with certain dyes as they contain a substance known as **chromatin.** In the resting or "interphase" nucleus the chromosomes are extremely elongated, vacuolated and rather indefinite in appearance. Each chromosome consists of two elongated parallel portions lying closely side by side. These "half" chromosomes known as **chromatids**, are made up of a string of characteristic particles of unequal size and arranged at unequal distances from one another. These particles are **chromomeres** and there is evidence that they are normally present in a permanent linear order on the chromosome. The chromatids have a relatively achromatic part known as the **centromere.** The position of the centromere varies in individual chromosomes, but is constant in the individual chromosomes of every nuclear group characteristic of an individual organism.

An organism grows by the addition of new cells. These new cells arise from previous ones by the process of **cell division,** or, as it is also known, **mitosis** or **karyokinesis.** Although mitosis is a continuous process it is convenient to divide it into four phases which pass imperceptibly into one another. The whole process is connected, essentially, with the nucleoplasm only.

1. **Prophase.**—Division is apparently initiated by

the **centrosome,** a small body lying just outside of the nuclear membrane. The centrosome divides into two portions, which move towards opposite poles of the cell. The chromosomes shorten and become coiled. This increase in thickness obliterates the individual identity of the chromomeres and the chromatids become rounded in outline. A large number of minute cell organs, the mitochondria, become apparent in the region of the centre of the cell. The daughter centrosomes have now arrived at opposite poles. Radiating from each centrosomic pole is a series of lines akin to those of a magnetic field. Each centrosome and ' lines ' form an **aster.** Continued shortening of the linin thread gives rise to a short tangled mass of chromatin. The nuclear sap begins to pass out from within the nucleus and the membrane eventually disappears. The number of chromosomes into which the nucleus resolves at mitosis varies in different animals, but is constant for each species—*e.g.*, man has forty-eight, the " fruit-fly " has eight, and the sweet pea fourteen chromosomes. The chromosomes now lie freely in the cytoplasm on the fibrillæ between the centrosomes. The fibrillar network is termed the **spindle.** This " ends " the prophase.

2. **Metaphase.**—The chromosomes now arrange themselves at the equator of the spindle to form an **equatorial " plate."** The chromosomes are attached to the fibrillar network by the centromere and the double nature of the chromosomes is apparent. Each chromosome then splits longitudinally into two equal **daughter chromosomes** (chromatids have separated), which separate. This stage passes imperceptibly into the next.

3. **Anaphase.**—The daughter chromosomes then move towards their nearest pole.

4. **Telophase.**—As the daughter chromosomes ap-

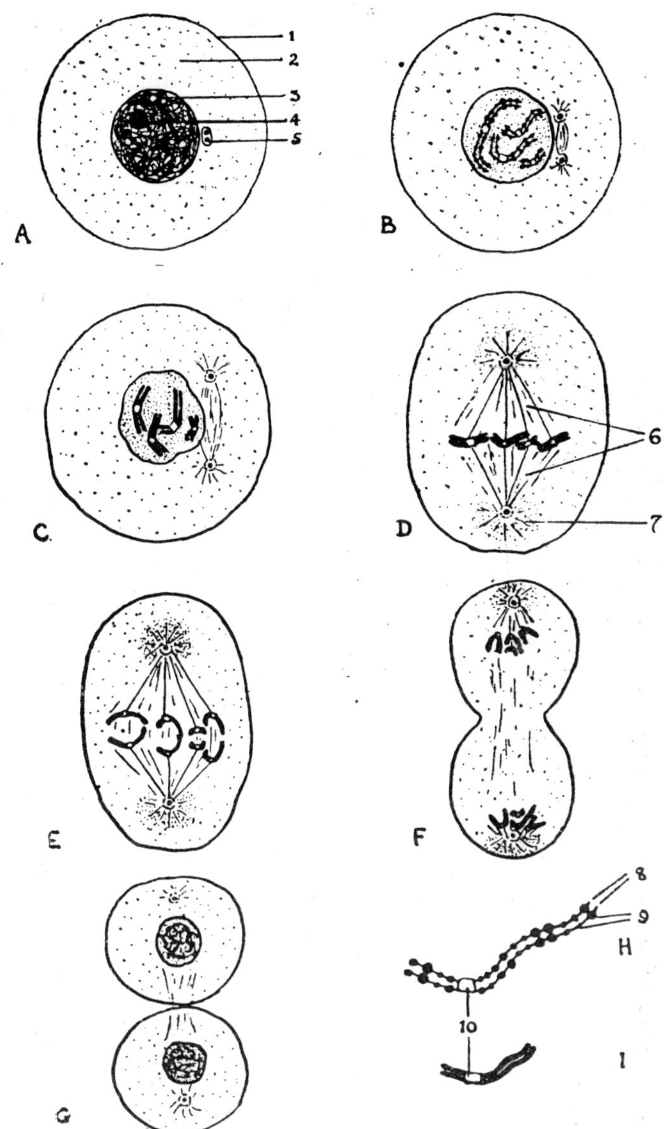

FIG. I.—DIAGRAM TO SHOW STAGES IN MITOSIS.

A, " resting " cell; B and C, early and late prophase; D, metaphase; E and F, early and late anaphase; G, cell division completed; H, chromosome at about prophase to show chromatids and chromomeres; I, chromosome at metaphase.

1, Cell membrane; 2, cytoplasm; 3, nucleus; 4, nucleolus; 5, centrosome; 6, spindle; 7, aster; 8, chromatids; 9, chromomeres; 10, centromere.

proach their respective poles the protoplasm constricts into two. The chromosomes in each daughter cell become elongated and threadlike and so appear to form a tangled mass around which a nuclear membrane forms to give a nucleus. The two daughter nuclei in their own new daughter cells then return to the resting condition.

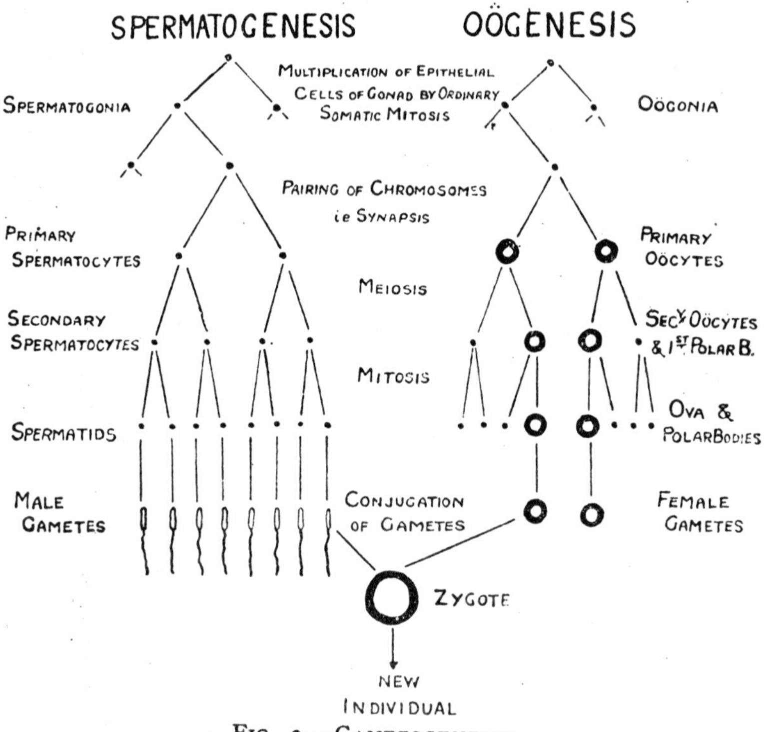

FIG. 2.—GAMETOGENESIS.

When a new animal is produced, the more usual (sexual) method is that the new individual arises from the union of two cells or **gametes**, one male and one female. Thus chromosomes from two individuals unite to form the number in the offspring. Hence, if the adults have eight chromosomes the offspring might be expected to have sixteen—eight from each parent. However, when the gametes are forming the number of chromosomes in them is reduced by half. Hence the offspring has still the specific number, but half of them are of maternal origin and the rest are paternal ones.

The process by which the number of chromosomes is halved is **meiosis.** The cells of the gonad or sex organ continue to multiply in order to keep the number of cells constant, while some of them undergo **maturation** into functional gametes. The whole process is known as **gametogenesis** (Fig. 2), or in the male **spermatogenesis** and in the female **oögenesis.** The primordial germ cells are set aside early in development and later migrate to the gonads. Here, they increase by many mitotic divisions to become **spermatogonia** and **oögonia.** Certain of them about to mature store food (the female oögonia to a greater extent) and become **primary spermatocytes** or **oöcytes.** These then undergo the meiotic or reducing division to form **secondary spermatocytes** or **oöcytes.**

During the prophase of meiosis the following stages can be discerned:—

1. Leptotene stage.—The chromosomes, when they appear, are single threads and not double, as in mitosis. Their granular appearance is due to the chromomeres. Commencing at the centromeres, the chromosomes associate in twisted pairs, and then shorten and thicken, giving the zygotene condition. Each pair consists of a chromosome from the male parent, and one from the female parent.
2. Pachytene stage.—The pairs of chromosomes show a differential condensation in various parts. The paired coils then begin to loosen, so leading to the

3. Diplotene stage. The further loosening of the pairs of chromosomes reveals that each one now consists of two chromatids. The paired chromosomes now separate except at certain points along their length, known as **chiasmata,** and at these points there is "crossing over" between elements of the two chromatids of each of the partner chromosomes. Thus groups of chromomeres may be exchanged, so giving new combinations in the reconstructed chromatids. This is of great importance when considering the chromosomes as bearers of hereditary factors.
4. Diakinesis. The chromosomes, which now have become spiral, move to the periphery of the nucleus, while still remaining in pairs.

The nuclear membrane now breaks down and metaphase and anaphase follow as in mitosis, except that **whole chromosomes separate** as the pairs come apart. Thus the secondary spermatocyte and oöcyte have only half the number of chromosomes present in the normal cells of the body. The next mitotic division follows immediately without the nucleus being reconstituted.

Each primary spermatocyte gives two secondary spermatocytes (reduced number of chromosomes). Each of the latter divides mitotically into two **spermatids,** each of which develops a tail and becomes a spermatozoon or male cell. The division of the primary oöcyte is unequal, producing a larger cell, the **secondary oöcyte,** and a small one, the **first polar body.** This is followed by an ordinary mitotic division (equal to that giving spermatids), which is also unequal, so that a large **mature ovum** and a polar

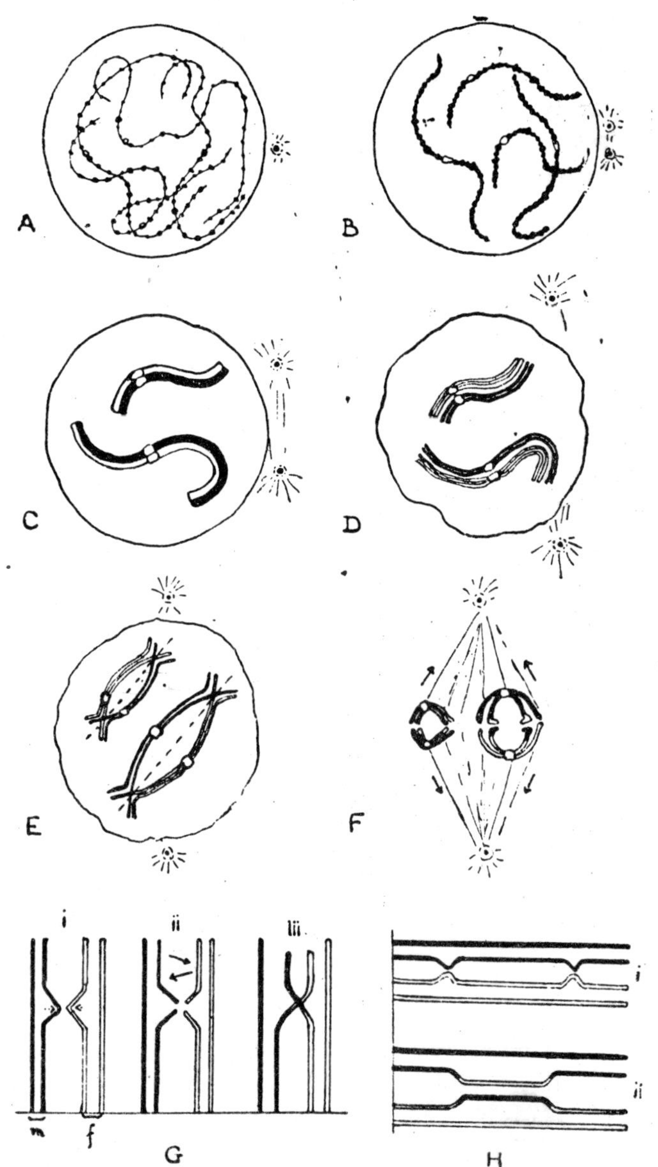

FIG. 3.—DIAGRAMS TO SHOW STAGES IN MEIOSIS.

A, Leptotene; B, zygotene; C, pachytene; D, early diplotene; E, late diplotene; F, anaphase; G, simple chiasmata near end of chromosomes; H, one of other types of chiasmata. Note: dotted lines in E indicate direction of splitting.

body are formed, and two polar bodies from the first polar body. Thus from one spermatogonium there arises eventually eight spermatozoa, whereas one onium produces two mature ova and six useless polar bodies.

The union of an ovum and a spermatozoon—or fertilization of the ovum—produces a fertilized cell or **zygote,** from which, by repeated mitotic divisions, a new individual is produced.

The chromosomes divide with great accuracy during mitosis. At fertilization new chromosome combinations are made. As the chromosomes are assumed to be the carriers of hereditary factors, reassortment of the factors is thus possible.

In many cases reproduction is only possible by the co-operation of two types of individual or **sex.** Each sex, **male** or **female,** produces a particular kind of reproductive body or gamete:—

1. Male gamete or **spermatozoon** is small and active. It consists usually of a head-piece and a tail for use in active movement. The head is made up almost entirely of nuclear material. No food is stored.
2. Female gamete or **ovum** is large and passive. The cytoplasm is filled with globules of reserve food for the use of the developing embryo.

The gametes conjugate or the egg is fertilized when spermatozoon and ovum fuse together. The resultant cell is a **zygote.** In many animals—aquatic types—the conjugation of gametes takes place outside of the bodies of the parents. In the higher types—mostly terrestrial—the male gametes or sperm are transferred by the male to the female during **coition.** Some animals possess both male and female reproductive organs in the one body, and such are said to be **hermaphrodite.**

When a zygote is formed, by the conjugation of gametes, the whole process is known as **sexual reproduction. Asexual reproduction** is said to occur when a portion of the body of an organism is capable of developing unaided into another adult organism. The production of a new organism from an unfertilized ovum is known as **parthenogenesis.** In such cases sexual reproduction usually alternates with parthenogenesis. Thus the female gametes may be of the ordinary sexual type or they may be capable of unaided development (parthenogonidia).

CLASSIFICATION

The animal kingdom is divided into groups, each of which contains members showing similar basic characters. Within a large group are smaller groupings of types exhibiting more specialized features. Hence, by this subdividing, numbers of individuals with similar specialized characters are grouped together, although each kind within this small group, or **genus,** has its own particular feature separating it off—as a **species**—from the other members of the genus. Thus the animal kingdom is subdivided into phyla, classes, orders, families, genera, and species. In addition, it is often found convenient to break up the above groups into sub-classes, sub-orders or tribes, and varieties.

Carl Linnæus (1707-1778) was a great Swedish naturalist to whose credit must go the final establishment of the **binomial nomenclature** system of classification (1735). Thus each organism is given two names—the **generic** or "family" name and the **specific** or "individual" name. The convenience of the binomial system may be judged by classifying a common organism.

The whole animal kingdom is divided into a number of large primary groups or **phyla**. One of these is the **Chordata**—animals having a supporting structure in the middle line of the back. In the majority of Chordates this central dorsal supporting rod is a chain of small bones or vertebræ, hence the class **Vertebrata** within the Chordata.

Within the Vertebrata or backboned animals are groups of animals with a number of common group characters. Thus the Vertebrata are divided up into classes: Pisces (thin scales on body); Amphibia (damp, bare skin); Reptilia (horny scales); Aves (feathered skin); and Mammalia (hair on the body). Each class is again divided into orders: the Mammalia, including the Insectivora (insect-eating types); the Ungulata (animals with hoofs); Carnivora (flesh-eaters); Primates (arboreal types—monkeys, apes, and man).

Of the Carnivora there are two parallel sub-orders: the Carnivora Fissipedia, with four separate limbs; and the Carnivora Pinnipedia—the seals, sea lions, and walruses, with the hind limbs bound together to form a "tail" flipper. Within the former sub-order are included, amongst others, the dog family, Canidæ and the cat family, Felidæ. There are various kinds of cats belonging to the same genus Felis, of which the lion, tiger, and domestic cat may be taken as examples. Each of them has its own particular characters, and hence is placed as a species having both the generic name Felis and a specific name, thus—*F. leo*, *F. tigris*, and *F. domesticus* respectively.

This method of classifying animals may be summed up in the following table:

General Terms.	*Specific Examples.*
PHYLUM.	CHORDATA.
SUB-PHYLUM.	VERTEBRATA.
CLASS.	MAMMALIA.
ORDER.	CARNIVORA.
SUB-ORDER.	CARNIVORA FISSIPEDIA.
FAMILY.	FELIDÆ.
GENUS.	FELIS.
SPECIES.	*F. leo.* *F. tigris.* *F. domesticus.*

The aim of such a scheme of classification is to endeavour to express what seems to be the natural relationships of animal to animal and group to group.

CHAPTER II

PROTOZOA

SARCODINA—FLAGELLATA

THE Protozoa is a phylum of simply organized animals in which each organism consists of a mass of protoplasm with a nucleus controlling its activities. Morphologically a protozoan cell is equivalent to one of the many cells which make up a human body.

The organisms are important pathologically, owing to their effect as parasites in man; and economically from their effect upon plants and animals from which man derives food and economic wealth.

The shape varies in the different types of Protozoa. Some possess no shape-retaining envelope; others have an outer layer of an elastic nature, thus limiting the amount of movement. Finally, many have a very firm envelope, or **pellicle,** which allows of no change of shape whatever.

The Protozoa, which are universally distributed, are divided into four main classes:

Class I., **Sarcodina,** characterized by the absence of any definite, persistent body form.

Class II., **Flagellata,** with whip-like locomotory organ(s)—a **flagellum.**

Class III., **Ciliata,** having a body covering of small, slender, hair-like locomotory organs—**cilia.**

Class IV., **Sporozoa,** a group derived from more than one type, but owing to their parasitic life they have the common feature of reproducing by means of **spores** in some phase of their complicated life-histories.

Class I. : SARCODINA

The body form is unstable owing to the absence of a rigid pellicle. Hence the protoplasm flows out in various directions forming streams of the living substance. These projections, or **pseudopodia,** can be withdrawn into the main mass of the cell, and can be formed in any position on the periphery. Members of the class are found in fresh water, the seas, and the soil. Of several orders within this class some examples are taken below.

Order : Lobosa.

Members of this order creep by means of broad, blunt—**lobate**—pseudopodia. One of the commoner forms is *Amœba* (Fig. 4).

AMŒBA.

Habitat.—Amœba is found creeping upon the surface of the debris on the bottom of fresh-water ponds. It is a greyish blob of translucent protoplasm about one-eightieth of an inch in diameter.

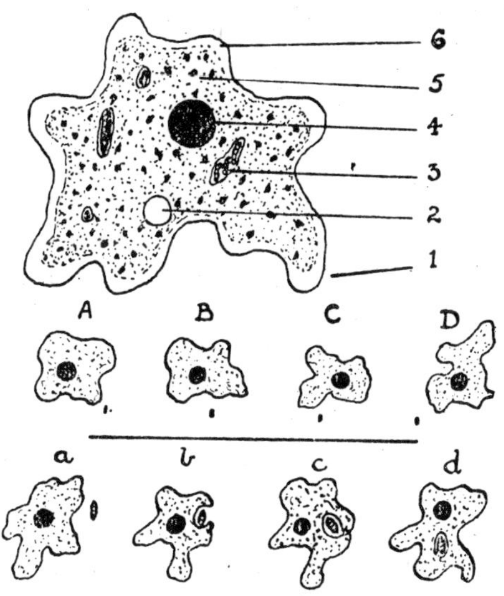

FIG. 4.—AMŒBA.

1, Pseudopodium; 2, contractile vacuole; 3, food vacuole; 4, nucleus; 5, endoplasm; 6, ectoplasm.
A-D, Locomotion (1 indicates fixed point): *a,b,c*, ingestion; *d*, assimilation; *c,b,a*, defecation (egestion).

Structure.—Upon closer examination two layers of protoplasm may be distinguished:

(*a*) **Ectoplasm,** the outer clear layer.

(*b*) **Endoplasm,** the inner and densely granular region whose granules are continually moving. Situated here also are the **nucleus** and the **contractile vacuole.** One or more **food vacuoles** may also be present.

Locomotion is by means of pseudopodia. One pseudopodium increases in size by a local liquefaction of the ectoplasm, which causes the endoplasm to flow into it by the contraction of the rest of the ectoplasm. Thus, this pseudopodium becomes the body of the organism which progresses in this manner. The ectoplasm does not flow in the same manner, but travels forward on the upper surface, downwards on the front pseudopodial surfaces, backwards on the under side, and upwards at the rear. This action is similar to that of the driving bands of a caterpillar tractor.

Nutrition.—The whole process of ingestion, digestion, and defecation is extremely simple. **Ingestion** —the taking in of food—is accomplished by the aid of the pseudopodia. The food consists of single-celled plants or animals and organic debris. The particle of food is surrounded, and eventually enclosed, by the embrace of two pseudopodia. Hence a space containing water and food is cut off between the two pseudopodia. As the pseudopodia fuse beyond the particle there is formed a **food vacuole,** which circulates in the endoplasm. **Digestive juices** are poured into the vacuole by the surrounding protoplasm, digestion takes place, and the dissolved food is absorbed by the protoplasm. The unused material is **egested** or **defecated** by a reversing of the ingestion stages.

Respiration.—The body surface absorbs oxygen and gives out carbon dioxide, by diffusion through the ectoplasm. The proportion between body area and surface area is an important factor in respiration. In small animals this relationship is such that adequate exchanges of gases in solution can be made without any increase of respiratory surface area, so necessary in larger animals.

Excretion.—Nitrogenous waste materials pass into solution and diffuse outwards through the ectoplasm.

Osmo-regulation.—Water is continually entering the protoplasm by osmosis from the dilute external medium, the ectoplasm acting as a semi-permeable membrane. There is an excess amount of water taken in and the contractile vacuole is formed by the localised collection of this excess, and thus prevents indefinite dilution of the body fluids. The excess water passes from the protoplasm, as the vacuole releases it on bursting, to the exterior.

Growth and Reproduction.—When the Amœba reaches its specific maximum size by the **assimilation** of food it then reproduces. This may occur in either of two ways—

1. *Asexual or Vegetative Reproduction.*

(*a*) The nucleus elongates, becomes dumb-bell shaped, and then pulls into two portions (amitosis). The cystoplasm also undergoes division, so that the result is a pulling into two portions of the original body. This whole process is known as **binary fission.**

(*b*) At the approach of unfavourable conditions—*e.g.*, winter—the Amœba may form around itself a hard resistant cell wall. Within this the protoplasm remains inactive—in a state of suspended animation. This condition is known as **encystment,** and in this state the Amœba is capable of withstanding very hard conditions. Upon the approach of better conditions the nucleus divides amitotically into several hundred parts in some cases, and each small portion lies near the periphery of the cytoplasm. A small amount of protoplasm aggregates around each nucleus, and so upon the bursting of the cyst a number of small Amœbæ, or **Amœbulæ,** emerge and grow to adult size. This production of many individuals from one is known as **multiple fission.**

2. *Sexual Reproduction.*

In some species of Amœba two individuals may **conjugate** or fuse together completely, the two nuclei and entities becoming one. Conjugation is usually followed by rapid fission.

Allied Forms.—Living along with the common Amœba—*A. proteus*—are usually a number of allied forms, which build or secrete a protective shelter:

Arcella secretes a chitinous case of a domed shape on one side, with a slightly concave floor to the dome. The opening is in the concavity, and through it the amœboid body can protrude.

Difflugia builds a club-shaped case of sand grains, the pseudopodia protruding from an opening in the narrower end.

Euglypha has a case similar in shape to that of Difflugia, but made of plates secreted by the animal itself.

Parasitic Forms.—Several relations of *A. proteus* have become **parasites,** and obtain their food from within the body of another animal or **host.** This parasitic group belongs to the genus *Entamœba,* of which the commoner forms are:

1. *E. blattæ,* found in the alimentary tract of the Cockroach.
2. *E. buccalis,* living in the human mouth.
3. *E. coli,* inhabiting the colon (intestine) of Man. It feeds mainly upon the swarms of bacteria present there, and is harmless to the host.
4. *E. histolytica* (or *dysenteriæ*) also lives in the human intestine. It attacks the intestinal wall, where its action causes **amœbic dysentery.** It feeds upon red corpuscles as well as upon bacteria. It may penetrate into the blood system of the host and be

carried to the liver, where its presence sets up abscesses.

Entamœbæ pass from host to host as dry cysts, which pass out with the fæces, the cysts then blowing about. Infection of the new host is purely a matter of chance.

Other members of the Sarcodina live in the sea-water. Such forms do not usually possess a contractile vacuole.

Order : Foraminifera.

The pseudopodia of the members of this order are very thin and delicate, anastomosing in places, and so form a reticulate fringe all around the main protoplasmic mass. Shells are present in these forms, and may be secreted by the animal—**calcareous, siliceous,** or **chitinous shells**; or small particles of sand material may be used—**arenaceous shells.** A great deal of morphological variation in the shell is to be seen. The completed shell is made up of a number of chambers, which may be arranged linearly, as in *Nodosaria*; or in a flat spiral, as in *Globigerina, Polystomella,* and *Rotalia.*

The function of the shell is to support the protoplasm rather than to protect it, as the protoplasm streams upon the outside in a thin layer, from which arise the reticulate pseudopodia. The outer protoplasmic layer is connected with that inside the shell by strands of protoplasm, which pass through openings in the shell. These openings may be in the form of small pores scattered all over the shell, which is then said to be of a **perforate type.** In other examples the connection is through large holes, usually aggregated to form a punctured plate, and the shell is then of an **imperforate type.**

Each species of the Foraminifera shows two forms

—some have a large central chamber to the shell, whilst others have a small one. These two types alternate, the large-chambered form arising from asexually produced gametes, whilst the small form is the result of development from the sexually produced zygote. Thus the Foraminifera show **dimorphism** (*i.e.*, two forms), a large or **megalospheric** form, and a small or **microspheric** type.

During the formation of the sexual or asexual re-

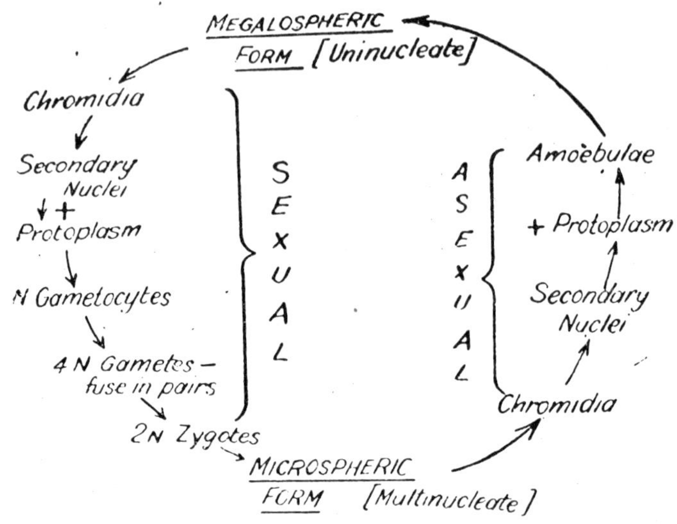

FIG. 5.—DIAGRAM TO ILLUSTRATE THE LIFE-HISTORY OF POLYSTOMELLA.

productive bodies (gametes or amœbulæ), the nuclear material is first broken up into small pieces, or **chromidia.** Then the chromidia aggregate to form a number of **secondary nuclei.** An outline of the life-history of the Foraminiferan *Polystomella* may be taken as typical of the order (Fig. 5).

The living Foraminifera float near the surface of the sea, and form part of the large heterogeneous assemblage of organisms—larval and adult—which is known as the **plankton.** Upon the death of the protoplasm the small shells of the Foraminifera sink toward the sea-bed. During the downward journey the sea-water slowly dissolves away the calcareous material. Hence, provided that the time the shells are in suspension is long enough—*i.e.*, according to the depth of the sea—there comes a point when the shell is entirely dissolved. There is a constant rain of the skeletal parts of organisms from the surface waters on to the sea-bed. In many regions of the sea there is a preponderance of Foraminifera in the plankton. Thus the sea-bed in such regions tends to be made up of Foraminiferan skeletons. One of the commoner and more abundant of this order is the form known as *Globigerina.* The deposition of Foraminiferan skeletons gives rise to **Foraminiferan ooze.** A concentration of Globigerina skeletons forms **Globigerina ooze,** which occurs at depths between one thousand and three thousand fathoms.

Order : Radiolaria.

The members of the order Radiolaria are also found in the marine plankton. They are characterized by having long, slender, **stiff, non-anastomosing pseudopodia,** a **siliceous skeleton,** and a **central capsule.**

The skeletonic structure of the Radiolaria is very complex, varied, and beautiful. The central capsule is typical of and exclusive to the Radiolaria. It is a spherical membranous layer embedded in the protoplasm, and is unconnected with the skeletal structures. The protoplasm is thus divided into two regions—viz.:

1. **Intracapsular protoplasm,** which possesses the nucleus of the organism, and is therefore concerned with reproduction.

2. **Extracapsular protoplasm** of a very vacuolated nature. All other life functions, apart from reproduction, are carried out in this region.

The action of the sea-water upon the sinking skeletons of the Radiolaria is not so swift as upon those of the Foraminifera. This is because the skeletons of the former are of a siliceous nature, and so **Radiolarian ooze** is found at greater depths than Foraminiferan ooze.

Class II. : FLAGELLATA

Each member of this class of the Protozoa has a definite shape throughout most of its lifetime. The organism possesses a thin horny cuticle or **pellicle** upon the outside. The pellicle, whilst being able to retain a definite shape, may still permit of a certain amount of temporary change in outline.

The locomotory organ is a long, thin, hair-like structure or flagellum. The flagellum may arise from the anterior of the body, which follows the locomotory organ. This type of flagellum is called a **tractellum.** In others the flagellum pushes the body of the organism through the water and is known as a **pulsellum.**

Flagellates are very widely and abundantly distributed, and are also the cause of some of the deadliest diseases of man and his domesticated animals. Amongst the members of this class are to be found some organisms which seem to combine plant and animal characteristics.

Euglena Viridis.

Habitat.—This organism can be taken as an example of the type with plant and animal characters. It is a form which is very common in stagnant water, especially such ponds as contain a large percentage of nitrogenous matter derived from organic sources. Large numbers of Euglena give rise to the green scum so often found forming a surface layer.

Structure.—Each organism is spindle-shaped, attaining about 0·15 mm. in length (Fig. 6A). The anterior end is blunt, whilst the posterior extremity is pointed. Within the thin pellicle is a layer of ectoplasm surrounding the endoplasm. At the anterior end the pellicle and ectoplasm are reflected inwards to form a funnel-like pit—the so-called "**gullet,**" which leads into a rounded cavity—the **reservoir.** Here also arises the single flagellum.

The **endoplasm** contains the following structures:

1. **Nucleus.**—A large spherical body situated in the posterior portion of the body.
2. **Chloroplasts.**—These are rod-like bodies containing the green pigment, chlorophyll, which is characteristic of plants. They radiate from a common centre so that a stellate structure is produced.
3. **Paramylum granules,** or grains of a **starch-like** food reserve.
4. **Stigma.**—This is a red pigment spot situated at the anterior of the body and to one side of the "gullet." It is sensitive to the stimulus of light, and hence is often erroneously termed the "eye spot."
5. **Excretory organelles.**

Movement.—Movement is carried out in two ways:

(*a*) **Locomotion.**—The lashing movement of the flagellum is transmitted to the organism's body so that the whole organism appears to "dither" and it rotates on its own axis as it moves through the water.

(*b*) The shape of the body is altered by waves of contraction and expansion passing up or down the body. This is typical euglenoid movement (*cf.* amœboid movement) (Fig. 6, C.).

Osmo-regulation.—The method of eliminating excess fluids is complicated. Four sets of structures take part in this excretion: the gullet, excretory reservoir, contractile vacuole, and a number of accessory vacuoles.

The fluid to be excreted is passed from the endoplasm into the **accessory vacuoles** which surround the **contractile vacuole.** They pass the fluid into the **contractile vacuole,** which gradually enlarges to its maximum size. The vacuole contracts and the fluid passes into the **reservoir,** which in its turn empties into the gullet.

Respiration and Excretion.—The exchange of gases concerned in respiration takes place by diffusion through the general body surface. Excretory products also diffuse outwards from the body.

Reproduction.—The organism divides by simple **longitudinal binary fission,** commencing at the anterior end after the loss of the flagellum. Some individuals encyst in a gelatinous envelope, wherein a number of divisions follow one another. In some species of Euglena conjugation between amœboid gametes has been observed.

Nutrition.—The mode of feeding in Euglena constitutes its most interesting feature. Normally, Euglena feeds **holophytically** (entirely like a plant) in the presence of a small amount of albuminoid material in solution. Holophytic nutrition is carried on by means of the chloroplasts. If the surrounding fluid is rich in dissolved organic material, then the chloroplasts become pale and food in solution is absorbed in a **saphrophytic** manner. Certain flagellates related to Euglena are able to take in solid food at times by means of the "gullet," thus exhibiting **holozoic** nutrition.

Trypanosomes.

Habitat.—The Trypanosomes form a family of extremely important flagellates. They are responsible

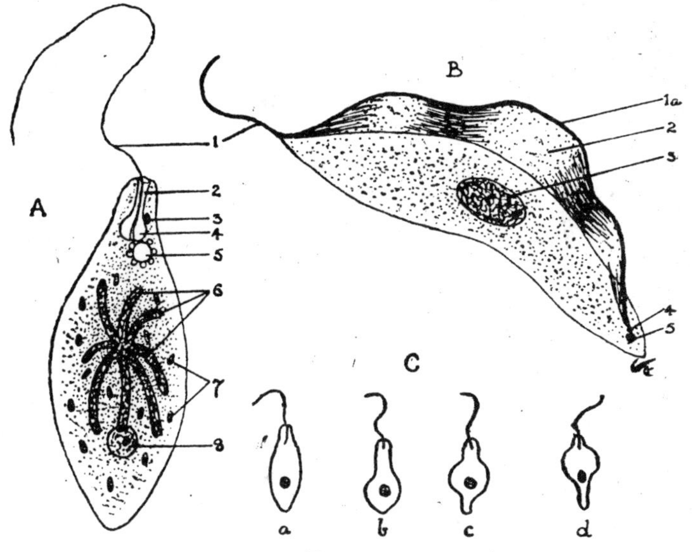

FIG. 6.

A. ENGLENA.—1, Flagellum; 2, "gullet;" 3, Stigma; 4, reservoir; 5, contractile vacuole; 6, chloroplast; 7, paramylum granules; 8, nucleus.
B. TRYPANOSOMÆ.—1, Flagellum; 1a, flagellum at edge of undulating membrane (2); 3, trophonucleus; 4, basal granule; 5, kinetonucleus.
C.—"Euglenoid" movement.

for a number of diseases affecting humans and their domestic animals, as the Trypanosomes are typically parasites of the blood of Vertebrates.

Structure.—A typical Trypanosome is about 0·001 inch in length, and of an elongated spindle shape (Fig. 6, B.). One end of the body is rather pointed and is prolonged into a single flagellum. The flagellum runs parallel with the cell wall and is connected to it by a thin sheet of protoplasm—an **undulating membrane.** The membrane, with its thickened edge, or **flagellum,** is usually thrown into a number of small undulations.

The cytoplasm is of a very finely granular nature, and contains no vacuoles of any sort. Lying in this cytoplasm is the very characteristic nuclear apparatus, consisting of:

1. **Trophonucleus.**—A centrally placed dense mass of chromatin. It is usually taken that this nuclear mass controls the food-taking activities of the cell.
2. **Kinetonucleus.**—This is a smaller mass of chromatin, usually situated towards the blunter end of the cell. This nuclear mass controls the movements of the organism.
3. **Basal Granule.**—The flagellum arises from the basal granule, which is always closely associated with the kinetonucleus. Owing tc the fact that division of the cell is initiated by the basal granule, it may be regarded as of the same nature as the centrosome of other animal cells.

Division takes place by longitudinal fission, first the basal granule, then flagellum, kinetonucleus, trophonucleus, and cytoplasm in the order given. Nothing resembling conjugation or sexual reproduction has been observed.

Trypanosomes are transferred from one vertebrate host to another by the agency of blood-sucking animals—*e.g.*, certain insects and leeches—according to the environment of the vertebrate host.

Trypanosomiasis is the general name given to diseases caused by Trypanosomes, but specific names distinguish the disease in various hosts.

"**Sleeping Sickness**" is a fatal disease in human subjects, and is caused by a Trypanosome—*T. gambiense.*

During the later stages of the disease the Trypanosomes make their way into the **cerebro-spinal fluid** of the patient, where the poisonous excreta, acting upon the central nervous system, give rise to the characteristic languor preceding death.

The more important Trypanosomes and the particular diseases they cause can be tabulated thus:

Disease.	*Host.*	*Transmitter.*	*Trypanosome Species.*
Sleeping sickness.	Man.	*Glossina palpalis.*	*T. gambiense.*
Nagana.	Domestic animals.	*G. morsitans.*	*T. brucii.*
Surra.	Horses, camels.	A horse fly (*Tabanus*), or stable fly (*Stomoxys*).	*T. evansi.*
Mal de caderas.	Horses.	Unknown.	*T. equinum.*
Dourine.	Breeding horses.	Direct; during coition.	*T. equiperdum.*
—	Rats.	Fleas.	*T. lewisi.*

Sleeping sickness is carried by the tsetse-fly (*G. palpalis*). The peculiar life-history of this fly makes it very difficult to attack during development. Hence the following points should be noted:

1. **Life-History of** *G. palpalis.*—The transmitting fly has a peculiar life-history. It favours the shady margins of fresh waters. Only one egg is fertilized at a time, and it **remains within the mother,** where it becomes a larva. It is born as an advanced **larva.** and almost immediately pupates in the earth beneath the bushes. The adult insect hatches from the **pupa.**

Hence this care of the young by the mother is an important factor in preventing the destruction of the transmitting insect in its younger stages (*cf.* mosquito in later pages).

2. **Destruction of** *G. palpalis*.—This is effected by clearing the shade-producing plants fringing the fresh waters. In addition, low shelters are erected wherein—being the only shade—the fly will deposit grubs, which can then be destroyed. This method is not possible when dealing with areas on the banks of long rivers.

3. **Segregation.**—The segregation of patients in fly-proof shelters would be effective but for the fact that wild animals probably act as a reservoir for the Trypanosomes. *T. gambiense* is known to be a natural parasite of at least one of the wild animals of Africa—namely, the Sitatunga antelope (*Limnotragus*). The destruction of this animal would only prove effective as a check when more precise knowledge is gained regarding other wild types which may be natural hosts of *T. gambiense*.

4. **Removal of People.**—The withdrawal of the population from the fly-infected margins of the waters is a very practical method. It has been carried out in Uganda on quite a large scale, where it has resulted in a considerable diminution of sleeping-sickness cases. (Compare with Mosquito and Malarial Fever, *vide infra*.)

Many of the Flagellata are parasites, and are usually found in the alimentary canals of their hosts. The insects particularly are the hosts of many flagellates (*Crithidia, Leptomonas*). Hence it would seem very probable that forms like the Trypanosomes were originally parasites of insects, and only secondarily have spread to the vertebrate host through the blood-sucking habits of their original host.

CHAPTER III

PROTOZOA (*Continued*)

CILIATA—SPOROZOA—CONCLUSION TO PROTOZOA

Class III. : CILIATA

THE Ciliata contains the most complex and highly organized members of the Protozoa. The majority of the class live a free aquatic existence, whilst others are to be found as parasites either within a host (**endoparasites**) or upon the outside of its body (**ectoparasites**).

A strong pellicle keeps the body shape constant. This outer layer may be sculptured, and a skeleton is present in some forms.

Characteristic locomotory organs are present in the form of **cilia**—short, fine, hair-like threads of protoplasm. In some types the cilia may form an even coating over all of the body. Such ciliates are said to be **holotrichous.** If cilia are absent in some regions, then the organism is of the **oligotrichous** type. In others the cilia are of varying lengths, and so the animal is **heterotrichous.**

The cilia are, primitively, arranged in parallel rows. This arrangement may be modified in two ways:

(*a*) **Undulating membranes** may be formed by the fusion of adjacent cilia in the same row (*cf.* undulating membrane of Trypanosomes).

(*b*) **Penicilliate membranelles** are made by the fusion of ciliary tufts from the adjacent rows, giving rise to a structure which may be compared with a fine camel-hair brush in which the hairs are adhering to one another.

The nuclear apparatus is complex, there being two nuclei to each organism. A large nucleus—the **macronucleus**—controls all the cell activities except reproduction. Situated near the macronucleus is a much smaller **micronucleus,** which is concerned with reproduction only.

A very common example of the Ciliata is the "slipper animalcule" or *Paramecium.*

Paramecium.

Habitat.—This ciliate is found in ponds of fresh water in which there are decaying organic remains—

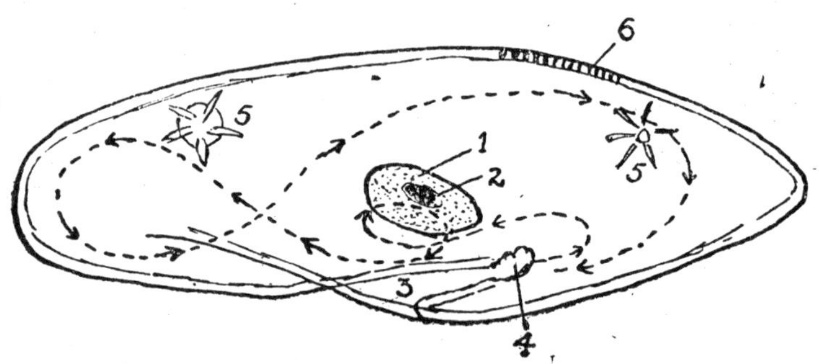

FIG. 7.—PARAMECIUM.

1, Macronucleus; 2, micronucleus; 3, vestibule; 4, gullet; 5, contractile vacuole; 6, trichocysts. The dotted line indicates the path taken by the food vacuoles.

leaves, etc. The animal feeds upon the bacteria which cause the decomposition of the dead organic material. A successful culture of Paramecia can be readily obtained by placing chopped hay in a beaker of water and boiling for two minutes. When cool, several drops of pond water, containing Paramecia, are added, and the whole infusion left for a time. Periodic examination shows that the fluid soon swarms with bacteria and various Protozoa, prominent amongst which is the genus *Paramecium* (Fig. 7).

Structure.—Paramecium is broadly spindle-shaped in outline, with a blunter anterior end, and slightly flattened ventrally. It is a holotrichous ciliate. Its body appears to be slightly twisted in the anterior region on account of the position of a groove. This depression runs from the left anterior side of the body, backwards and under the ventral surface. It deepens towards the middle of the body, and at about that level dips more steeply, so forming a circular funnel which is bounded at its inner end by the endoplasm. The depression is the **peristome** or **vestibule** and leads into the **"gullet,"** which opens into the endoplasm by the so-called mouth. Such names as "gullet," "œsophagus," etc., as applied to the Protozoa are inappropriate, as such structures do not compare morphologically with the parts of the higher animals originally called by those names.

Two layers of protoplasm are discernible under higher magnification.

1. **Ectoplasm.**—This, the outer layer, has a tough pellicle which is firm enough to retain the shape of the cell, but yet slightly elastic, so allowing of transient indentation. The pellicle is sculptured into rectangular depressions, but these may become hexagonal owing to the twist in the body. In the centre of each depression is a hole through which two cilia project. Upon the ridges which separate the depressions are groups of openings.

Below the pellicle is a thick layer of **cortical ectoplasm.** Embedded here at right angles to the body surface are many short spindles of denser protoplasm known as **trichocysts.** These structures react to violent stimuli—*e.g.*, tannic acid—and at such times elongate, forming long threads which shoot through the openings on the pellicle's ridges. Their exact function is still obscure, but it has been suggested that they are for defensive and offensive purposes, or are, according to more recent work, for attachment.

The cilia originate in the ectoplasm from basal les. They have axial threads surrounded by layers of protoplasm which are continuous with the pellicle. Two characteristic **contractile vacuoles** are situated in the dorsal ectoplasm, one towards each end of the organism.

2. **Endoplasm.**—This inner layer of protoplasm is a homogeneous granular mass. The following structures are present in the endoplasm:

(*a*) **Food vacuoles** in various stages of digestion.

(*b*) **Nuclei.**—There are two nuclei present—a large macronucleus, and a much smaller micronucleus in a depression in one side of the former.

Locomotion is effected by the action of the cilia, which are arranged in parallel rows. The rows follow the slight spiral twist of the anterior of the body. Undulations pass in a diagonal direction as the ciliary rows bend down one after the other. The effect is similar to that produced by gentle gusts of wind rippling a field of corn. The beat of the cilia can be reversed, driving the animal backwards. Owing to the twist of the body and of the rows of cilia the animal's path is in the form of an elongated spiral, and at the same time its body rotates upon its own longitudinal axis.

Nutrition.—Bacteria form the major part of the food of Paramecium. The cilia of the peristomal region set up a current which draws the bacteria towards the deeper posterior part of the depression. Upon the roof of the gullet the cilia have fused to form an undulating membrane. The action of this membrane drives the water, with contained bacteria, down the gullet, at the base of which pressure is set up. The bacteria are thus concentrated at the base of the gullet, where the pressure causes the endoplasm to bulge inwards. This bulge—containing water and many bacteria—is nipped off by constriction of the endoplasm, and so a food vacuole is formed.

The food vacuoles travel through the endoplasm in a definite direction—carried, in fact, by the definite streaming of the protoplasm (**cyclosis**). During the passage of the food through the endoplasm digestive fluids change the food, and the necessary materials are absorbed in solution. Any waste matter left is thrown out by the temporary anus, which opens into the gullet, whose current is temporarily reversed.

Excretion and Respiration.—The inward diffusion of dissolved oxygen and the outward diffusion of carbon dioxide and nitrogenous waste take place directly through the ectoplasm.

Osmo-regulation.—There are two contractile vacuoles in the endoplasm, towards the dorsal side of the animal, one being situated at each end. From each vacuole six to ten formative canals radiate. These canals initiate new vacuoles when the full ones have collapsed, discharging their waste solutions through a pore in the pellicle. The vacuoles fill up and collapse in a rhythmic manner, the rhythm of the two vacuoles alternating.

Reproduction.—Normally Paramecium divides by **asexual** binary fission. The macronucleus splits amitotically, whilst the micronucleus divides by mitosis. A groove appears in a transverse plane at the middle of the body. By the deepening of this groove the body splits into two, the anterior portion regenerating a posterior, and the posterior an anterior piece. Each daughter cell then grows to its maximum size and again divides. This takes place within a few hours in a well-fed culture.

Conjugation also occurs at certain times. This

usually follows rapid division and the falling off of good conditions, when a period of depression seems to set in. The **conjugants**—*i.e.*, individuals taking part in conjugation—are smaller than the normal individuals. Two conjugants come together side by side with their ventral surfaces together. Degeneration of pellicle and ectoplasm at the point of contact puts the two endoplasmic masses into contact with one another. The macronucleus takes no part what-

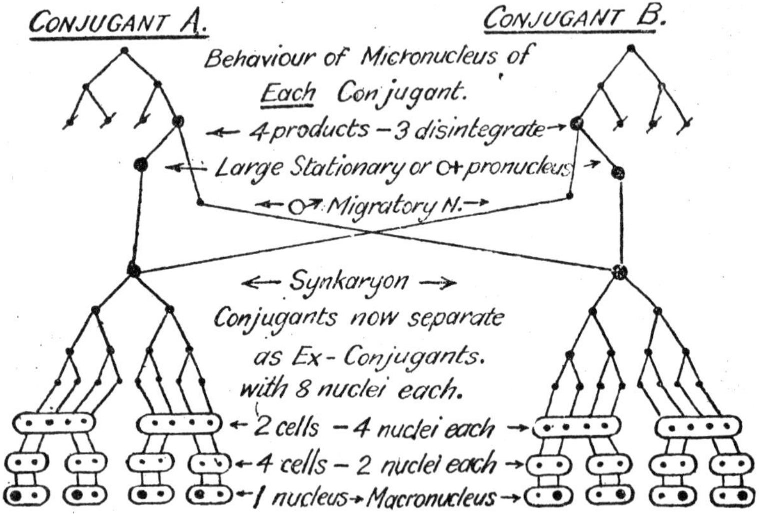

FIG. 8.—DIAGRAM TO ILLUSTRATE CONJUGATION IN *Paramecium caudatum*.

soever in conjugation, but gradually disintegrates and so can be disregarded. The behaviour of the micronucleus is important, and can be studied in detail elsewhere. The diagram (Fig. 8) summarizes the changes during conjugation.

It will be noticed that only one product of the division of the original micronucleus survives, and that it divides unequally. The smaller **migratory nucleus** passes across to, and fuses with, the **stationary**

nucleus of the opposite conjugant. Rapid division of the **synkaryon** of each exconjugant gives eight nuclei. This is followed by two quick divisions of each exconjugant, giving rise to four small cells each with two nuclei. In each case one of these nuclei per cell enlarges and becomes the future macronucleus. Thus from two conjugants eight cells are produced, which possess renewed vitality.

Vorticella.

Habitat and Structure.—There are a number of other ciliates besides Paramecium which occur frequently in fresh-water ponds. *Vorticella* may be taken as an example of another type of ciliate. During most of its life this organism is attached by means of a stalk, hence cilia are not needed for locomotory purposes, but are aids to nutrition. Thus the cilia are confined to the peristomal region, and the organism is said to be a **peritrichous** ciliate.

The body of Vorticella is bell-shaped, with the "handle" prolonged downwards as a stalk. The mouth of the bell points upwards, and in the protozoon is occupied by a disc. A little way inwards from the lip of the disc is a groove, which gradually deepens as it almost completes a circumference. The deeper end of the groove is continued downwards as the "gullet." Cilia line the peristome's inner wall, protruding freely into the water, whilst the "gullet" has an undulating membrane.

A pellicle, ectoplasm, and endoplasm can be discerned. The inner region of the ectoplasm shows a number of striations running in a longitudinal direction. These are **myonemes,** and they collect at the top of the stalk, down which they pass as a very open spiral of contractile elements. It is the contraction of this **contractile fibre** which causes the sudden retraction of the animal—a movement characteristic of Vorticella. Coinciding with the contraction of the stalk the oral disc region is retracted by the use of special myonemes.

The macronucleus is crescentic in outline, and lies with its greatest dimension parallel with the long axis of the body. The micronucleus is small, and lies towards the posterior of, and close to, the macronucleus.

Within the endoplasm is also a contractile vacuole, which communicates with the vestibule region by means of a permanent opening into a reservoir.

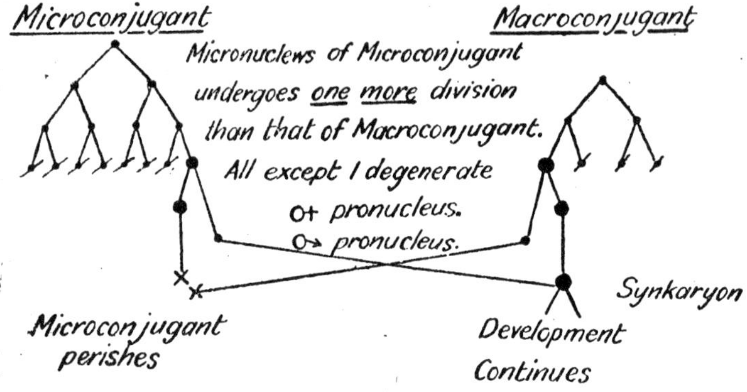

FIG. 9.—DIAGRAM TO ILLUSTRATE CONJUGATION IN VORTICELLA.

Pulsation of the contractile vacuole is rapid, driving the fluid into the reservoir, which in its turn voids the material by means of slow contraction.

Reproduction.—The reproductive processes in Vorticella make an interesting comparison with those in Paramecium.

Binary **longitudinal fission** takes place, thus giving two individuals upon the one stalk, one of which remains there. The other develops a circlet of aboral cilia by which it swims. After a while it settles down and produces a stalk for itself. Thus two daughter cells are produced which are equal in bulk.

By repeated binary fission, or by budding, there are produced smaller individuals which are conjugants resembling a normal product in all respects but size. Conjugation takes place in essentially the same way as in Paramecium, a small conjugant (**microconjugant**) conjugating with a normal-sized individual (**macroconjugant**). The difference, however, lies in the fact that one exconjugant (microconjugant) does not continue as a separate individual but is absorbed by the macroconjugant. Diagram 9 should be compared with that for Paramecium.

In addition to free living forms, there are a number of ciliates which are parasites in the alimentary canals of many animals.

Class IV.: SPOROZOA

The Sporozoa is a group of parasitic Protozoa. The organization of the individuals of the class is extremely simple. Each member of this group forms **spores** at some period of its life-history. However, their life-histories are usually very complex, especially as many of them can only complete their full life-cycle by commencing life in one host and continuing it in an organism of a different group from the first host. The food is always absorbed in solution by the whole of the body wall.

The class must be regarded as a heterogeneous assemblage of members of the other protozoan groups, which, owing to their evolving as parasites, have developed many similar characters. Owing to their parasitic habit members of this class are extremely important, as they cause diseases in organisms useful to man, and in man himself.

Two examples of the class Sporozoa will be dealt with here: *Monocystis*, as this is very easily obtained; and *Plasmodium*, the cause of malaria in human subjects.

Monocystis.

If a freshly killed earth-worm (by chloroform) be opened along the dorsal side of the anterior of the body, a clump of cream-coloured organs will be exposed. These organs are known as the **seminal vesicles,** and contain the male reproductive cells. Monocystis is a parasite within the seminal vesicles of the earth-worm, so that a microscope slide smear of seminal fluid should show whether the worm is infected or not. The parasites may be present in one or more of the stages outlined in the life-history below.

Two species of the genus Monocystis are found in the earth-worm:

1. *M. agilis,* a small form occurring as a free parasite in the seminal fluid.
2. *M. magna,* a larger form, which, unlike the other, is quite visible to the naked eye as a very small white thread adhering to the opening of the vesicles (*i.e.*, the vasa deferentia).

Life-History.—It is convenient to start the life-cycle of the organism with what is termed the **trophozoite** stage—*i.e.*, the feeding and growing individual. In such an organism there is clear, firm **ectoplasm,** bounded by a thin cuticle, and containing towards its inner margin a network of contractile fibres or myonemes. By means of these muscle fibrillæ the organism exhibits "euglenoid movement." The **endoplasm** is finely granular, and contains paramylum granules, whilst a large nucleus is situated within this central mass. To one end of the trophozoite of *M. magna* is a small knob or **epimerite,** by means of which the organism adheres to the wall of the vesicle.

At maturity two individual trophozoites come together and secrete a common cyst around themselves.

Within this common cyst further development takes place. The nucleus of each cell by repeated division gives rise to many nuclei, which arrange themselves on the periphery of the protoplasm. Each secondary nucleus then becomes surrounded by, and is cut off in, a small amount of protoplasm. Thus from each of the individuals in the common cyst a number of **gametes** are formed. The gametes fuse in pairs, one of each pair being derived from opposite parents which came together to form the common cyst.

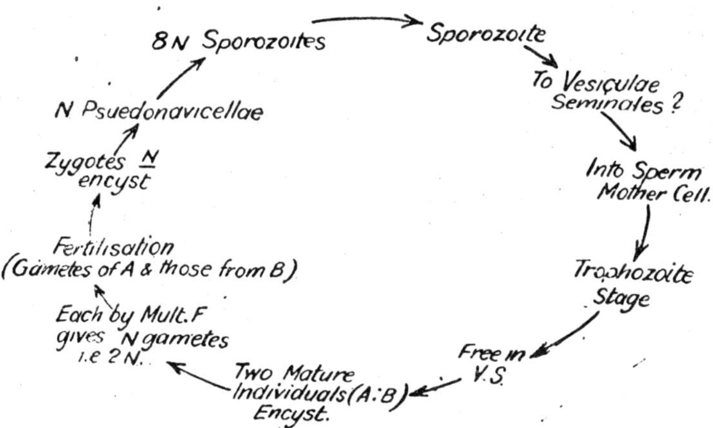

FIG. 10.—DIAGRAM TO ILLUSTRATE LIFE-CYCLE OF MONOCYSTIS.

The fusion of two gametes gives rise to a **zygote,** which is variously called a **sporont** or a **spore**. Each zygote encysts in a small case of its own, and gives rise to the form called a **pseudonavicella.** Within this small cyst the protoplasm divides, and gives rise to eight sickle-shaped **sporozoites,** each with a central nucleus. Hence there can be found large cysts containing many pseudonavicellæ, each of which has eight sporozoites

New worms are infected by the sporozoites, which attack the sperm clumps. Here they live within the sperm mother cell, growing at the expense of the developing sperms. Thus trophozoites of Monocystis are often found clothed with the sperm tails—all that remains of spermatozoa—so giving the parasite a ciliated appearance.

The actual method whereby the sporozoites are transferred from one worm to another cannot be definitely stated. It may be by one or more of the following methods: during coition; in the cocoon with the worm's eggs; or by the medium of worm-eating birds, through which the sporozoites pass unharmed.

Malaria.

The dread malarial fever was up to the beginning of this century one of the worst scourges of the tropics. Now, thanks to the pioneer work of such men as Sir Ronald Ross, Laveran, Grassi, and others, its violence has been considerably reduced.

The life-histories of three species of malarial parasites have been fully worked out. As they are similar in their essentials, a general idea of their life-cycle can be gained from the following summary. The generic name of the parasite has varied from time to time—*Plasmodium, Laverania, Hæmamœba.* The last name is now usually applied to the family to which the parasite belongs, whilst *Plasmodium* is now recognized as the generic name of that member of the family *Hæmamœba* which causes malarial fever in man.

There are three recognized forms of the malarial disease, so named according to the period which elapses between the recurrent attacks of fever. Each of these kinds is caused by a separate species of Plasmodium:

1. **Tertian malaria,** caused by *Plasmodium vivax,* the fever recurring every forty-eight hours.
2. **Quartan fever,** the period between the fever

attacks being seventy-two hours, and the parasite *P. malariæ*.

3. **Tropical fever or pernicious malaria,** wherein the fever occurs at irregular intervals. It is caused by *P. falciparum*.

The life-cycle of the malarial parasite may be divided into two sections. The first part is spent in the blood of man, whilst the cycle is completed in one of the mosquitoes—*e.g.*, genus *Anopheles*.

A. **The Cycle in Man.**—The progress of the parasite has been divided into convenient stages:

1. SPOROZOITE.—When the human subject is bitten by a malaria-carrying mosquito, sporozoites are injected into the blood stream along with the saliva from the insect. Each sporozoite is a narrow spindle-shaped body with a central nucleus. The human subject develops no symptoms for ten days. All sporozoites are found to have disappeared from the blood stream after about half an hour from the time of infection. They have reached the liver, where they invade the cells there and undergo rapid division —**Schizogony**—so that each sporozoite produces about one thousand small cells or **merozoites.** This cycle is the pre-erythrocytic phase—*i.e.*, before invading the red blood corpuscles (erythrocytes). During this phase the parasites are immune to quinine, mepacrine or any natural immunity of the host. This multiplication phase may continue in the liver whilst merozoites are being released in the blood.

2. TROPHOZOITE.—Each merozoite attacks a red blood corpuscle, in which it becomes amœboid, growing at the expense of the corpuscle. This growing amœboid stage is termed the **trophozoite** phase. Each trophozoite often accumulates fluid within its body, giving rise to the well-known signet-ring shape.

The full-grown trophozoite next becomes a **schizont**

—*i.e.*, a cell which reproduces by **schizogony** or splitting. Each schizont splits in several (eight to twelve) small nucleated masses known as merozoites, which burst the blood corpuscle and lie free in the blood stream. During the trophozoite stage granules of waste material—**melanin**—collect in the cell, and at schizogony they are left in the blood stream. It is the action of this melanin upon the body of the host which causes the fever.

3. MEROZOITES AND REPEATED SCHIZOGONY.—Each merozoite attacks a fresh blood corpuscle, becomes a trophozoite and then a schizont, so producing more merozoites. This process of schizogony recurs indefinitely. Every time the schizonts split the toxic melanin is set free, causing the fever, which recurs at intervals corresponding with the time taken for the completion of the schizogony cycle.

4. GAMONTS.—Eventually, however, certain of the merozoites which enter fresh blood corpuscles behave differently from those which form schizonts. At the end of their trophic phase they do not divide, but become free from the corpuscles and float in the blood stream. These individuals are known as **gamonts** or **gametocytes**—*i.e.*, cells which will eventually produce gametes. Two distinct types of gamonts can be discerned:

1. **Female Gamonts or Macrogametocytes.**—These cells are the larger of the gamonts, with the nucleus placed towards one side, and near to the surface of the protoplasm. The cytoplasm is laden with reserve food material.
2. **Male Gamonts or Microgametocytes.**—In these cells, which are rather smaller, the large nucleus is centrally placed.

The further development of the gamonts does not

take place within the human body. The formation of gametes from mature gamonts can be demonstrated if a small quantity of blood in which they are living is allowed to cool upon a glass slide. This development takes place normally within the mosquito—*i.e.*, a **cold-blooded** animal. Hence the reason for the gamete formation under artificial conditions.

B. **The Cycle in the Mosquito.**—When a mosquito draws in the blood of a malaria patient, included in the meal are gamonts, trophozoites, and/or merozoites. If the mosquito is one of the *Culex* types, then all material drawn into its stomach is digested. If, however, the insect is an Anopheles mosquito, then the reduction of temperature stimulates the gamonts, whilst all other stages of the parasites are digested along with the blood corpuscles.

5. MATURATION OF GAMETES: (1) *Macrogametocyte.* —The nucleus here divides into two, one half being extruded. The macrogametocyte by this process becomes a mature **macrogamete** or female **cell.**

(2) *Microgametocyte.*—Fission of the nucleus of the microgametocyte gives rise usually to six smaller elongated masses of chromatin. The cytoplasm at the periphery of the sphere elongates into a number of threads (equal in number to the nuclei already formed). Each nucleus passes into a protoplasmic thread. These threads by lashing violently tear away from the central mass of residual protoplasm. Each nucleated thread of protoplasm is a **microgamete.**

6. FERTILIZATION.—When a microgamete approaches a macrogamete the latter attracts the former, which dashes violently into the macrogamete. The complete fusion of the cytoplasm and nuclei takes place, so giving rise to a zygote. The zygote of this parasite, unlike the majority of other zygotes,

is active. Such an active fertilized cell is known as an **oökinete,** or motile zygote.

7. Development of Zygote (an Oökinete).—The zygote burrows through the stomach wall of the mosquito and comes to rest just under the outer membrane covering the stomach. Here it encysts and the cytoplasm and nucleus undergo fission, giving rise to a number of nucleated masses (**sporoblasts**). Each sporoblast by multiple fission results in spindle-shaped **sporozoites,** of which there are enormous numbers. Masses of residual protoplasm remain.

The delicate cyst enclosing the mass of sporozoites ruptures, setting them free. They eventually reach the salivary glands by way of the blood stream. These sporozoites are then injected into a human being when an infected mosquito bites. Thus the life-cycle of the parasite is completed.

Many textbooks contain a detailed account of the malaria parasite, etc. The essentials, however, are presented here. It is often very convenient to be able to summarize such a life-cycle in the form of a diagram. The student will find that the method used in this book—namely, **written** diagrams—can be used more readily than a pictorial diagram in order to give a basis of a life-history. This cycle for the malarial parasite may be summarized as shown in Fig. 11.

In order to be able to deal adequately with a disease which is transmitted from one principal host to another by means of an intermediate host, it is, of course, necessary to know certain facts about the latter. One of the most important is a knowledge of the life-history of the carrier and the weak links in it, so that a successful attack may be made upon the parasite before reaching the principal host.

Thus an outline of the life-history of the mosquito

gives the necessary data upon which the methods of attacking the disease are made. (Compare with tsetse fly and sleeping sickness.)

The mosquito spends the younger stages of its life in ponds and any small collections of sluggish or stagnant water. A favourite place is the rain-water

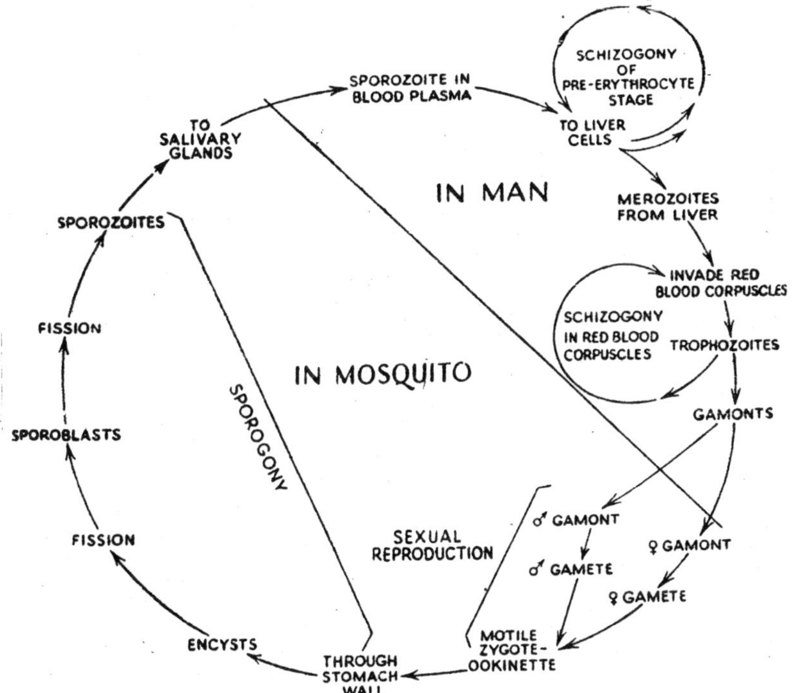

FIG. 11.—DIAGRAM TO ILLUSTRATE THE LIFE-CYCLE OF PLASMODIUM.

butt so common in front of the English cottage. The malarial parasite is transmitted by the **female** *Anopheles* mosquito only, the male being a vegetarian.

The life-history of a mosquito may be summarized as follows:

1. *Eggs.*—Between 200 and 300 eggs are laid by the

female, and massed together to form a saucer-shaped raft. The eggs are firmly glued together with their long axes at right angles to the surface of the raft. A lid is provided at the base of each egg, so that the young larva enters directly into the water.

2. *Larva*.—The larva has a well-developed head provided with a pair of eyes, a pair of short antennæ, and three pairs of bristle-covered jaws. The thorax is composed of three broad segments, while there are ten abdominal segments. From the eighth abdominal segment there projects a short tube closed at the outer end by five movable flaps. The larva uses free air for respiration, and not dissolved oxygen from the water. In order to obtain the air the larva wriggles towards the surface of the water, pushes the respiratory siphon through the surface film, and opens the protecting flaps. It remains in this position, suspended by the surface tension of the water film, whilst air is drawn into its respiratory system. Then, on closing the flaps, the larva swims about for a period before replenishing its air supply. As the larva grows it casts its skin. Eventually the larval stage is replaced by the pupal period.

3. *Pupa and Imago*.—This period is one of change, the larval organization breaking down and being rebuilt into the adult systems. No feeding takes place, although the pupa is active. The larval respiratory siphon is replaced by a pair of respiratory trumpets situated upon the anterior dorsal side of the thorax. A fringe of fine bristles prevents the water from entering the respiratory trumpets when the pupa is submerged. After a few days of pupal life the adult or **imago** stage emerges from a split on the dorsal side of the pupal skin. The mosquito uses the skin as a raft until, its wings becoming hardened, it flies away to complete its life-cycle.

There are several characteristics by which the

Anopheles mosquito can be distinguished from the *Culex* genus. The male mosquitoes can be distinguished by their plumed and bushy antennæ

1. Imago

Anopheles.	*Culex.*
At rest the body is carried at an angle of 45 degrees with the surface on which insect stands. Posterior region further away. No abdominal scales.	*At rest* the body is held parallel with the surface. Scales on abdomen. Maxillary palps shorter than proboscis.

2. Ova

Egg raft rather loosely made. Eggs tend to separate.	Egg raft more circular than that of *Anopheles* and firmly made.

3. Larva

During intake of air the body of the larva lies parallel with the surface film of water.	The larva hangs head downwards whilst exchanging oxygen and carbon dioxide.

4. Pupa

Slightly larger pupa. Short "trumpets." Strongly curved abdomen.	Longer respiratory trumpets. Abdomen slightly flexed, but practically at right angles with surface of water.

Methods of attacking Malaria.—Obviously, prevention here is better than attempts to cure the disease. Thus the main line of attack is directed towards the parasite before it reaches man. It will be seen that a reduction in the number of mosquitoes will have a corresponding check upon the spread of malaria. The mosquitoes are destroyed in various ways, amongst which the following methods are more important:

1. Drainage.—Areas of stagnant water and swamps can be drained in many cases, thus reducing the number of breeding-places for the mosquito. Sluggish drainage, ditches, dykes, etc., can be periodically cleaned of the aquatic vegetation. Hence, the conse-

quent speeding up of the water flow will result in the removal of the eggs, larvæ, and pupæ towards rivers and seas, where they perish.

2. Use of Oil.—In many cases it is impossible or inconvenient to drain swamps and lakes. The pouring of oil upon these stagnant waters gives satisfactory results in such cases. Paraffin oil is sprayed upon the water, and so a thin oil film forms at the surface. The strength of the surface tension in the case of water is sufficient to bear the weight of the larva of the mosquito; that of the oil, however, is too weak. The larvæ swim to the surface and push their respiratory siphons through towards the air. Under normal conditions they are supported in this position by the surface tension, and with no muscular effort on their part. When oil forms the upper surface the mosquito larva, after reaching the air with the end of its siphon, ceases its muscular activity, but the surface film of oil being too weak to support its weight, the larva descends involuntarily. Thus the position of the larva can only be maintained by continuous muscular action, which soon exhausts the animal. When the larva descends normally, the terminal flaps close over the aperture of the siphon. The unexpected involuntary descent in oil-covered water does not allow of time to shut the siphon, so that oil trickles in and eventually blocks up the siphon. Thus combined exhaustion and suffocation due to the blocking up of the siphon cause the death of the larva. The oil acts in a similar manner

upon pupal stages, quickly blocking up the respiratory trumpets.

3. Small Ponds, Tanks, etc.—In the case of water-butts, cisterns, and other tanks of fresh water, covering them prevents the female mosquito from depositing any eggs. Fishes, which are particularly fond of the larvæ and pupæ, are used in ornamental fountains in many places.
4. Nets.—In places where, owing to prevailing conditions, the above methods are not practicable, mosquito netting and clothing are used to keep the insects from the human body.

CONCLUSION TO PROTOZOA

From this brief survey of some of the types of Protozoa certain extremely important points emerge.

1. **Nature of Cell Organization.**—The Protozoa are usually referred to as "unicellular" organisms. A cell, according to the original definition of Schwann, is "a mass of protoplasm containing a nucleus," which controls the activities of that protoplasm. The higher animals are made up of large numbers of such cells. A protozoon is therefore equivalent in structure—*i.e.*, **morphologically**—to one cell of a multicellular organism.

When, however, the **work** of a single cell from a multicellular organism is considered the problem becomes more complex. Each unit of a multicellular organism performs one kind of work for which it has been specialized. Hence, a nerve cell, a muscle cell, a bone-forming cell, a kidney cell, and a liver cell, cannot change their particular work and function as another type of specialized cell. On examining a protozoön from the standpoint of work performed it is clear that it is capable of divers kinds of action. The **one** nucleated mass respires, ingests, moves, excretes, and reproduces **for itself alone** in most cases. It may have an intricate life-history as in some many-celled organisms. This suggests that a protozoan organism must be regarded as equivalent **physiologically**—*i.e.*, in work performed—to a whole multicellular organism.

Cells were first seen and described as parts of a many-celled organism—*i.e.*, a cell is to be regarded as a **part** of, and **not** as a **whole,** organism. Although a protozoön may be said to be a cell morphologically, it cannot be regarded as part of an organism, but is, of course, a whole individual in itself. Furthermore, a **potential whole organism** such as a zygote is also a cell morphologically. Thus the term **cell** can be applied to three types of organization:

(*a*) A **part** of an **organism**—*i.e.*, a cell in its original sense;
(*b*) A **potential whole organism**—*e.g.*, a zygote; and
(*c*) A **physiologically whole individual**—*i.e.*, a protozoön performing many functions.

To avoid this confusion the following two terms have been suggested and are used by many biologists:

1. A **cellular organism** is one in which the body material is divided into many small unit portions. Each portion is nucleated and has a particular function to perform—*e.g.*, man, frog, worm.
2. A **non-cellular** organism has its body substance undivided; one nucleus (or sometimes nuclei) controls the activities of such an organism.

Thus the Protozoa may be regarded as **non-cellular,** rather than as unicellular, animals.

2. **Specialization.**—In certain protozoan types numbers of individuals live together, so that such a colony

must be regarded as the individual. Thus a step towards cellular organization seems to be made. The majority of the individuals are still of a plastic nature, and keep their own identity. The functions of the colony, however, are being divided up. Hence in such forms as Volvox certain individuals specialize and reproduce for the whole colony. This specialization is carried still further and separate types of reproductive individuals arise, males and females. Each type is modified to subserve its particular function. Thus in the Protozoa can be traced the initiation and development of syngamy and sex.

3. The importance of the Protozoa to man is clear, as they are the causes, directly or indirectly, of many of his diseases and economical reverses.

CHAPTER IV

METAZOA

THE examples of Protozoa already studied have dealt with single individuals whose construction is the same as that of one unit cell of a multicellular (or cellular) organism. The products of protozoan fission usually separate and become new entities, each product retaining its plasticity through not specializing.

All other members of the animal kingdom above the Protozoa are grouped together as the **Metazoa.** They begin life as a single cell, a zygote, but the products of the fission of this cell do not separate. Repeated fission thus gives a large mass of cells, which is the body of the Metazoön. There is a definite limit to this continued fission, which gives an average maximum size, specific for each Metazoön. With this increase in size there is, of course, the need of dividing up the various life activities. Hence organs and systems are established so that the result of the efforts of one particular group of cells is at the disposal of other cell groups. Thus are the various vital activities divided out, each activity being performed more efficiently by very specialized cells.

Such a large mass of cells requires support, which is supplied by **skeleton-**forming cells. The actual product of these cells varies in the different animal groups. The outer layer of cells becomes protective, so that exchange of gases through the body wall is difficult. The proportion of free surface area to body volume is adversely affected and, so **respiratory** and **excretory** systems appear. Food is ingested in a special region, and many complicated organs arise in order to deal adequately with the food. All of these structures are connected with a special food tube or **alimentary canal,** which is usually open at both ends. As the alimentary tract is not able to take the food direct to every part of the body, the essentials of such food are conveyed to the tissues by a **circulatory system.** So, eventually, there is built up a body composed of numerous systems, all dependent upon, and linked up with, one another, the **nervous system** co-ordinating them.

The cells of the various body systems have lost their plasticity through specialization. Hence such cells do not possess the power to reproduce the whole individual organism and they die after a certain period of life. However, the reproduction of the individual is provided for very early in development as certain cells which do not specialize are set aside and are therefore plastic. These cells grow and multiply by fission, the products remaining together as a **gonad.** All other cells which have developed from the zygote, other than those of the gonad, are collectively known as the **soma.**

There is a large range of organization shown in the

bodies of the Metazoa. In the lower and more simple types the body is made up of two layers of tissues. Such types are said to be **diploblastic.** These two layers are:

1. **Ectoderm,** a protective layer, and one from which the nervous tissues develop.
2. **Endoderm,** essentially the **lining** of the food tube.

Other Metazoa, however, have a third layer of tissue intercalated between the ectoderm and endoderm. This layer is the **mesoderm,** and animals possessing it are of the **triploblastic** type. In the mesoderm all skeletonic and muscular structures originate.

During the development of a triploblastic metazoön a split occurs in the mesodermic mass, giving an inner and an outer mesodermic layer. The split gives rise to the space known as the **cœlom.** Whilst the inner layer of mesoderm applies itself to the endoderm and forms the muscles of the alimentary canal, the outer mesodermic layer fuses to the ectoderm and forms the muscles and skeleton of the body wall. There are thus two main spaces in the body of a triploblastic cœlomate:

1. **Cœlom,** the result of a split in the mesoderm, and in this space is suspended the alimentary tube and its accessory organs, muscles, etc.
2. The **enteron** or cavity of the alimentary canal. There may or may not be a posterior opening.

Phylum: Cœlenterata.

One of the lower groups of the Metazoa is that known as the **Cœlenterata.** The members of this phylum have three diagnostic characters:

1. Two-layered body wall (*i.e.*, diploblastic).
2. **Cœlenteron.** This is the only cavity in the body and is that of the food tube. The name cœlenteron was given as it was supposed that this space combined the properties of both cœlom (cœl) and enteron. This, however, is not the case, as a true cœlom is formed by the splitting of the mesoderm, which is not present in these organisms.
3. Possession of **cnidoblasts** or stinging cells.

The majority of the Cœlenterates occur in the seas, either as fixed or floating forms. The phylum is divided into three main classes:

1. **Hydrozoa.**—Hydra and many small colonial forms—*e.g.*, Obelia.
2. **Scyphozoa.**—Large jelly-fishes—*e.g.*, Aurelia.
3. **Anthozoa.**—Sea anemones and true Corals.

Class I. : HYDROZOA (HYDROMEDUSÆ)

The members of this class are, with one exception, marine. The life-cycle can be divided into two generations in the more typical members: a fixed asexual form, the **hydroid,** and a free-swimming sexual **medusoid** form. The surface of the enteron in both forms is smooth and has **no gastric ridges** or **filaments,** which are typical of the other two classes. In the Hydromedusæ the hydroid generation is more emphasized than the medusoid individuals.

One genus of this class is the " Fresh-water Polyp," *Hydra* (Fig. 12). It is important at the outset to realize that Hydra differs from the other members of its class in several essential features. In *Hydra* there is no medusoid generation, the members are solitary and do not form colonies, as do most other hydroid forms of the Hydromedusæ. These differences are traceable to the fact that *Hydra* is a freshwater form, and thus has many difficulties with which

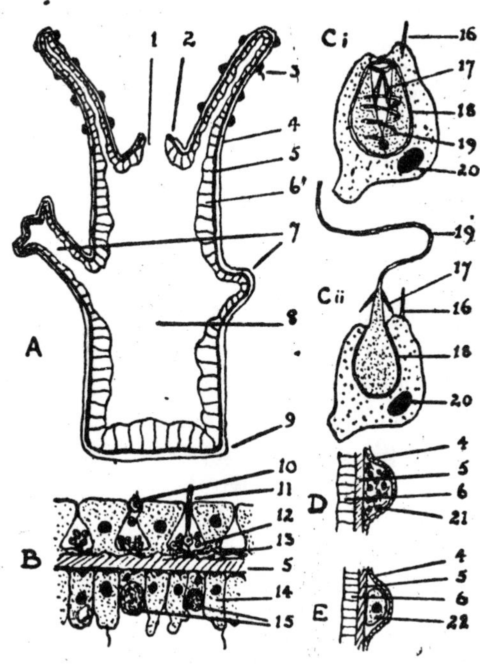

FIG. 12.—HYDRA.

A, Diagram of vertical section; B, L.S. body wall; C, cnidoblast: (i) at rest, (ii) discharged; D, testis; E, ovary.

1, Mouth; 2, hypostome; 3, cnidoblast battery; 4, ectoderm; 5, mesoglœa; 6, endoderm; 7, bud development; 8, enteron; 9, "foot"; 10, cnidoblast; 11, nerve and sense cell; 12, interstitial cells; 13, contractile fibres of epithelial cell; 14, amœboid and flagellate endodermal cells; 15, "goblet" gland cells; 16, cnidocil; 17, barbs; 18, nematocyst wall; 19, thread; 20, nucleus; 21, male gametes; 22, ovum.

to contend—drought, frost, swift seaward currents, etc. The study of Hydra, however, gives a general idea of the structure and principles upon which other hydroid forms are built.

Hydra.

Habitat and Structure.—*Hydra* is quite commonly found in fresh-water ponds and ditches. It varies in size owing to its great power of contraction and expansion. Thus it is about the size of a pin's head in the retracted state; ¼ inch and thread-like when expanded.

Its structure is extremely simple. The body shape is that of a hollow cylinder to which there is only one opening in the centre of one end. The complete end is the **basal disc** or "**foot,**" by which the animal attaches itself. At the opposite end is the **mouth**—a small aperture situated upon a raised cone—the **hypostome.** Arising from the base of the hypostome are a number of hollow **tentacles** (six to eight). The spaces of the tentacles are in direct communication with the single body cavity—the **enteron.** The body wall is composed of two layers of cells—**ectoderm** and **endoderm,** with a cell-less jelly layer, the **mesoglœa,** in between them.

1. Ectoderm.—This outer layer consists of several kinds of cells:

(*a*) *Epithelial Cells* (*Myo-epithelial or Musculo-epithelial Cells*).—The two last names, however, cannot strictly be used, as they tend to confuse the student with muscular structures, which are, of course, mesodermal in origin. The epithelial cells are conical in outline, with the base to the outside of the animal. Their narrower ends are prolonged into **contractile fibres,** which lie parallel with the longitudinal axis of the body.

(*b*) *Interstitial Cells.*—In the spaces between the apices of the epithelial cells are numerous small spherical cells known as interstitial cells. They are undifferentiated, and form a reserve of material from which cells can specialize in order to replace worn or damaged tissue. They also give rise to the gametes.

(*c*) *Cnidoblasts, nematoblasts* or stinging cells are found scattered among the epithelial cells. They arise from interstitial cells which migrate into the enteron and so pass to the endoderm cells in the upper part of the body. They then pass through to the ectoderm of the tentacles where development is completed. There are several types of cnidoblasts, but all are essentially similar in general structure. They are of an offensive and defensive nature and are often in groups, this being so in the tentacles in particular.

Each cnidoblast is a pear-shaped cell, the narrower end of which is level with the outer ectodermal surface. Within this cell is a pear-shaped sac—the **nematocyst** whose outer end is closed by an operculum. In some types of cnidoblasts barbs are present on the neck of the nematocyst.

(*d*) *Sense and Nerve cells* of a very primitive nature are found in the ectoderm. The nerve cells form a basal network, receive stimuli from sensory cells, and pass on an "order" to epithelial cells, etc. So is the reaction to stimulus obtained.

2. ENDODERM.—The endodermal cells line the enteron. They are tall and columnar, and each possesses a large vacuole. The free ends of the cells —*i.e.*, lining the enteron—may develop temporary pseudopodia or flagella. The opposite ends—*i.e.*, the walls nearer to the ectoderm—have their substance drawn out into **contractile fibres**, which, how-

ever, are arranged around the circumference of the cylindrical body. Scattered among these columnar ells are a number of goblet-shaped **gland cells,** which rete digestive enzymes.

Between the ectodermal and endodermal layers ere lies the **mesoglœa.** This is a thin, gelatinous, ructureless layer, and, as it has no definite cell structure, it must not be confused with a true mesoderm.

Locomotion.—The body of *Hydra* possesses the power of great elasticity. Expansion and contraction are the result of the activity of the contractile fibres of both endoderm and ectoderm. Contraction of the ectodermal processes with relaxation of endodermal fibres results in the body becoming shorter and wider. Endodermal contraction and ectodermal relaxation produce an elongated and narrow form.

Hydra searches for food in the immediate vicinity by circling its tentacular region around, with the basal disc as centre. It moves from place to place either by somersaulting or in the manner of a looper caterpillar. It can also glide on its basal disc or swim freely by movements of its tentacles.

Nutrition.—Water fleas and other small creatures form the food of *Hydra.* The food is entrapped by the tentacles and paralysed by the cnidoblasts. The actual mechanism by which the nematocyst thread is everted may be complicated. One explanation is that the stimulation of the **cnidocil** causes the cnidoblast to contract, so increasing pressure on the fluid-filled nematocyst. This increased pressure causes the explosive evagination of the thread. As a result of recent research, another explanation has now been given of this action. When the cnidocil or trigger projection is stimulated, contractile elements in the protoplasm of the cnidoblast cause the operculum to open and the contact of the water with the coiled filament within the nematocyst, causes swelling by imbibition and the complete liquefaction of the filament. The extruded liquid spurts out in a fine jet, which immediately solidifies as a stinging thread. As the barbs emerge and separate their points wound the epidermis of the prey and into the wound the thread is thrust. The toxic substance of the thread numbs the prey and the tentacles take it to the mouth and so into the enteron.

The flagella of the endodermal cells lining the enteron set up currents of water which sweep small particles of food into the enteron. Within the enteron digestion takes place in two ways:

1. Part of the food is attacked and dissolved by the gastric enzymes secreted by the goblet-shaped gland cells. The dissolved material is then drawn into the endodermal cells.
2. Small portions of the food can be ingested by the cells with pseudopodia, after the same fashion as ingestion takes place in *Amœba*.

Fæces are driven out through the mouth by a sudden contraction of the body.

Respiration and **excretion** take place from the general body surface.

Reproduction: 1. ASEXUAL.—(*a*) Transverse or longitudinal **fission** occurs.

(*b*) *Budding.*—In the middle region of the body at one point rapid cell multiplication—initiated by interstitial cells—takes place. Hence such a region tends to bulge outwards. This continues and gives rise to a finger-like projection whose lumen is in direct continuation with the enteron. This digitate outgrowth is a **bud.** The free end of the bud develops a circlet of small knobs which give rise to tentacles. A hypostome arises within the tentacular ring, and here the mouth eventually breaks through. Constriction of the basal region of the bud nips off this asexually produced individual from the parent. Sometimes the primary bud is retained for a considerable time and may give rise in turn to a secondary bud. Thus a colonial organization is approached.

2. SEXUAL.—Reproduction by means of sexual gametes occurs in autumn in *H. fusca* (brown *Hydra*); in spring and summer in *H. viridis* (green) and *H. grisea* (white).

These animals are usually hermaphrodite. One ovary only develops on the lower part of the body, while several testes may arise upon the upper region.

(*a*) *Development of Ovum.*—The interstitial cells aggregate in one spot and by growth cause the ectoderm to bulge. One of these interstitial cells enlarges enormously at the expense of the others, which are used as food. The large cell—an **oöcyte**—stores much food material, thus causing the ectoderm to rupture. After maturation the ovum surrounds itself with a gelatinous envelope and is ready for fertilization (Fig. 12, E).

(*b*) *Development of Spermatozoa.*—The initial stages of development—ectodermal swelling and aggregation of cells—resemble those of the ovary. However, each interstitial cell becomes a spermatocyte, giving rise to four tailed sperms (Fig. 12, D). The spermatozoa are freed into the water by the rupture of the ectoderm, and fertilization takes place. The zygote encysts, and in this condition is able to withstand those adverse conditions—drying up or freezing—which kill the adult forms.

As both gonads on the same individual do not ripen together, cross-fertilization is usual.

Related Forms.—The marine forms related to *Hydra* are colonial. Large numbers occur in pools, etc., attached to various objects, in the intertidal zone. One of these types is the genus *Obelia*.

Obelia.

The colonial forms arise as the result of the retention of buds which develop in a manner similar to those of *Hydra*. The point of origin of such new individuals follows a definite plan, which varies in each genus, so a typical colony mosaic arises.

The central stem of the colony consists of a tube whose walls have typical ectoderm and endoderm layers and mesoglœa. At various points buds from this tube give rise to **hydranths** (*Hydra*-like individuals). The hydranths of *Obelia* are arranged alternately upon the central tube. The bases of the upright tubes continue along the surface upon which the colony grows. The tubes of the whole colony are collectively called the **cœnosarc.** The meandering base is known as the **hydrorhiza.** Less numerous than the hydranths, and found chiefly in the proximal parts of the colony, are cylindrical bodies—the **blastostyles.** Each **blastostyle** is really an altered hydranth which specializes in reproducing asexually the medusoid individuals. The ectoderm, endoderm, and mesoglœa are continuous throughout the whole colony.

The ectoderm secretes a hard, horny case. This will, of course, follow the course of the ectoderm. Thus this **perisarc,** as it is called, conforms to the contour of the colony. The perisarc forms cups around the hydranths and blastostyles, such cups being **hydrothecæ** and **gonothecæ** respectively.

(*a*) *Hydroid Individual.*—The hydranth of *Obelia* resembles an individual *Hydra* in essential points. The points of difference between them are:

1. An *Obelia* hydranth has twenty-four tentacles.

2. Each tentacle has a solid core of endoderm.

3. The ectoderm possesses special contractile cells, separate from the ordinary epithelial cells, which, therefore, have no fibres, as those of *Hydra*.

4. The hypostome is enlarged as the **oral cone** and encloses a large space—the oral region of the enteron.

5. The middle of the basal disc has an aperture through which the enteron of each hydranth communicates with the lumen of the cœnosarc.

The buds on the blastostyle resemble those of *Hydra* in the first stages. However, as development proceeds the oral surface is invaginated and approaches the basal or aboral surface. The latter becomes wider and convex upon the outer side. The oral surface thus is concave, with the mouth in the centre. This individual is then freed and passes into the water, where, while swimming freely, it reaches maturity.

(*b*) *Medusoid Individual.*—The body resembles the head of a mushroom, with a mouth in the position of the stalk. Such a structure is an **umbrella.** The convex surface, the **exumbrella,** is uppermost during life. In the centre of the concave **subumbrella** surface is a downward projecting tube—the **manubrium**—at the end of which is the **mouth.** Numerous tentacles fringe the edge of the medusa. A small ledge of tissue—the **velum**—forms an inward projecting shelf at the circumference.

The mouth leads into the manubrial tube, which opens into a **central body cavity** (an enteron). This cavity is small, and from it **four radial canals** (at 90 degrees to each other) pass outwards to the periphery, where a **ring canal** joins their ends together. The central cavity, the four radial canals, and the ring canal are the remains of the enteron of a hydranth type of individual. Excessive growth of the mesoglœa in the four primary quarters of the umbrella has displaced the endoderm-lined enteron, except in the places which remain as the central cavity and its canal system. Elsewhere the endoderm has no cavity between its layers, but is reduced to an endodermal lamella, continuous, of course, with that lining the enteron system. The whole of the outside of the body is covered with ectoderm.

The medusa moves by muscular contraction, which forces the water out from the subumbrella cavity. These muscular contractions are co-ordinated by two special concentrations of nerve cells forming two **nerve rings** at the edge of the umbrella. This is a rudimentary nervous system. Cutting the rings paralyses the medusa.

Balance is maintained by eight **statocysts** situated at the base of the tentacles. Two statocysts are placed in the quarter of circumference bounded by two adjacent radial canals. A statocyst consists of a hollow vesicle lined with hair-like projections. A number of small calcareous bodies—**statoliths**—are enclosed. The rolling of these bodies stimulates the hairy projections, thus setting up impulses to which the medusa responds.

Medusæ are of opposite sexes. The gonads do not develop for some time after the medusa is freed from the blastostyle. Each gonad is placed half-way along a radial canal. At a point over the gonad the radial canal sends down a small endodermal pit. The gametocytes originate in the ectoderm of the manubrium, and migrate—by way of endoderm and radial canals—to the endodermal pits of the canals. Here they pass through to the ectoderm, where they form a knob-like projection. The ova and sperm, when ripe, are shed into the water by rupture of the ectoderm, and fertilization takes place.

The hydranth of *Obelia* is said to be of the **calyptoblastic** type, because it is surrounded by a hydrotheca. Other Hydromedusa hydranths have no hydrothecæ, the perisarc ending at the base of each polyp. These cupless types are known as **gymnoblastic** hydranths.

The medusa of *Obelia* has a rather flattened umbrella, and is called a Leptomedusa. The medusæ of colonies with gymnoblastic hydranths are much more convex aborally, forming a bell-like umbrella, known as Anthomedusæ. Thus among the commoner Hydromedusæ of the intertidal zone two types can be distinguished, characterized by differences in hydroid and medusoid generations:

Order I.: **Gymnoblastica** or **Anthomedusa**—

(*a*) Hydranths without hydrothecæ.
(*b*) Bell-shaped medusæ.
(*c*) Gonads on manubrium of medusæ.

Examples: *Tubularia, Clava, Hydractinia.*

Order II.: **Calyptoblastica** or **Leptomedusa**—

(*a*) Hydranths with hydrothecæ.
(*b*) Saucer-shaped medusæ.
(*c*) Gonads on radial canals of medusæ.

Examples: *Obelia, Campanularia.*

Other members of the Hydromedusæ are *Millepora*, the stone coral; *Physalia*, the Portuguese man-o'-war; and *Porpita.*

Class II.: SCYPHOMEDUSÆ (SCYPHOZOA)

The Scyphozoa also show an alternation of generations between a sexual, free medusa and an asexual fixed hydroid form. The former is the dominant generation in this class, however (*cf.* Hydrozoa). The hydroid individual is very small and solitary and is known as a **Hydratuba** or **Scyphistoma.** This begins with a typical Hydra-like form, and then small slices are cut off from the free ends. Each slice becomes eventually a jelly-fish of very large dimensions.

The enteron of a jelly-fish is lined with endoderm, which gives rise to thin thread-like projections known as **gastric filaments.** The four radii of the manubrium are pulled out to form oral arms. No velum is present. In other essentials these large jelly-fishes resemble the medusæ of *Obelia.* Their size is due mainly to enormous developments of mesoglœa. The ectoderm covers the outside, and the endoderm lines a central digestive cavity and its connected canal system. *Aurelia* is one of the common members of this class.

Class III. : ANTHOZOA

There is no alternation of generations in the life-history of members of this class. They exist only in the hydroid form.

This class includes the sea anemones and corals. The enteron has its surface area increased by groups of **mesenteries** varying in size. The body wall is in-tucked, so forming a tube leading to the centre of the enteron. This tube is the **stomodeum.** Some of the mesenteries join the stomodeum. Tentacles are also present. The stomodeum can be closed, its walls approximating, and so forming a slit. A small round aperture, however, usually remains connecting the enteron to the exterior. This small aperture is the **siphonoglyphe.** The class is divided into two main types:

Sub-class I.: **Alcyonaria.** Characters:

(*a*) Eight mesenteries only.
(*b*) Eight hollow pinnate tentacles.
(*c*) One siphonoglyphe on closure of stomodeum.
(*d*) Muscles on mesenteries, on side facing siphonoglyphe.

Common examples: *Alcyonium,* Dead-men's Fingers; *Tubipora,* the Organ-pipe Coral; *Corallium rubrum,* the Red Coral of commerce; *Gorgonids*, the Sea-fans *Pennatulids*, the Sea-pens.

Sub-class II.: **Zoantharia.** Characters:

(*a*) Tentacles in multiples of six.
(*b*) Mesenteries in pairs and in multiples of six.
(*c*) Two siphonoglyphes.
(*d*) Muscles on inner side of each pair of mesenteries.

Examples: Anemones and Corals.

The corals secrete a hard calcareous skeleton. The skeleton of each hydranth consists of a cylinder, with thin plates of material projecting inwards. The circular layer is laid down in the main body wall, whilst the radiating laminæ arise in the mesenteries.

CHAPTER V

PLATYHELMINTHES

TURBELLARIA—TREMATODA—CESTODA

NEMATHELMINTHES

ASCARIS

UNDER the phylum Vermes, or worms, were formerly included a number of metazoan groups. These groups, however, differ very widely from one another, and the old group Vermes is now divided into a number of more compact and definite phyla.

The more important of the five phyla are:

1. **Platyhelminthes.**
2. **Nemathelminthes.**
3. **Annulata.**

Phylum : PLATYHELMINTHES

This group is also known as the Flat-worms, and consists of soft-bodied, bilaterally symmetrical animals, whose bodies show no segmentation. The main characters of the group are:

1. Triploblastic body—*i.e.*, ectoderm, endoderm, and mesoderm. The body cavity or cœlom is not present, but the spaces between the body wall and the organs are filled with a loose packing of connective tissue, or **parenchyma.**

2. A peculiar excretory system of branched tubules ending in characteristic **flame cells.**

3. The egg usually contains stored food in the form of yolk, and the whole—*i.e.*, fertilized egg and yolk—enclosed in a hard protective shell. The yolk is manufactured in accessory female organs—the **vitelline glands**—whilst the activity of a **shell gland** produces the protective envelope.

The phylum Platyhelminthes is divided into three main classes:

1. **Turbellaria**—free forms.
2. **Trematoda** } parasitic types.
3. **Cestoda** }

Class I. : TURBELLARIA

The members of this class have a ciliated epidermis and lead a free-living existence. A number of them are to be found frequently on the muddy bottoms of fresh-water ponds, etc. They are then known as fresh-water Planarians, the commoner forms being the genera *Planaria* and *Dendrocœlum*.

The body is bilaterally symmetrical, showing a dorsal and ventral surface, right and left sides, a blunt anterior end, and a more pointed posterior extremity. The animal moves in the direction of the long axis of the body. This is effected by the movement of the cilia, producing a typical even gliding motion.

Eye spots are present anteriorly, whilst the mouth opens at about the centre of the ventral surface. The genital opening is situated ventrally near to the posterior end.

The **alimentary** system has only one opening—the **mouth**—there being no anus present. The mouth opens into a muscular **pharynx,** lying posterior to the former. The pharynx, which lies in a sheath, is protrusible. From the pharynx cavity there arises the **intestine,** which is divided into three branches. One branch runs towards the anterior and in the middle line, while the other two branches turn and pass backwards, one on each side of the pharynx. Each branch sends off smaller tubules, which ramify in the body tissue. All branches end blindly.

A typical **excretory system** of flame cells is present (see next type).

The **nervous system** consists of an anterior concentration of nervous tissue, two lateral cords, and finer branches.

The **reproductive system** is important. The animal is **hermaphrodite.** A comparison of the reproductive organs of Turbellaria, Trematoda, and Cestoda should be made. Points marked with an asterisk should be compared in the three groups.

1. *Male System.*—(*a*) **Testes,** numerous small, rounded bodies lying along each side of the body. Each testis has a small duct.

(*b*) All the ducts join a **vas deferens.** There is a right and left vas deferens (plural, vasa deferentia). The vasa deferentia unite in the posterior region of the body.* From this point a common median duct enlarges to form a muscular, protrusible **penis.** A slight enlargement of the median duct gives a storage place for sperms—the **vesicula seminalis.**

2. *Female System.*—(*a*) Two **ovaries** or **germaria,*** small rounded bodies,* lie at the anterior end of the body, one per side.

(*b*) From each ovary an **oviduct** passes backwards. The two oviducts unite posterior to the genital opening as a common oviduct. This median duct runs into the **genital atrium** or **cloaca**—*i.e.*, a depression into which both male and female organs open.

(*c*) Numerous branched tubes—the **vitelline glands**—open into the lateral oviducts.*

(*d*) The **uterus** is a median rounded chamber connected with the genital cloaca.* Here fertilized eggs are stored ready for deposition.

(*e*) A thick-walled **muscular sac** * also arises from the genital atrium.

Class II. : TREMATODA

The members of this group are parasites—either ectoparasites or endoparasites. The body is devoid of cilia, whilst the cellular epidermis or ectoderm changes, and becomes a non-cellular horny layer or "cuticle"—a change necessitated by the parasitic habitat. An excellent example of this important group of parasites is found in the liver fluke—*Fasciola hepatica* or *Distomum hepaticum* (Fig. 13).

Fasciola hepaticum (Distomum hepaticum).

The liver fluke inhabits the larger bile ducts in the livers of sheep. It causes "liver rot," a serious, often fatal, disease attacking sheep pastured in damp meadows. The diseased animal becomes dropsical, the wool falls off, and fatal wasting sets in.

The parasite is about 1 inch in length, $\frac{1}{2}$ inch broad, and $\frac{1}{32}$ inch thick. In outline it resembles a privet leaf, with a blunt projection corresponding to the stalk of the leaf. Externally the body shows bilateral symmetry, although this is not so within.

The "stalk-like" projection marks the anterior end, and also has the **mouth** situated at its extremity. The mouth opening lies in the centre of a muscular **oral sucker.** Just posterior to the mouth-bearing

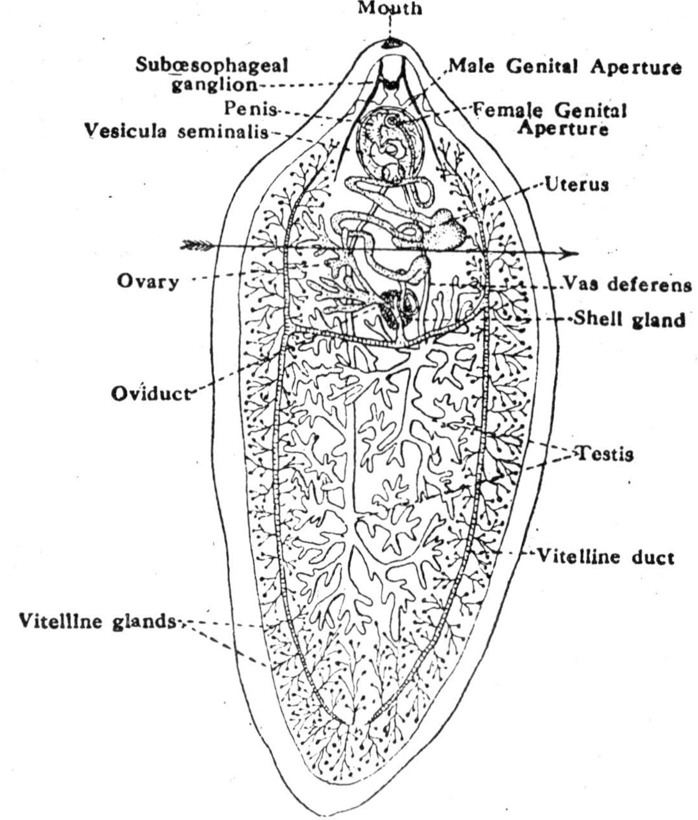

FIG. 13.—VENTRAL VIEW OF THE LIVER FLUKE (*Fasciola hepatica*), SHOWING THE REPRODUCTIVE SYSTEM. (×4.)
(From Gilchrist and von Bonde's "Practical Zoology.")

projection and on the ventral surface there is a larger **posterior sucker.** Lying slightly anterior to the posterior sucker is the **genital pore.** At the posterior end of the body is a small opening—the **excretory pore.**

Alimentary Canal.—The mouth leads into a muscular **pharynx,** from which arises a short passage—the **œsophagus.** When the œsophagus reaches the level of the posterior sucker it bifurcates into a left and a right main branch.* Each branch runs backwards to one side of the middle line, giving off a number of diverticula into the body tissue. There is no anus.

Excretory System.—This system is well developed and very typical of the Platyhelminthes. The whole system resembles the branching of a tree from a main trunk. The finer tubules are collected to form a main central duct which opens by the posterior **excretory pore.** The smaller canals are formed of a series of "drain-pipe cells" or **porocytes.** Each cell has a cavity running through it, and the connecting up of the cavities of adjacent porocytes forms the lumen of a tubule. The porocytes have no excretory function. Each of the finer tubules ends in two or three typical **flame cells.** Each cell is club-shaped and has irregular prolongations in contact with the surrounding tissue. The cavity of a tubule continues as an enlarged tubular space in the flame cell.

Projecting from the cell into the enlarged lumen of the tubule there are several flagella. Their flickering movement, from which the cell derives its name, sets up a current. The waste substances in solution are removed from the surrounding tissue by the projections of the flame cell. The substances then pass into the lumen of the tubule and so are driven down to the main duct by the flagellar movements.

Nervous System.—There is an anterior concentration of nervous tissues in the form of a **circumœsophageal ring** thickened laterally to give two **ganglia** and a mid-ventral ganglion. Nerves pass from these ganglia to the various parts of the body. The chief nerves are a pair of **lateral** ones, which give branches to the sides of the body. There are no special sense organs.

Reproductive Organs.—The liver fluke is hermaphroditic.

1. *Male Organs.*—(*a*) The **testes,*** two in number and composed of ramifying tubules, occupy the middle portion of the body. One testis lies to the posterior of the other.

(*b*) A **vas deferens** runs forward from each testis.*

(*c*) The **vesicula seminalis** is an elongated sac formed by the union of the vasa deferentia.

(*d*) The vesicula seminalis passes into a narrow tube. This is the **ejaculatory duct.**

(*e*) The walls of the tube become muscular, and this forms the **cirrus or penis,** which opens into the **genital cloaca** or **atrium.**

2. *Female Organs.*—(*a*) The single **ovary** * is a branched tube lying to the right-hand side, and in front of, the anterior testis.*

(*b*) A short **oviduct** arises from the ovary.

(*c*) The **vitelline glands**—numerous, rounded follicles—occupy the lateral zones of the body.

(*d*) The vitelline glands open into a **main lateral vitelline duct** on each side.* At a point about one-third of the body length from the anterior each lateral duct sends inwards a **transverse vitelline duct.** The two transverse ducts join at about the middle line and form a small sac or **yolk reservoir.** From this point a short **common median vitelline duct** runs forward to join the oviduct.

(*e*) A number of unicellular **shell glands** open into the end of the oviduct, which is termed an **oötype.**

(*f*) The **uterus** arises at the junction of the oviduct and median vitelline duct.* It runs forward as a wider convoluted tube, for storage of shell-covered eggs, and opens into the genital atrium near the cirrus.

(g) From the point where oviduct and vitelline ducts meet, a short tube—**Laurer's canal**—passes to the dorsal surface. It acts as an overflow for excess yolk cells, and possibly for surplus eggs.

Life-History.—*Distomum hepaticum* can only complete its full life-cycle by the agency of another host besides the sheep. The latter is the **principal** host, whilst the **intermediate** agent is a species of water snail—*Limnæus truncatulus*. The whole cycle can be divided into a number of stages:

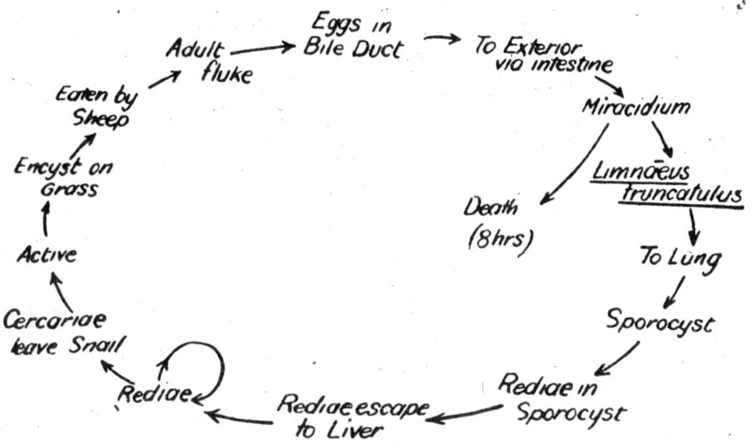

FIG. 14.—DIAGRAM TO ILLUSTRATE THE LIFE-CYCLE OF *Distomum hepaticum*.

1. The eggs are laid in the bile ducts of the sheep, and from there pass through the intestine, protected from the digestive juices of the host by their shell, and so to the grass in the fæces of the host.
2. After a few weeks, according to temperature and moisture, there hatches from the egg a larva known as a **miracidium.** It has a ciliated body 0·12 mm. long, with a conical anterior projection. Two flame cells, an

eye spot, and nerve ganglion are present. This larva swims about actively and is attracted by the small water snail. If a suitable intermediate host is not found within about eight hours the larva perishes. A successful miracidium attaches itself to the snail's skin and proceeds to bore its way into the tissue, aided by the anterior cone. The parasite eventually reaches the large blood spaces of the snail's lung.

3. Here the larval organization degenerates and the parasite becomes a sac containing germ cells. This is the **sporocyst** stage. The germ cells undergo repeated fission, giving rise to masses of germ cells. Each mass, at first rounded, elongates and forms the next stage.

4. **Redia.**—Each redia is an elongated vermiform organism with two posteriorly placed lateral projections and a blind gut—pharynx and intestine—opening at the front end. A small reproductive opening is present to one side of the anterior end. The space between gut and body wall is filled with masses of germ cells, which in turn develop into rediæ. Several generations of rediæ may thus be produced, usually while the parasite is in the snail's liver.

5. Eventually, instead of more rediæ, **cercariæ** are developed. Each cercaria has an elongated body which has a posterior indentation from which a stout tail arises. An oral sucker surrounds the mouth, which leads into the pharynx and a bifurcated but unbranched intestine. A ventral sucker is also present, so that the cercaria is organized on the same general plan as the adult fluke.

The cercariæ leave the snail and swim with jerky motions. The tail eventually drops off and the animal creeps to the top of a blade of grass. Here, by secretions of special glands, it encysts. Within the cyst gradual change produces a structure like the adult organism. When the grass and cyst is eaten by a sheep the latter is digested, but the parasite wanders to the liver, where it attains its adult form and becomes sexually mature.

The association of "liver rot" and damp pasture is at once clear owing to the presence of *Limnæus truncatulus* on such land. Preventive methods lie in drainage, removal of sheep to dry pasture, or turning of ducks, etc., on to the infected area in order that they may feed on the snails.

Form related to Distomum.—*Schistosoma* (or *Bilharzia*) *hæmatobia* is a distomid parasite living in the veins of the human body, and producing a serious disease. This Trematode has a long and narrow body, while the sexes are separate. The lateral regions of the body are folded over the ventral surface, so forming a slit cylinder. The mature female lives permanently within the groove of the male. The adult worms favour the venous blood stream. Hæmaturia (*i.e.*, blood in the urine) is a conspicuous symptom of the disease, which occurs frequently in Egypt (90 per cent. population infected), Africa, and Asia.

The egg has its shell prolonged into a spine at one end. Eggs reach the small veins of the bladder, and there, aided by the spine and muscular contraction, become free in the urine. The life-cycle is continued in a water snail (genus *Isidora*), but there are no redial stages. When the cercariæ are freed, they infect new human hosts by burrowing through the skin to the bloodvessels.

Class III. : CESTODA

The **Tape-worm** is the name commonly used to describe members of this class of Platyhelminthes.

They are essentially parasites, like the Trematodes, but differ from the latter in a number of distinctive features. The Cestoda have elongated, tape-like bodies without alimentary canals. Their bodies are subdivided so as to form a chain of small pieces, which enlarge as the posterior is approached. Each piece is a **proglottis** (plural, proglottides), and contains a complete set of hermaphrodite reproductive organs. Thus the whole worm may be regarded as a chain of sexual individuals which have been produced by asexual budding in one direction.

The tape-worms have a typical **bladder-worm** stage which infects the intermediate host. The adults are found in the intestines of Vertebrates. *Tænia* is a common genus of tape-worm, and will serve to illustrate the structure and history of these organisms.

Tænia Solium.

The adult individual lives in the intestine of man, where it reaches a length of many feet. The worm is attached to the intestine wall by means of a definite head end. The **head** or **scolex** is rounded and of the size of a small pin-head. Arranged at the equatorial region and at the opposite points of the two main diameters are **four suckers.** The anterior extremity forms a conical **rostellum,** at the base of which is a double **ring of hooks.** Both suckers and hooks are used for the attachment of the worm to the intestine.

The head narrows to form a short **neck,** which at its flattened posterior end buds off the proglottides. As new proglottides are formed the older ones are pushed away from the head, so that the older and matured proglottides are at the posterior extremity of the worm.

There is **no alimentary canal,** the nourishment being absorbed through the surface of the body. The **excretory system** is made of flame cells and ducts, as in the other Platyhelminthes. The main ducts of this system run down the sides of the chain of proglottides. These two **lateral ducts** are connected across by a **transverse duct** at the **posterior** side of **each** pro-

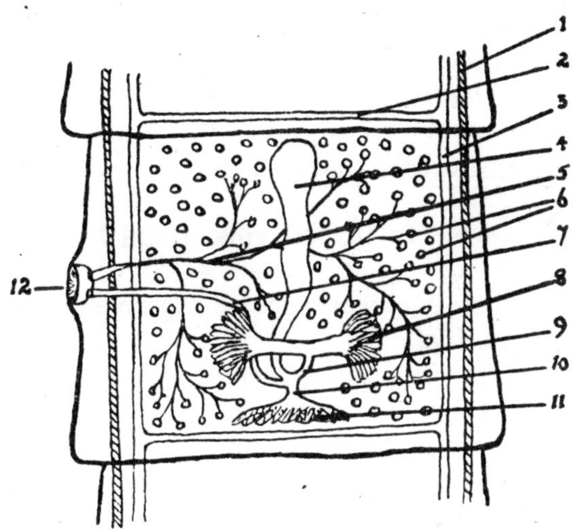

FIG. 15.—PROGLOTTIS OF TÆNIA.

1, Lateral nerve; 2, transverse excretory duct; 3, lateral excretory duct; 4, uterus; 5, vas deferens; 6, testes; 7, vagina; 8, ovary; 9, oviduct; 10, vitelline duct; 11, vitelline gland; 12, genital atrium.

glottis. The transverse duct of the posterior proglottis has a median excretory opening. The **nervous system** consists of an anterior circular concentration of nervous tissue and a number of longitudinal nerves. Two of these are much larger than the others and lie just external to the lateral excretory ducts.

Each proglottis contains a set of hermaphrodite **reproductive organs.** (Fig. 15.)

1. *Male Organs.*—(*a*) **Testes,** numerous small spherical bodies scattered in the parenchyma of the body. They occupy the outer zone, particularly the two sides and anterior of the proglottis.

(*b*) Each testis has a slender tubule leading away from it. These small tubules join eventually to form a main **vas deferens,** which runs transversely across the central part of the proglottis. The vas deferens opens into a shallow lateral **genital** atrium by means of a small **non-muscular papilla.***

2. *Female Organs.*—(*a*) The **ovary** is situated centrally in the posterior half of the proglottis. It is somewhat dumb-bell shaped, having right and left digitate portions.

(*b*) A transversely placed **yolk gland** lies between the ovary and the transverse excretory duct.

(*c*) The short backward-projecting **oviduct** joins a short **vitelline duct.**

(*d*) From the junction point of oviduct and yolk duct a blind tube, the **uterus,** passes forward almost to the anterior margin of the proglottis.

(*e*) A set of **shell glands** surround the union point of uterus, oviduct, and yolk duct.

(*f*) The **vagina,*** or main female duct, connects the oviduct-yolk duct junction with the genital atrium.

The spermatozoa pass from the genital atrium up the vagina, and fertilization takes place at the opening of the oviduct. Yolk and shell are then added and the complete egg passes into the uterus.

The gradual maturing of the reproductive organs can be seen if selected proglottides from before backwards are examined. After fertilization is accomplished the sex organs, except the uterus, disappear. The uterus becomes extended with shell-covered embryos. Each egg case now contains the embryo which has developed from the zygote since the packing of the fertilised egg in the uterus. When the mature proglottis is shed from the host, it is little more than a mass of embryos each in its shell case. These proglottides pass out with the fæces of the host.

Life-History.—*Tænia solium* has as its intermediate host the pig. The proglottides dry up and set free the encysted embryos whose further development is arrested at this point. In this encysted state, the organism can withstand very adverse conditions. Only when these resistant embryos are swallowed by a pig does further development take place.

1. In the alimentary canal of the pig the shell is dissolved away, and a small spherical structure is left. This hollow sphere of cells has six hooks, and is known

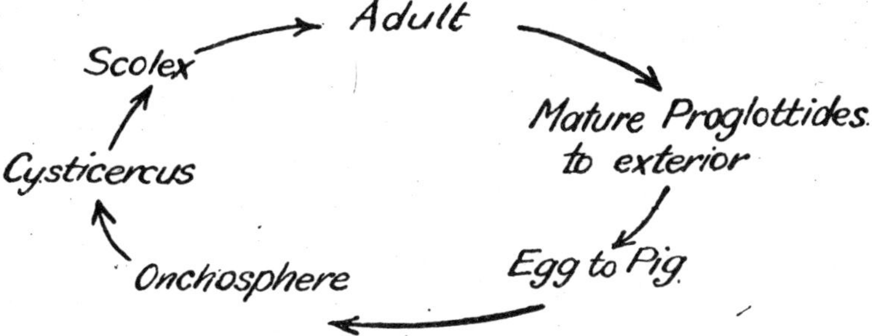

FIG. 16.—LIFE-HISTORY OF TÆNIA.

as the **six-hooked embryo** or **onchosphere.** The onchosphere bores through the alimentary canal wall to the bloodvessels. By the blood stream it is carried around the body. The embryo settles in various parts of the host—*e.g.*, muscles—where it loses its hooks and increases in size.

2. The wall of this sphere invaginates at one point, so forming a pit on whose inner wall four suckers and a ring of hooks develop. This is the **bladder-worm** or **cysticercus stage** (*C. cellulosæ*). The presence of bladder-worms causes " measly pork," which is now, fortunately, not so common as it used to be. The cysticercus larvæ can be readily killed by cooking the

pork sufficiently. However, if the pork is eaten in an "underdone" state, then the worms, which can survive a considerable amount of heat, will finish their life-cycle.

3. When ingested by man the worm is stimulated, causing the head to be everted. The bladder portion is digested and the scolex attaches itself to the wall of the intestine, where it commences to bud off proglottides.

Other Tape-Worms.

T. saginata, which is found in man, has no crown of hooks. The cysticercus is found in the ox. Adult, 30 feet.

T. serrata is one of the commonest tape-worms of the dog. The bladder-worm occurs in rabbits, hares, and mice.

T. cœnurus, found particularly in dogs protecting sheep, has a bladder-worm, *Cœnurus cerebralis,* in the brain of hoofed animals, particularly sheep, where it causes "sturdy" or "staggers." The bladder-worm stage is very large (up to 2 inches or more in diameter) and **many scolices** are produced from the one cysticercus.

T. echinococcus is another worm infecting the dogs of Iceland, Australia, and parts of South America particularly. The worm is very small in the adult stage (2 to 6 mm.), and consists of three or four proglottides only. However, they usually compensate for lack of size by being present in enormous numbers. The bladder-worms occur in ox, sheep, pig, and occasionally in man. This stage is usually very large, reaching a diameter of 6 to 7 inches. The bladder buds off smaller bladders or **brood capsules,** which in turn produce **many scolices** each. All the scolices come to lie free in the large parent cyst. As the host's tissues attempt to wall off such a cyst in tough connective tissue the whole thing is known as a **hydatid cyst** containing hydatid "sand." The cysts often develop in important organs like the liver, so becoming very dangerous to the host. Hydatid cysts are particularly dangerous in man.

T. caninum (*Dipylidium caninum*) is found in the dog and cat. The bladder-worm is very small (cysticercoid larva) and is found in the dog louse (*Trichodectes*) or flea (*Pulex*). Sometimes the adult occurs in man, due no doubt to the human flea (*P. irritans*) carrying the bladder-worm stage.

Bothriocephalus latus, one of the larger tape-worms (30 feet), is found in man, particularly in districts where much fresh-water fish is eaten, as the cysticercus occurs in perch (*Perca*) and burbot (*Lota*).

The damage caused by tape-worms is due, not to the appropriation of food, but to the toxic nature of the metabolic products of the parasite, acting upon the host. Vermifuges (extract of male fern) followed by purgatives are used to rid the host of the parasite. Care must always be taken to ascertain that the **scolex** has been passed **out,** as otherwise another chain of proglottides quickly develop.

NEMATHELMINTHES

The members of this phylum are characterized by having an elongated cylindrical body. They are often known as the **round-** or **thread-worms.** The most important class in the phylum is the **Nematoda.** This comprises the round-worms in the strictest sense of the term. Numerous species occur in the sea, fresh water, and the soil, but the more important forms are endoparasites.

Nematoda.—As an example of the class the common round-worm of man (*Ascaris lumbricoides*) may be taken. This outline of the organization of the human parasite can be applied to *A. suillæ* of the pig and *A. megalocephala* of the horse.

Ascaris lumbricoides.—The worms inhabit the human intestine. The female measures between 8 to 15 inches in length and ¼ inch in diameter. The male is very much smaller.

When examined fresh, the body is ivory-brown in colour and marked by four longitudinal streaks. Two of these, pure white in colour, mark the dorsal and ventral meridians, and are called the **dorsal** and **ventral lines.** The other two marks are broader than those mentioned, and brown in colour. They are the **lateral lines.**

The **mouth** is placed in an anterior terminal position, and is surrounded by **three** lips. One lip is **median** and **dorsal,** the other two being **ventro-lateral.** The **excretory pore** is a minute opening placed upon the ventral side about 2 mm. from the anterior end. The **anus,** which is ventrally placed about 3 mm. from the pointed posterior end, is a transverse slit with thickened fleshy lips. In the male the posterior extremity of the body is recurved ventrally. Here the anus also acts as the reproductive aperture, and from it project a pair of slender chitinous **penial setæ.** In the female the anus and reproductive openings are separate. The reproductive opening or **gonopore** in the female opens upon the ventral surface about one-third of the body length from the anterior.

T.S. body wall shows the following tissue layers:

1. Transparent elastic **cuticle.** This gives the animal a segmented appearance owing to the cuticle being wrinkled transversely.

2. **Syncytial Ectoderm.**—An ectodermal layer in which the cells have no definite boundaries, the nuclei only indicating its cellular origin. Such a mass of

tissue is a **syncytium.** The ectoderm along the two lateral, the mid-dorsal, and mid-ventral lines projects inwards to form a longitudinal ridge. These ridges give rise to the external appearances known as the four longitudinal lines (see above).

3. The next layer—**longitudinal muscles**—is divided into four blocks of tissue by the four inwardly projecting ectodermal ridges. Each muscle fibre is of a peculiar structure and is spindle-shaped in outline. It is divided into two parts. A long, narrow, boat-shaped spindle of a contractile nature contains an amœboid mass of undifferentiated protoplasm. In transverse section such a fibre resembles a letter **V**, which contains protoplasm within the angle of its arms.

The alimentary canal consists of a **triangular pharynx** and **œsophagus** lined by an **ectodermally** secreted **cuticle,** which is continuous with that of the body. The œsophagus opens to the **intestine,** which is flattened dorso-ventrally, and bounded inside and outside by a thin cuticle. The tube continues as a much narrower **rectum** opening by the anus. The food drawn into the alimentary canal consists of semi-fluid material from the host's intestine. As the food is already digested there is no need of digestive secretions in the parasite. Absorption takes place in the intestine.

A **body cavity** is present, but as it is bounded by the muscle layer on the outside and only by cuticle on the inner side (on A.C.) it is not a true cœlom.

The **excretory system** is peculiar to the Nematodes. Two long tubes traverse the lateral-line ridges of ectoderm. These tubes unite anteriorly and open by the excretory pore already mentioned. The tubes end blindly at their posterior ends, and there is no trace of cilia or flame cells. Each tube is made of **one** enormous **cell** hollowed out.

The **nervous system** consists of a circumpharyngeal ring giving off nerves to the anterior and posterior. The two largest nerves run in the mid-dorsal and mid-ventral line. They are connected by semicircular commissures, which occur alternately right and left. A number of **sensory papillæ** at the base of the lips are the only definite sense organs.

The **reproductive organs** are quite characteristic of the group.

1. *Male Organs.*—(*a*) The **testis** occupies a large portion of the body cavity. It is composed of long and very slender coiled thread.

(*b*) At its posterior end the testis gradually widens to form a **vas deferens,** which, however, cannot be differentiated clearly externally.

(*c*) The vas deferens widens to give a tubular **vesicula seminalis.**

(*d*) This opens into the rectum by a narrow muscular **ductus ejaculatorius.**

(*e*) A pair of **muscular sacs** containing the bases of the penial setæ open on to the dorsal wall of the rectum near the anus.

The sperm do not have tails, but exhibit amœboid movement when coition has occurred.

2. *Female Organs.*—The female genital organs are built upon the same plan as in the male.

(*a*) **Two** coiled thread-like **ovaries** each pass into a uterus of about the same diameter.

(*b*) The two uteri unite to form a small **median vagina,** which opens to the surface by the **gonopore.**

The eggs, which are produced at the rate of 15,000 a day, are fertilized in the upper portion of the uterus. The zygotes are protected by a chitinous shell and pass from the host in the fæces. Infection of the new host is direct.

Other Nematodes.

A large proportion of the Nematodes are free living, spending their lives in salt or fresh water, damp earth, etc. Others are parasitic during the whole or part of their life, and they vary in size from 1 mm. (Anguillula) to 6 feet (Filaria). Selected examples are mentioned below.

1. *Anguillula aceti*, the vinegar-worm, found in vinegar, and *A. rhabditis*, inhabiting the soil, are examples of free-living forms.

2. *Tylenchus scandens*, the cockle-worm, causes "ear cockles" in corn. In the larval stages they live freely in the soil, but pair in, and remain in, the developing ears of corn.

Of the parasitic forms the following examples are more well known:

3. Some of the Nematodes spend the larval stages in the free state, becoming animal parasites in the adult stage. *Ancylostomum duodenale*, the miner's-worm or hook-worm, is a small intestinal parasite of man. The eggs pass out by the fæces. The larvæ live in the damp earth for a time and reinfect a host by the mouth or by boring through the skin.

4. The guinea-worm, *Dracunculus* (*Filaria*) *medinensis*, is a human parasite common in the tropics. The larval stage is passed in the body of a small aquatic Arthropod *Cyclops*.

5. *Filaria bancrofti* is another of the Nematode parasites of man in the tropics. It inhabits the lymph vessels and causes the disease known as elephantiasis arabum, in which the limbs swell enormously.

6. *Oxyuris vermicularis* is the species which most commonly causes "worms" in children.

7. *Trichina* (*Trichinella*) *spiralis* is a minute worm (1 to 3 mm.) which lives in the pig, the rat, and sometimes in man. The adults settle down in the volun-

tary muscles of the host, and are present in enormous numbers. One ounce of infected pork is estimated to contain 85,000 encysted worms. If one ounce of this "measly" pork was eaten, the result would be the development of millions of new adults. The host's muscles undergo calcareous degeneration and the morbid symptoms of "trichiniasis" arise.

CHAPTER VI

Phylum: ANNULATA

Chætopoda.

POLYCHÆTA—OLIGOCHÆTA

THE phylum Annulata includes the marine worms, the earthworms, and the leeches, among other types.

The class *Chætopoda* is the most important, and consists of the earthworms, fresh-water, and marine annelid worms.

Class: CHÆTOPODA

The body of the chætopod worm is made up of a number of practically similar **segments** or **metameres**. Each segment consists of a portion of the body wall, with a set of appendages or other locomotory apparatus, a section of the gut, a nerve ganglion, a piece of the cœlom, excretory tubes, and blood-vessels. An organism so constructed is said to have a metamerically segmented body. The segments are separated from one another by internal **septa** or thin sheets of tissue between the body wall and the alimentary canal. Externally the segmentation is marked by a number of grooves, each of which is in the same transverse plane as a septum. Each segment bears a number of stiff bristles—the **chætæ** or **setæ** *—which assist in locomotion.

The Chætopoda have a well-developed closed vascular system. Segmentally arranged excretory organs or **nephridia** are present. There are two sub-classes of the Chætopoda.

Sub-Class I.: Polychæta.

The members of this sub-class show the more primitive characters. The sexes are separate, the gonads being of a simple character and metamerically repeated. The locomotory organs are in the form of well-developed outgrowths of the body wall. Each outgrowth, or **parapodium,** has numerous strong **setæ** or bristles. A definite head, with eyes and tentacles, is usually present. A clitellum (see next sub-class) is never developed. Nearly all the Polychæta are marine and have a definite larval form (trochophore) which metamorphoses into the adult. *Nereis* may be taken as a common example showing the characters of the Polychæta.

Nereis.—*Nereis* is found quite commonly under stones upon the southern coasts of England. It is known as the "Rag Worm," or the "Red Cat," and is used as bait by fishermen. It varies in colour within the same species at different times according to the stage of sexual maturity. It is, however, usually of a pale, iridescent, greenish colour. The body is long and cylindrical (though with a slight dorso-ventral flattening), tapering towards the posterior end.

The **head** is quite distinct and consists of two parts:

1. **Prostomium,** bearing upon its dorsal surface four **eyes,** and a pair of stout cylindrical **tentacles** on

* Both words are used, meaning bristle: *chætæ* from the Greek and *setæ* from the Latin.

the centre of the anterior margin. A pair of much stouter **palpi** project from the outer margin of the anterior of the segment. The prostomium is a very small segment which really overhangs the mouth opening. The mouth is situated on the next segment, the prostomium forming a dorsal oral lip, somewhat triangular in outline, with the apex pointing forward.

2. **Peristomium.**—This segment completely surrounds the mouth, which is in the form of a transversely elongated slit upon the ventral portion of the peristomium. No parapodia are present, but two pairs of slender **peristomial tentacles** are present on each side. (Fig. 17, A.)

The remaining segments of the worm do not vary much in external features. Each segment bears a pair of lateral parapodia which are adapted to creeping and swimming movements. Each parapodium has a dorsal notopodium and a ventral neuropodium. Each of these parts has a number of lobes and setæ. (Fig. 17, B.) A very strong bristle, the **aciculum,** is buried in both the neuropodium and notopodium.

The nephridia open by small pores near the ventral margins of the parapodia.

The **alimentary canal** is a straight tube. The mouth opens into a wide **buccal cavity** which passes into a muscular **pharynx,** both being lined with cuticle. The former has numerous chitinous denticles or "teeth," whilst the latter possesses a pair of large serrated "jaws" or mandibles. The œsophagus is a straight tube which continues as the intestine. The intestine is constricted as it passes through each septum.

The structure of the nervous and excretory systems of *Nereis* corresponds to those of the earthworm (to be described later) in essentials.

It is in the reproductive elements that *Nereis* differs most widely from the earthworm. *Nereis* is unisexual; the ova or sperms, as the case may be, develop as localized proliferations of the cœlomic epithelium. The gametes mature whilst floating in the cœlomic

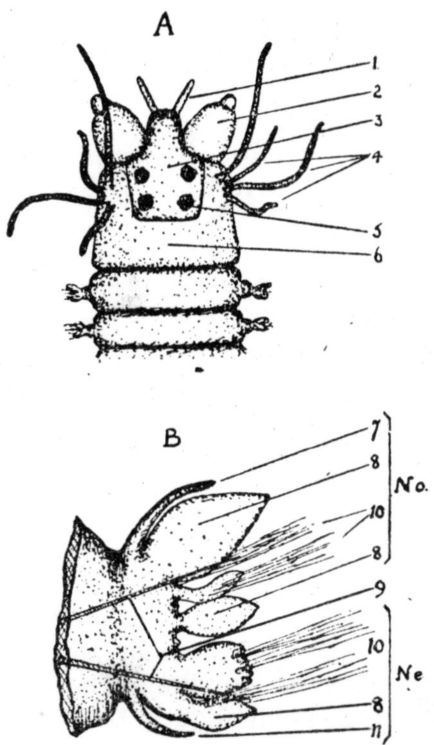

FIG. 17.—NEREIS.

A, Diagram of head region; B, parapodium from a middle segment of the body.

1, Tentacles; 2, palp; 3, prostomium; 4, peristomial tentacles; 5, "eye" spots; 6, peristomium; 7, dorsal cirrus; 8, parapodial lobe; 9, acicula; 10, setæ; 11, ventral cirrus; No., notopodium; Ne, neuropodium.

fluid, and are freed by a temporary opening in the body wall. The gonads cannot be discerned at periods when breeding does not take place.

Sub-Class II.: Oligochæta.

The members of this sub-class are hermaphrodite, productive system is rather complicated. and testes are compact, whilst there are 'er more than two pairs of either type. Parapodia are replaced by a smaller number of simple setæ embedded in each segment. There is no definite head. A characteristic clitellum is present. Most of the forms are terrestrial, or live in fresh water. No metamorphosis takes place. The common earthworm is usually taken as an example.

Lumbricus.—The body of the earthworm is in the form of a long narrow cylinder, but pointed towards the anterior and posterior ends. The dorsal surface is darker than the ventral side. The body is composed of approximately 150 segments. The **prostomium** is small, and lies anterior and dorsal to the crescentic mouth slit on the first complete segment —the **peristomium.**

The **setæ,** or bristles, are embedded in **setal sacs**— pairs per segment, there being two pairs of and two pairs of **ventro-lateral** setæ. The setæ can be extended from or withdrawn into the sacs by means of muscles. The earthworm uses the setæ, which point slightly towards the posterior, for locomotion.

Besides the setæ various other external structures and openings must be noted:

1. Segments **32** to **37** inclusive. A glandular thickening of the epidermis forms the **clitellum,** which varies in prominence according to the state of sexual activity.
2. **Spermathecal pores** open in the **grooves** between segments **9** and **10** (one pair) and **10** and **11** (one pair) at the level of the lateral setæ.

3. **Segment 14.** Two small openings of the **oviducts** on the ventral side.
4. **Segment 15.** A pair of slit-like openings with fleshy lips mark the ventral external aperture of the **vasa deferentia.**
5. **Nephridiopores**—from the excretory tubes—are very small pores situated just in front of each pair of ventro-lateral setæ, on every segment except the first three and the last.
6. **Dorsal pores** are minute median openings found in the groove behind segment 8, and in every subsequent one. They open into the body cavity, and through them cœlomic fluid oozes. This fluid contains a substance which is lethal to bacteria. It, along with a secretion from the skin glands, keeps the surface of the body moist.

The Gut.—The alimentary canal is a straight tube with a number of wider regions anteriorly. These anterior enlargements have displaced the intersegmental septa in some cases. The mouth leads into the **buccal cavity** (segs. 1 to 3), which widens to the muscular **pharynx** (segs. 4 and 5). From here a thin narrower **œsophagus** (segs. 6 to 14) passes backwards. It bears a pair of **œsophageal pouches** (seg. 11) and two pairs of **œsophageal glands** (seg. 12). These secrete calcium carbonate, which is passed into the œsophagus.

From the œsophagus the tube widens into a thin-walled **crop** (segs. 15 and 16), which opens into a muscular-walled, horny-lined **gizzard** (segs. 17 and 18). The remainder of the gut is the **intestine,** a thin-walled, narrow tube opening by the anus. The mid-dorsal region of the intestine is thrown into several folds, and all infolded as the **typhlosole.**

The cœlomic surface of the intestine, particularly in the typhlosole, is covered by yellow **chlorogogenous**

tissue. These cells are really those of the inner cœlomic epithelium, which have altered, to subserve the function of excreting material in the form of yellow granules. The excretory matter remains in the cells which are shed into the cœlom.

Food is ground up in the gizzard—a process probably aided by small stones.

A section through the body of *Lumbricus*, from the outside to the gut lumen, shows the following typical arrangement:

Body wall:

1. Thin **cuticle.**
2. **Epidermal** columnar **epithelium** with glandular and sensory cells interspersed.
3. **Circular muscle layer.**
4. **Longitudinal muscle layer** of fibres collected into bundles, which are aggregated into larger muscle blocks bound together by connective tissue.
5. **Outer cœlomic epithelium** of pavement cells.

6. **Cœlomic space** (nephridia, blood-vessels, nerve cord, etc.).

Gut wall:

7. **Inner cœlomic epithelium** of chlorogogenous cells.
8. **Longitudinal muscle** fibres.
9. **Circular muscle layer.**
10. **Endodermal epithelium** of ciliated columnar cells.

Nervous System.—A pair of **suprapharyngeal ganglia** ("brain") are joined to the **ventral nerve cord** by a pair of **circumœsophageal commissures.** The ventral cord is really two cords fused along their inner sides (see T.S.). The middle and upper parts of the cord are occupied by longitudinal nerve fibres, whilst nerve cells fill the lower and outer parts. Along the dorsal median line the fibres have been bound into three bundles surrounded by a protective sheath. These are the **giant fibres.**

In each segment there is an enlargement of the

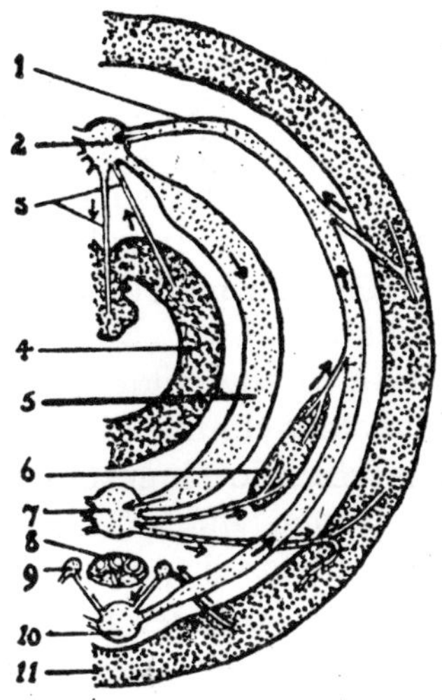

FIG. 18.—LUMBRICUS.

Diagram to show path of blood in a segment. Pseudo-hearts (5) in segments 7-11 only.

1, Parietal vessel; 2, dorsal vessel; 3, vessels supplying and draining gut; 4, gut wall; 5, pseudo-heart; 6, nephridium; 7, sub-intestinal vessel; 8, nerve cord; 9, lateral neural vessel; 10, sub-neural vessel; 11, body wall.

nerve cord—a segmental ganglion—from which arise segmental nerves.

Excretion.—The excretory organs are **nephridia,** of which there are a pair in all segments (except first three and last). A nephridium is a tube opening internally into the cœlom, externally to the exterior and through which excreta is passed. The internal opening—the **nephrostome**—is ciliated, and opens into the segment immediately anterior to the one in which the rest of the tube lies. Thus the tube leading from the nephrostome passes backwards through a septum. The tube, varying in diameter, is thrown into three loops, bound by connective tissue. The first portion is narrow, and consists of a perforation through a row of cells (intracellular), each cell resembling a drain-pipe. The last two portions are lined by whole cells (intercellular) and invested by muscle fibres. The waste products pass into the nephrostome—owing to ciliary current—and so to the exterior by the nephridiopore. Material in solution is also taken from the blood capillaries which lie in the surrounding connective tissue.

The disintegration of the chlorogogenous cells and of the bacteroidal cells lining the cœlom, releases excretory particles which are ingested by amœbocytes present in the cœlomic fluid. These amœbocytes together with the enclosed particles are able, by amœboid movement, to wander between the cells of any tissue. They may eventually reach the outside of the body and fulfil their excretory function, or they may accumulate in small nodules, known as **brown bodies,** in the cœlom, from which they are eventually lost through the dorsal pore.

Phagocytes in the blood also take up waste matter, and become **yellow cells,** which then migrate through the gut wall and pass out with the fæces.

Vascular System.—*Lumbricus* has a closed system of red blood. The hæmoglobin, however, is dissolved in the blood plasma or fluid, and not contained in corpuscles, as in the higher animals. The blood passes forwards along a contractile **dorsal vessel.** This vessel supplies the gut, and also drains it, directly. The blood from the rest of the body passes to the dorsal vessel indirectly. The anterior end of this vessel breaks up into finer branches upon the pharynx. In each of the segments 7-11 inclusive, a pair of contractile vessels (**pseudo-hearts**) encircle the œsophagus and join a **ventral** or **sub-intestinal** vessel, which is suspended below the gut by a mesentery. The blood passes backwards in the ventral vessel, which sends branches to the body wall and nephridia, where purification takes place. A pair of **lateral neural** vessels lie one at each side of the nerve cord, below which is the **subneural** vessel. In each segment a pair of semicircular **parietal** vessels carry the blood from the subneural vessel to the dorsal vessel. The parietal vessels receive branches which drain the nephridia and skin.

Reproductive Organs (Fig. 19).—*Lumbricus* is hermaphrodite, the sexual organs being concentrated towards the anterior of the body.

1. *Male Organs.*—(*a*) **Testes,** two pairs of digitate bodies hang into segments 10 and 11 from the posterior side of the anterior septum.

(*b*) Part of the cœloms of segments 10 and 11 (median ventral region) are enclosed to form vesiculæ seminales. The **anterior vesicula seminalis** has a median portion (seg. 10), two lateral **anterior horns** (seg. 9), and two **posterior** lateral **horns** (seg. 11). The **posterior** vesicula has a **median** portion (seg. 11) and a pair of **posterior** horns (seg. 12). The testes lie inside the vesiculæ seminales.

(*c*) Just opposite to each testis and on the posterior wall of the segment a **ciliated funnel** or **rosette** leads into a short duct. The two ducts on each side join to form a **vas deferens,** which opens to the exterior on segment 15.

2. *Female Organs.*—(*a*) A pair of **ovaries**—pear-shaped bodies—occupy a position in segment corresponding to that of the testis.

(*b*) In the posterior wall of segment 13 and immediately opposite the ovaries a pair of **oviducts** open. These tubes pass into segment 14, where a lateral swelling on each gives a sac—the **receptaculum ovorum.** The oviducts open on the ventral wall of segment 14.

(*c*) A pair of sacs—the **receptacula seminis** or

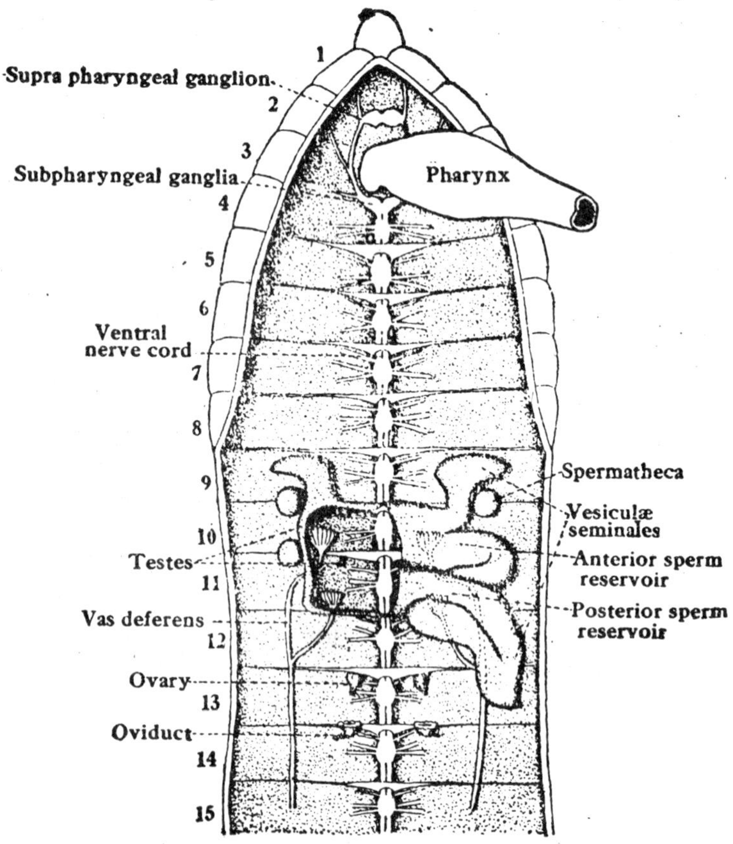

FIG. 19.—NERVOUS AND REPRODUCTIVE SYSTEMS OF EARTHWORM (*Lumbricus*).
(From Gilchrist and Von Bonde.)

spermathecæ—for storing sperm from another worm lie in each of segments 9 and 10.

Coition.—Earthworms are not self-fertilizing. Two worms come together by their ventral surfaces, with heads pointing in opposite directions. They are held thus by special genital setæ and secretions from the clitellum. Spermatozoa pass from one worm to the other from the male apertures, along a series of depressions produced by the acriform muscles, to the spermathecæ of the opposite individual. The worms then separate.

The clitellum secretes a cocoon, which is worked

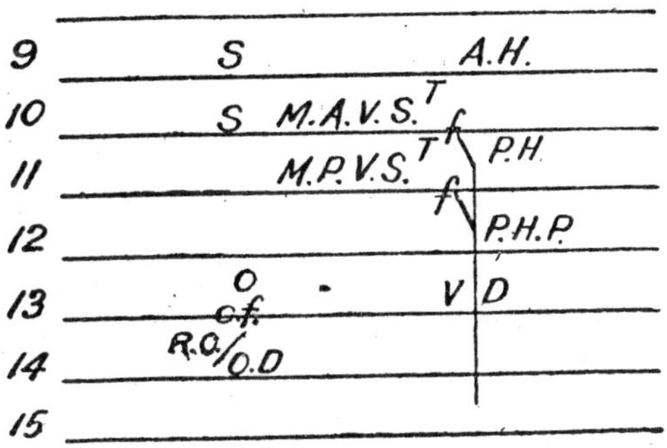

FIG. 20.—DIAGRAM OF REPRODUCTIVE ORGANS OF *Lumbricus*.

S, Spermatheca (rt. side only shown); M.A.V.S., median ant. ves. sem.; A.H., anterior horn M.A.V.S.; P.H., posterior horn M.A.V.S.; M.P.V.S., med. posterior ves. sem.; P.H.P., posterior horn M.P.V.S.; T, testis; f, rosette; V.D., vas deferens; O, ovary; o.f., oviduct funnel; O.D., oviduct and rec. ovorum (R.O.).

N.B.—All structures except M.A.V.S. and M.P.V.S. are paired.

forward. As the cocoon, which contains a nutrient fluid, passes segment 14, ova, previously collected in the receptacula ovorum, pass into it. A sperm packet, or **spermatophore,** is added from the spermathecæ and the cocoon closes, when it passes over the head. Although several ova may be deposited in each cocoon, only one usually completes development.

CHAPTER VII

ARTHROPODA

CRUSTACEA—INSECTA—ARACHNIDA

THE Arthropods form a large and important phylum, which includes many common marine, fresh-water, and terrestrial animals. Many members of the phylum are important to mankind—by providing food; by the destruction of food material and other articles; and by being disease carriers.

The structure of the Arthropod has advanced considerably upon that of the Annelid. Their characteristic features may be summed up thus:

1. A metamerically segmented body.
2. Central nervous system consists of a dorsal " brain " and ventral chain of double ganglia.
3. Each segment usually bears a pair of well-developed appendages. Each appendage is made up of a number of limb segments (**podomeres**) separated by movable joints.
4. The outside of the body is protected by an exo-skeleton of chitin, which may be reinforced by lime deposits.
5. The true cœlom has shrunken, and only remains as a vestige in one or two organs. Its place has been taken by wide extensions of the blood system. One of these large spaces acts as a body cavity in which the organs are suspended. This is the **hæmocœlic** body cavity, and is in communication with the rest of the circulatory system.

There are five important classes in the phylum:

Class I., **Onychophora**: This includes Peripatus, a very primitive arthropod type.

Class II., **Crustacea**: Crayfishes, crabs, shrimps, wood-lice, etc., are included here.

Class III., **Myriapoda:** Centipedes and millipedes.

Class IV., **Insecta:** The true insects (six legs)—*e.g.*, cockroaches, flies, beetles, butterflies, and bees.

Class V., **Arachnida:** Spiders, scorpions, mites.

Class: CRUSTACEA.

Characters.—1. Five anterior segments and prostomium form the **head**, the rest giving thorax and

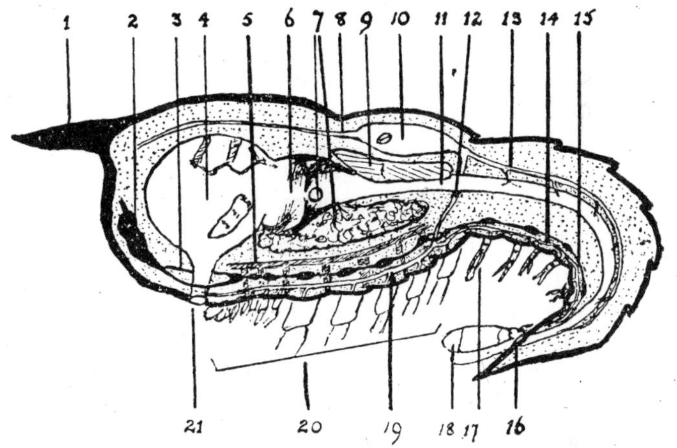

FIG. 21.—MEDIAN SECTION OF CRAYFISH.

1, Rostrum; 2, supraœsophageal ganglion; 3, circumœsophageal connectives; 4, proventriculus; 5, endophragmal skeleton; 6, filter chamber; 7, digestive gland and its opening into mesenteron; 8, ophthalmic artery; 9, gonad; 10, heart; 11, hind gut; 12, sternal artery; 13, dorsal abdominal artery; 14, ventral abdominal artery; 15, nerve cord and ganglia; 16, anus; 17, abdominal appendages; 18, telson; 19, ventral thoracic artery; 20, cephalo-thoracic appendages; 21, mouth.

abdomen. Sometimes the thoracic segments fuse and with the head form a **cephalothorax.**

2. Appendages are typically **biramous,** with a jointed base, the **protopodite;** an inner ray, the **endopodite;** and an outer, **exopodite.** Of these

appendages there are typically two pairs of antennæ and three pairs of post-oral mouth parts.

3. The body is covered by a chitinous exoskeleton often reinforced by lime deposits. Each segment is marked in the exoskeleton.

4. Respiration is either by the body surface or by gills—thin outgrowths of the thoracic wall or appendages.

5. The first and last regions of the alimentary canal are lined with chitin. Median portion gives digestive glands.

6. True cœlom is retained only in the cavities of the excretory and reproductive organs.

7. Open blood system.

8. No cilia are present in any part.

Potamobius

The fresh-water crayfish *Potamobius astacus* (*Astacus fluviatilis*) is common in European rivers, particularly those draining chalky districts.

External Characters.—Two regions are readily distinguished—an anterior **cephalothorax** and a posterior **abdomen.** The abdominal segmentation is still apparent. Each abdominal segment has a convex dorsal plate (tergum), a ventral flat **sternum,** and two triangular lateral **pleura.** In addition a pair of appendages arise from the sternum near its junction with each pleuron. (Fig. 22, B.)

The **telson** is a backward-projecting flat structure to the posterior of the last true abdominal segment, and has no appendages.

In the thorax and head the terga and pleura have fused together to give a solid **carapace.** This is divided by a transverse **cervical** groove into a head portion and a posterior thoracic region. Each side of the carapace forms an overhanging projection—the gill cover or **branchiostegite.** From the anterior of the carapace and in the median line a **rostrum** projects. The cephalothorax, whilst showing no segmentation dorsally, is clearly made of metameres,

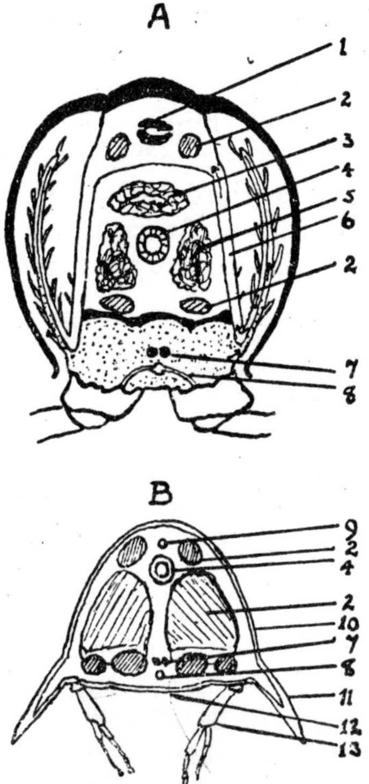

FIG. 22.—CRAYFISH: SECTIONS THROUGH BODY—A, THORAX; B, ABDOMEN.

1, Heart; 2, muscles; 3, gonad; 4, hind gut; 5, digestive gland; 6, efferent branchial sinus leading to pericardial sinus; 7, ventral nerve cord; 8, ventral artery and branches; 9, dorsal abdominal artery; 10, tergum; 11, pleuron; 12, sternum; 13, biramous appendage.

as is evidenced by the separate sterna and pairs of appendages on the ventral side. (Fig. 22, A.)

The entire body of the crayfish consists of twenty segments and the telson. Of these, six, including the prostomium, form the head, eight the thorax, and six the abdomen. Each appendage develops as a biramous structure, although the final proportion of parts differs in the various limbs.

The endopodite usually has five podomeres—namely (from the base), **ischiopodite, meropodite, carpopodite. propodite,** and **dactylopodite.** The outer ray—exopodite—is a more slender-jointed process. The basal joint of each limb—protopodite—is divided into **coxopodite** and **basipodite** regions. The appendages of segment 9 (third thoracic) are usually taken as showing the typical structure.

The appendages are grouped thus:

HEAD.		THORAX.
Antennules, Antennæ	Sensory.	Maxillipeds I.-III.—Foot-jaws.
Mandibles, Maxillæ I. and II.	Foot-jaws (Gnathopods).	Chelipeds.
		Walking legs, I.-IV.

Six abdominal segments and telson.

The last pair of abdominal appendages—**uropods**—have very much flattened biramous parts, and, together with the telson, form the extremely powerful **tail-fan.**

The muscles are attached to the inside of the exoskeleton. In the ventral thoracic region, ingrowths of hard material form the **endophragmal skeleton.** The abdomen can be flexed or straightened by **flexor** or **extensor** muscles attached anteriorly to the endophragmal skeleton and posteriorly to the abdominal segmental plates. This abdominal flexion is carried out very quickly and, when the tail-fan is spread, results in a backward darting movement by the crayfish. Locomotion is also carried out by the thoracic walking legs aided by the movement of the abdominal appendages (swimmerets).

Digestive System.

The mouth opens between the mandibles and leads by means of a short, wide **gullet** into the **proventri-**

culus (often misnamed "stomach"). This region consists of a spherical anterior **mill chamber** and a small posterior **filter chamber.** The former is provided with stout cuticular plates for food-crushing; the latter with bristles for straining the food before allowing it to pass on. From the filter region a short, thin-walled tube—the **mesenteron**—passes into a long, straight **hind gut** opening by the **anus.** All of the alimentary canal, **except** the **mesenteron,** is lined with chitin, and is moulted with the rest of the skeleton.

On each side of the mesenteron a large, lobed, yellow gland—the **digestive** gland (hepato-pancreas)—is in communication with the gut lumen. These glands secrete juices which digest all classes of food material. The food also passes into the glands themselves to be digested and absorbed.

Bloodvessels.—A hexagonal **heart** lies in a pericardial sinus beneath the central posterior region of the carapace. From the anterior of the heart five arteries pass forwards:

1. Median **ophthalmic** artery passing over the proventriculus to supply the eyes and other head organs.

2-3. A pair of **antennary arteries** arising one on each side of the ophthalmic and running forwards and outwards. Just after leaving the heart an inner **gastric** branch supplies the proventriculus, whilst the main vessel continues to the antennæ and green gland.

4-5. A pair of **hepatic arteries,** arising to the outside of the antennary arteries, supply the digestive glands.

From the posterior angle of the heart a very short vessel leaves and immediately divides into:

1. **Dorsal abdominal artery** running backwards above the hind gut, which it supplies.

2. **Sternal artery** passing downwards to the ventral side. It passes through a loop in the nervous system, under which it divides into:

(*a*) Ventral abdominal artery to the abdominal limbs.

(*b*) Ventral thoracic artery supplying the appendages of the cephalothorax.

The blood passes from the open ends of the finer arterial branches (capillaries) into the larger **sinuses,** where it bathes the various organs. Eventually the blood is collected from all parts of the body into the **sternal sinus** lying within the space formed by the

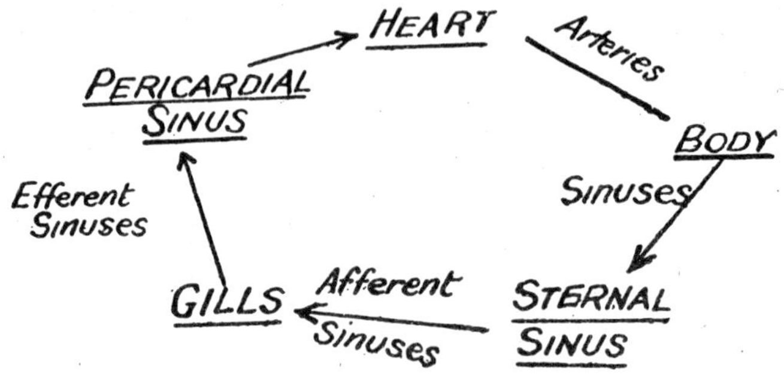

FIG. 23.—DIAGRAM OF THE BLOOD CIRCULATION IN CRAYFISH.

endophragmal skeleton and the sterna. The blood passes from here to the gills by **afferent branchial** sinuses, is purified, and returns by means of **efferent branchial** sinuses to the **pericardial sinus** and heart.

The blood contains a copper compound—**hæmocyanin**—which functions exactly as does hæmoglobin. It combines readily with oxygen (oxyhæmocyanin) and becomes an opalescent blue in colour.

The gills are found in a lateral chamber on each side of the cephalothorax and covered by the branchiostegite. The gills vary in position, some being upon epipodites (podobranchs), others on the joint of limb and body (arthrobranchs), and others upon the inner thoracic wall of the gill chamber (pleurobranchs).

Excretion.—The excretory organs or **green glands** lie at the base of the antennæ, upon whose basal joints their ducts open. Each gland *in situ* is a cushion-shaped mass, but is composed of three regions:

(*a*) **Saccule**—in the centre—a small bladder of yellowish hue with partitions growing inwards from its wall.

(*b*) **Cortical portion** of green anastomosing canals leading from (*a*) to

(*c*) **White portion,** consisting of a spongy tube (due to ingrowths of the wall). This leads into a thin-walled **urinary sac** which opens by a duct on the proximal segment of the antenna.

The saccule is a small remnant of the true cœlom.

Nervous System.—The nervous system of *Potamobius* is of the annelidan type. A **supracœsophageal ganglion** (brain) is connected to the **subœsophageal ganglion** by **circumœsophageal connectives.** The ventral cord then continues along the median ventral line. In the thorax the cord is double and has segmental ganglia. The first thoracic ganglion lies immediately behind the subœsophageal mass. The cords between ganglia 5 and 6 in the thorax are separated to allow of the passage through of the sternal artery.

The eyes are compound, and made up of a large number of separate elements (**ommatidia**), each of which has a **cornea** and a **crystalline cone** set in a tube of pigment. Below the cone are the actual **sensory** cells. In the crayfish the pigment may be contracted or expanded.

In bright light the pigment extends deeper round

the ommatidia, so that each ommatidium perceives its own portion of the image. Thus an external object is perceived "piecemeal" and the image of the object as a whole is rebuilt into one by the sensory cells. This type of eye (apposition eye) is characteristic of many crustacea and day-flying insects and gives simple **mosaic** vision.

In conditions of darkness the pigment contracts so that rays of light from several corneal facets reach one and the same group of sensory cells. This type of eye (super-position eye), which is found in many night-flying insects, gives a brighter, though less sharp, image.

Statocysts are situated in the coxopodites of the antennules, and each consists of a sac lined with sensitive setæ, on which lie sand grains.

Reproduction.—The sexes are separate, the male being the larger. The generative organs of the female open at the base of the second walking leg, whilst those of the male open at the base of the last walking leg. The first two pairs of abdominal appendages in the male are altered to assist in coition.

1. *Female Organs.*—The ovary is composed of two lateral anterior and one median posterior lobes. There is an interior cavity—a remnant of the true cœlom—into which the eggs are shed. From this space a pair of short wide oviducts lead to the external openings on the coxopodites of the second walking legs.

2. *Male Organs.*—The trilobate testis is shaped like the ovary. A pair of much-coiled vasa deferentia lead to the exterior. The spermatozoa have a discoid centre, from which radiate stiff processes.

Coition.—Breeding occurs in September and October. The female is thrown upon her back and the sperms are deposited on the ventral surface of the female's body by being passed along the male's tubular first abdominal limbs, and pushed by the second pair working in the tubes of the first. The sperm remains as white masses around the oviducal openings of the female until the eggs, which are laid in November, are fertilized. The eggs are then attached by stalked shells to hairs on the abdominal limbs of the female. The young crayfishes, which are very like their parents, remain attached in this position by means of their chelipeds for some time. This is an adaptation to overcome the disastrous effect of strong currents, which may carry the young to unfavourable conditions.

Class : INSECTA

Characters.—1. Body of well-defined head, thorax, and abdomen. The head, devoid of external segmentation, usually has compound eyes, **one** pair of antennæ (*cf.* Crustacea), a pair of mandibles and two pairs of maxillæ. The thorax consists of three segments, each with a pair of walking legs, while the second and third segments usually have a pair of wings also. The abdomen is composed of from seven to eleven segments, and has no appendages.

2. No hepato-pancreas, but salivary glands are present.

3. The respiratory system is absolutely typical of the class. A system of tubules—**tracheæ**—take the **air direct** to all parts of the body.

4. Poorly developed circulatory system with a dorsal tubular heart.

5. The excretory system is connected with the alimentary canal.

6. Sexes separate. Development often complicated by metamorphosis.

Example: The Common Cockroach.

Periplaneta (The Cockroach).

The Cockroach (*P. americana* or *P. orientalis*) is usually taken as an example of the class Insecta, owing to its large size and the fact that it is not as highly specialized as many other types.

The head is set at right angles to the thorax and abdomen.

Head.—The head is covered by the following plates and two large compound eyes to the dorsal and lateral side:

(*a*) **Epicranium,** the region between and behind the eyes.
(*b*) **Clypeus,** forming the front of the "face."
(*c*) Two lateral **genæ,** one per side.
(*d*) A pair of long antennæ are borne in sockets just below the eyes.
(*e*) Inside the bases of the antennæ are a pair of white plates—the **fenestræ**—whose exact function is unknown.
(*f*) The **labrum** (upper lip) is articulated to the ventral margin of the clypeus.

The mouth appendages consist of:

1. Pair of **mandibles,** which work horizontally, and are made of thick chitin. Their cutting edges are sharply serrated.

2. A pair of **first maxillæ,** flexible accessory jaws. Each maxilla consists of two basal segments—**cardo** and **stipes**—and from these arise an outer five-jointed **maxillary palp** and an inner double structure composed of a hard serrated inner **lacinia,** and a soft outer **galea.**

3. The **labium,** or lower lip, is really formed from the fusion of the basal joints of the second maxillæ along the median line. In structure each half of the labium resembles that of a first maxilla. The two

basal segments have fused to form a **submentum** and a **mentum,** and the two portions together form the **ligula.** Each side bears anteriorly an inner glossa

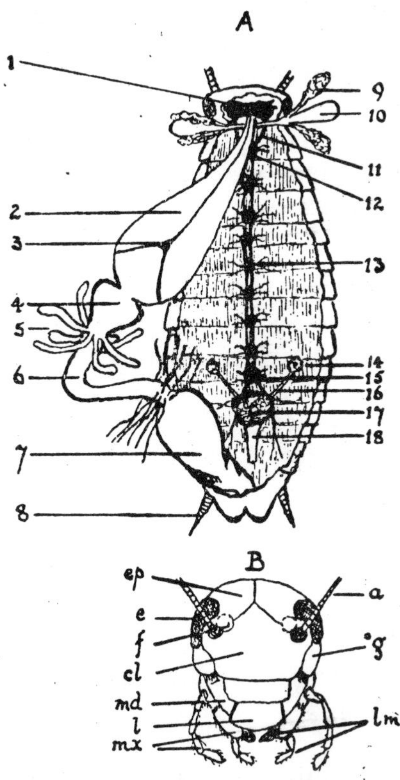

FIG. 24.—COCKROACH.

A. GENERAL DISSECTION (MALE).—1, Supraœsophageal ganglion; 2, crop; 3, visceral nerves; 4, gizzard; 5, hepatic cæca; 6, mesenteron; 7, colon leading to rectum; 8, anal cerci; 9, salivary gland; 10, salivary reservoir; 11, circum-œsophageal commissures; 12, subœsophageal ganglion; 13, ventral nerve cord with segmental ganglia; 14, testis; 15, sixth abdominal ganglion; 16, vas deferens; 17, "mushroom" gland; 18, ejaculatory duct.

B. HEAD (FRONT VIEW).—*a*, Antenna; *cl*, clypeus; *e*, eye; *ep*, epicranium; *f*, fenestra; *g*, gena; *l*, labrum; *lm*, labium and labial palp; *md*, mandible; *mx*, maxilla and maxillary palp.

and an outer **paraglossa** (*cf.* galea of Maxilla I.). The outer portions consist of a **pair** of three-jointed **labial palps.**

The head appendages of the members of the order to which the cockroaches belong (Orthoptera) are

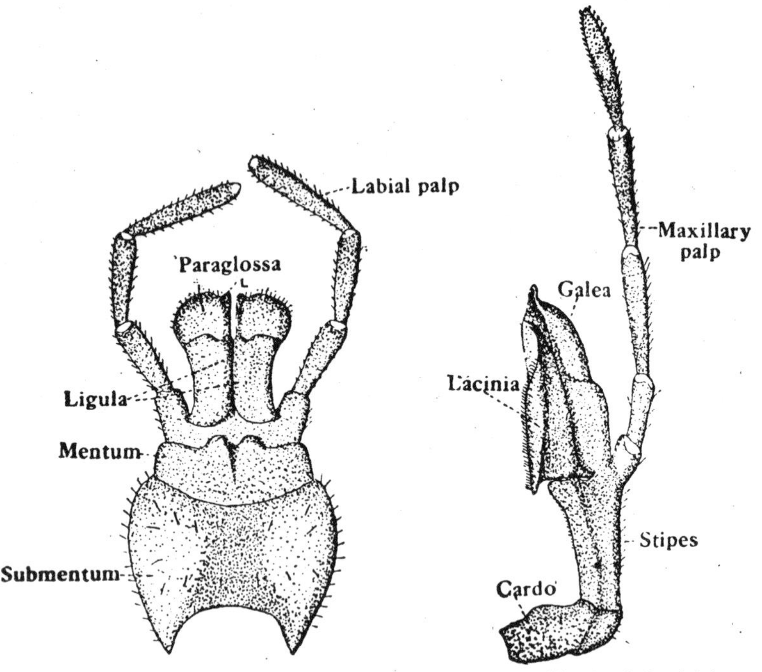

Second maxillæ (labium). First maxilla (of left side).

FIG. 25.—THE COCKROACH (*Periplaneta americana*).
The part of the second maxilla marked L is the glossa, which corresponds to the lacinia of the first maxilla.
(From Gilchrist and Von Bonde.)

of the above type, and as such are held to be of the more primitive type for the Insecta. Other insects have very highly specialized mouth parts derived from the basic orthopteran type.

Thorax.—The head is joined to the thorax by a slender **neck** covered by thin cuticle. The thorax is composed of three segments—**prothorax, mesothorax,** and **metathorax**—each of which is composed of a dorsal chitinous **tergum** and a ventral **sternum.** There is no fusion of terga here, as there is in *Potamobius.*

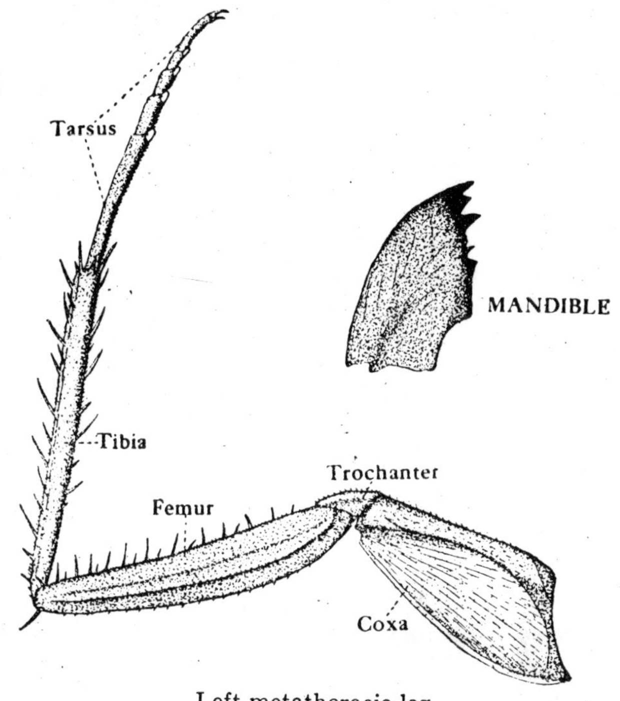

Left metathoracic leg.

FIG. 26.—APPENDAGES OF THE COCKROACH.
(From Gilchrist and Von Bonde.)

The tergum of the prothorax is larger than the others.

Each segment bears a pair of walking legs on its ventral side. Each leg is made up of a proximal podomere, the **coxa**; second, **trochanter** (very small); third, **femur** (narrow); fourth, spinose **tibia**; and fifth, the **tarsus.** The tarsus has six short segments, the last—**pulvillus**—being provided with a pair of claws.

The second and third thoracic segments each bear a pair of wings. The wings of the female *P. orientalis* are vestigial. The wings, delicate folds of chitin, are articulated in the anterior dorsal corners of the segment. The first pair of wings are thick, and known as **elytra.** They protect a second membranous pair of flying wings which, at rest, lie folded under the elytra.

Abdomen.—The thin, flexible sterna and terga of the abdomen overlap one another from before backwards. Although the abdomen is composed of ten segments, only eight can usually be seen, as the segments 8 and 9 are telescoped and hidden. Segment 10 is produced as a deeply notched thin plate. At the sides of this segment are a pair of many-jointed **cerci.** In the male segment 9 bears a pair of slender unjointed **styles,** whilst in the female segment 7 has its sternum produced backwards into a boat-shaped **genital pouch.**

Alimentary System.—The mouth opens into the pharynx, into which open the **salivary ducts.** Each **salivary gland** is a ramifying tubular structure divided into two main lobes, and associated with each gland is a **salivary reservoir.** The ducts from both glands and reservoirs unite and open by a common median duct into the pharynx. From the pharynx the **œsophagus** gradually enlarges to form a large, thin-walled **crop.** This is followed by a small conical **gizzard** (proventriculus) lined by toothed chitinous plates. The gut up to here is lined with chitin, and known as the **stomodeum.** The central portion of the food canal is, however, not lined with chitin, but has glandular walls. This is the **mesenteron,** and is, with its appended cæca, the only digestive region.

From the anterior end of the mesenteron eight blind-ended tubes arise. These are the **hepatic cæca,** which secrete a digestive fluid. The posterior margin of the mesenteron, where it joins the intestine, is marked by the attachment of a number of slender **Malpighian tubules,** which **excrete** the waste products. The intestine terminates in the **rectum,** the walls of which are corrugated. The tube from the region of the Malpighian tubules to the anus is known as the **proctodeum** and is lined with chitin.

Respiratory System.—The oxygen is taken direct to the various parts of the body by means of a ramifying system of air tubes or **tracheæ.** The tracheæ are lined with chitin; the lumen of each tube is always open, as the walls of the tubes are supported by spiral thickenings. The tracheal system communicates with the exterior by means of **stigmata** or **spiracles.** These openings are protected by hairy fringes. In the cockroach there are pairs of stigmata between thoracic segments 1 and 2, and between 2 and 3; also a pair open between the tergum and sternum of the first eight abdominal segments.

Blood System.—Correlated with a direct supply of air to the tissues there is a very poorly developed blood system. The contractile heart is an elongated tube lying along the dorsal median line of the thorax and abdomen. It is closed behind and divided into a number of chambers which are perforated by pairs of lateral valvular **ostia.** The heart is controlled by **alary** muscles. The anterior end of the heart is produced as the anterior **aorta.** The blood then bathes the tissues by means of sinuses. The blood collects into the perivisceral sinus, and so into the pericardial sinus and heart.

Nervous System.—This system is made up of a **supraœsophageal ganglion,** a pair of **circumœsophageal commissures,** a **subœsophageal ganglion, three thoracic** and **six abdominal ganglia.** The thoracic and abdominal ganglia are really of a double nature and connected by a double ventral nerve cord. Each ganglion gives off segmental nerves, whilst the last one supplies the posterior of the body.

The eyes are compound; the antennæ, palpi, and anal cerci are tactile organs, and certain antennal setæ have an olfactory function.

Reproductive Organs.—The sexes are separate.

1. *Male Organs.*—A pair of small **testes** (abd. segs. 4 and 5), dorsally placed, are connected to a pair of slender **vasa deferentia,** which lead to the **vesiculæ seminales.** The pair of vesiculæ, which lie close together and have numerous cæca, together form the "mushroom-shaped gland." A median ejaculatory duct with muscular walls opens to the exterior just below the anus. Around the genital aperture are a number of chitinous **gonapophyses** used during coition.

2. *Female Organs.*—Each of the two **ovaries** is a digitate structure, each "finger" or **ovariole** consisting of ova in various stages of maturation. The two lateral oviducts join, and open by a median aperture on the sternum of the eighth abdominal segment. A pair of **spermathecæ** open ventrally in the middle line between sterna on segments 8 and 9. On the ninth sternum a pair of branched **colleterial glands** open and secrete the egg cases.

The eggs are laid in cases, which resemble a "Gladstone bag" in shape. Each case contains sixteen ova and a quantity of spermatozoa from the spermathecæ. The young which hatch out resemble the adults in most respects, except that the former are wingless and sexually immature. The wings appear after several moults.

A study should be made of the various insect groups, particularly with reference to the adaptations of the mouth parts in the various types.

Class: ARACHNIDA

This class includes the spiders, scorpions, mites, and ticks. In most cases there is a cephalothorax and segmented abdomen, but some types have both regions amalgamated. No antennæ are to be found in the adult arachnid.

The first pair of appendages are **cheliceræ;** the second pair **pedipalpi,** and behind these are **four pairs** of walking legs.

The more common groups of Arachnids are as follows:

I. Scorpionida.

Here a cephalothorax and elongated abdomen, with a terminal sting, are present. The cheliceræ are small, but the chelate pedipalpi are very large.

Respiration takes place by means of **lung books** in pairs on the ventral surface of abdominal segments 3, 4, 5, and 6. A lung book is a depression on the body surface and into this cavity a number of " leaves " project. Each " leaf " is richly supplied with blood, and so a large respiratory surface is obtained.

This order includes the Scorpions.

II. Araneida.

The body consists of cephalothorax and unsegmented abdomen, which is usually soft and rounded. The cheliceræ are provided with poison glands. " Lung books " are present at the anterior of the abdomen, whose hind end possesses **spinnerets** secreting the silken web threads. These are the true Spiders.

III. Acarida (Acarina).

No body divisions present. Mouth parts altered for biting or piercing. A tracheal system may be present. *Demodex folliculorum* (" blackhead ") lives in the sebaceous gland ducts on the human face. Allied species cause "mange" in cats and dogs. *Sarcoptes scabei* burrows in the human skin and causes "itch." The ticks (*e.g.*, *Ixodes*) are larger than the mites. They hang on to their host by means of the barbed mouth parts, and become gorged with blood—*e.g.*, dog, sheep, and cattle ticks.

CHAPTER VIII

MOLLUSCA

THE Molluscs have soft unsegmented bodies without jointed appendages. They are often referred to as Shellfish, and included in the group are such organisms as Cockles and Mussels, Oysters, "Winkles," Snails, Slugs, and Cuttlefish. The body produces on its outside a shell of calcium carbonate deposited in an organic foundation of conchin. The shape of the shell varies in the different groups of Molluscs. It may be of two portions, as in the Mussel; or it may be a spiral shell of one piece, as in the Snail. The Mollusca are divided into three distinct groups:—

1. **Lamellibranchiata.**—Both fresh-water and marine forms with a bivalve shell, a bilaterally symmetrical body and no distinct head. Mussels, Oysters, etc.

2. **Gastropoda.**—They possess unsymmetrical bodies with a well-developed head, which usually bears tentacles and eyes. There is always present a rasping **radula** in the mouth. The alimentary canal and its associated organs form a **visceral hump** on the dorsal surface of the body. Moreover, the visceral hump has become twisted into a spiral. This spiral twist, together with a general torsion of the body to the right-hand side forwards, results in the anus being near the mouth, and in the development of

a spirally coiled shell. In the Slugs (marine and terrestrial) the shell may be vestigial or absent, Examples: Limpet, Periwinkle, Whelk, Sea Slugs. Land Slugs and Snails, and the Fresh-water Snails.

3. **Cephalopoda.**—They are bilaterally symmetrical and free-swimming Molluscs. They feed voraciously on Crustaceans, and are themselves the food of the toothed Whales. The typical "foot" (*vide infra*) has divided up into eight or ten sucker-bearing arms arising from around the mouth. Part of the foot forms a tubular **siphon,** through which water may be expelled quickly from the mantle cavity. Thus the Cephalopod is driven through the water.

The shell is vestigial in some members of the group (cuttlefish "bone" for birds), and is absent in others. A special "ink gland" discharges a black pigment (sepia) into the water. This ink cloud assists in the escape of the cuttlefish from enemies. The fossil Ammonites are related to the living Cephalopod known as the Pearly Nautilus.

General Anatomical Features of Molluscs.

The diversity of structure makes it difficult to understand the details unless a member of each group is studied. However, certain general features are summarized below.

(i.) Molluscs have unsegmented bodies and are without appendages. They are bilaterally symmetrical except the Gastropoda.

(ii.) On the ventral surface of the body there is a characteristic muscular "**foot.**" It is usually a locomotor structure, but its form varies with the habits of the various types of Molluscs. In the Gastropod it forms a flat "sole" on which the animal creeps (Snail, Whelk). In the fresh-water Mussel it "ploughs" through the mud, while the Cockle is able to take short jumps by protruding its "foot."

In the Cephalopod it forms the tentacles, while in the sedentary Molluscs it is much reduced (Oyster).

(iii.) A dorsal fold of skin—the **mantle**—is produced towards the head in the Gastropod. Thus a respiratory chamber is formed. Lateral mantle folds arise in the Bivalve, giving two "coat" flaps between which and the body the gills develop. As the shell is produced by secretion from the mantle the shape of the mantle determines that of the shell. The shell is added to by the mantle edge as the Mollusc grows.

(iv.) Respiration is carried on in most Molluscs by means of **gills.** In Bivalves the gills form large ciliated plates in the mantle cavity. The cilia set up a respiratory current which also brings in food material. In the Gastropods and Cephalopods the gills are plume-like. Water-testing organs (osphradia) are usually present. In the terrestrial Gastropods (snails and slugs) the large mantle cavity has no gills, but is richly supplied with bloodvessels. This respiratory chamber or "lung" is open to the exterior near the edge of the shell.

(v.) There are three chief pairs of nerve ganglia—the cerebrals controlling the head, the pedals for the "foot," and the pleurals for control of the viscera. The ganglia are interconnected by commissures. There is no indication of a ventral nerve cord concentration such as is characteristic of most other Invertebrates.

(vi.) In the Bivalve the head is poorly developed and the mouth adapted for using microscopic particles of food. Other Molluscs have a very typical **radula** in the mouth of a well-developed head. The radula is on the floor of the mouth, and it resembles a pliable file coiled up. These rasping "file teeth" cut the food, or may be used to bore into hard substances such as shell. In addition to a radula the Cuttlefish has a pair of parrot-like jaw plates forming a " beak."

CHAPTER IX

CHORDATA

Amphioxus

The phyla represented by the examples already studied belong to the sub-kingdom Invertebrata. A feature common to the Invertebrates is the absence of any internal skeleton. The supporting structure, if present, is in the form of an exoskeleton.

The other sub-kingdom is that known as the **Chordata.** The name is derived from the fact that all members of the group have a definite internal supporting rod known as the **notochord,** or **chorda dorsalis.** In the lower types of chordates the notochord persists throughout the whole life of the animal, whereas in the more highly organized types this structure only appears during the early embryonic stages. In the latter types the chorda dorsalis is replaced by a linear series of small bones known as **vertebræ.** Thus this type of chordate belongs to the group known as the **Vertebrata**—a group in which most of the Chordates can be placed.

The chief characters of the Chordata are as follows:

1. Dorsally placed **notochord,** which usually remains during early life only, but may persist.

2. The wall of the pharynx is perforated by a series of paired lateral clefts, which may persist throughout life (*e.g.*, fish), or may only occur in the larval or embryonic condition (*e.g.*, frog and man). Such pharyngeal openings are known as **branchial** or **gill clefts.**

3. The main bloodvessels lie along the dorsal wall of the cœlom.

4. The central nervous system is developed from a dorsal tubular structure. The lumen of this tube may swell in the anterior region. This system of cavities is the **neurocœle**.

5. The development of a portion of the body posterior to the anal opening gives rise to a typical **tail.** Hence lateral flexibility of the notochord or vertebræ is necessary for swimming.

The sub-kingdom Chordata is divided into four phyla:

1. **Hemichordata.**—They possess what is usually regarded as a modified notochord, which is in the form of a slender dorsal diverticulum of the alimentary canal—*e.g.*, *Balanoglossus*.

2. **Urochordata.**—In members of this group the notochord is confined to the tail region, and, moreover, is only found in the larvæ. The adults, however, have retrogressively metamorphosed in many respects, including the atrophy of the notochord—*e.g.*, **Ascidians** or **Sea Squirts.**

3. **Cephalochordata.**—The notochord persists and extends to the very anterior or head region of the body—*e.g.*, *Amphioxus*.

4. **Vertebrata or Craniata.**—The notochord is replaced by a vertebral column, while the anterior swollen end of the nervous system (brain) is enclosed in a protective hard box (cranium)—*e.g.*, Fishes, Amphibians, Reptiles, Birds, and Mammals.

AMPHIOXUS

A. lanceolatus (Fig. 27) is a small animal, about 1½ to 2 inches long, with a slender spindle-shaped body, which is laterally compressed. It lives in the shallow sandy seas of the coast, living most of the day buried in the sand with the anterior only projecting.

External Features.—There is no definite head marked off from the rest of the body.

1. **Dorsal fin,** a low fold of tissue running along the median dorsal line from end to end.

2. **Caudal fin,** a continuation of the dorsal fin, passing round the posterior end of the body. The caudal fin is deeper than the dorsal fold.

3. **Ventral fin,** an anterior continuation of the ventral lobe of the caudal fin, extending along the posterior third of the body.

4. In front of the ventral fin the under side of the body is flattened. This flat portion has a continuous ridge or fold as each lateral border. Each of these ridges is a **metapleural fold** or **lateral fin.**

5. Through the semi-transparent skin it is seen that the body is made up of a number of V-shaped

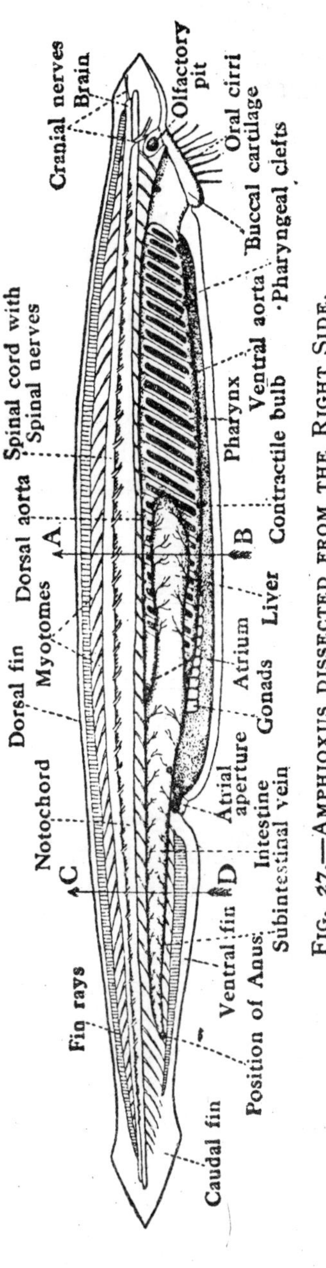

FIG. 27.—AMPHIOXUS DISSECTED FROM THE RIGHT SIDE.
(From Gilchrist and Von Bonde.)

regions. Each region is a muscle of the body wall (**myomere**). The myomeres are separated by **myocommata**—septa of connective tissue. The myomeres on opposite sides alternate (myotome=myomere).

6. The **anus** is a small opening on the left side of the body near the junction of the caudal and ventral fins. Behind the anus the body is known as the **tail**—such a structure containing no part of the alimentary canal.

7. The anterior opening of the alimentary canal is surrounded by a cup-shaped **vestibule.** The edge of the vestibule lies just under the anterior end of the body, and is fringed by numerous tentacles or **cirri,** and is known as the **oral hood.** The wall of the hood is marked with radiating ciliated grooves, which set up a current, driving the food particles towards the mouth. The mouth is surrounded by a ridge—the **velum**—bordered with approximately twelve **velar tentacles.**

8. Between the anterior of the ventral fin and the posterior ends of the metapleural folds is a small opening—the **atriopore**—through which a current of water escapes.

The body is covered with a layer of columnar epithelial cells, some of which have sensory hairs. The cuticle, secreted by this **epidermis,** is thin. Beneath the epidermis lies the **dermis,** a layer of soft connective tissue.

Digestive and Respiratory Systems.—The mouth leads to the pharynx, a wide and laterally compressed section of the enteric canal, occupying the anterior portion of the body. The walls of the pharynx are perforated by a large number of oblique gill slits or branchial apertures. These slits place the pharyngeal cavity in communication with a large cavity—the **atrium**—which surrounds the anterior region of the gut. The posterior end of the pharynx narrows and continues backwards, as a straight tubular intestine, to the anus. A diverticulum is given off from the ventral side of the forepart of the intestine. This blind pouch, or **hepatic cæcum,** extends forwards and to the right side of the pharynx. It is lined with glandular epithelium, which secretes the digestive fluid.

Along the median dorsai line of the pharynx is a ciliated groove which secretes mucus. This is the **epipharyngeal groove.** Another groove of similar structure—the **endostyle**—lies along the mid-ventral line. The endostyle and epipharyngeal grooves are connected anteriorly by a pair of ciliated **peripharyngeal bands.** These grooves entrap the minute particles of food brought in with the respiratory current. Such particles are then passed down to the intestine.

The **gill slits** run obliquely down each side of the pharynx. Although these slits originate as segmentally arranged structures—*i.e.*, one pair per segment—in the adult condition the slits outnumber the segmental myomeres, due to secondary splitting of the former. The inner portions of the gill bars—*i.e.*, the portions between adjacent clefts—are covered by ciliated epithelium (endodermal); whilst the outer sides—*i.e.*, in the atrial cavity—are covered with a non-ciliated epithelium of ectodermal origin. This difference is due to the fact that the atrium, which surrounds the lateral and ventral walls of the pharynx, is lined with ectoderm. The cavity has been cut off by the fusion of the distal ends of the two metapleural folds. The atrium communicates with the exterior by the posteriorly placed atriopore. The cavity has no anterior opening.

The **gill bars** or **branchial lamellæ** are supported by branchial rods near their outer sides. The supporting rods unite dorsally by means of loops between adjacent bars. Ventrally the rods end freely, forked ends alternating with simple ends. The forked rods—**primary branchial rods**—supporting **primary lamellæ,** are the original segmentally formed bars. The **secondary branchial rods** and **lamellæ** are those which have arisen later, dividing the primary segmental clefts each into two. The branchial clefts are again complicated by the joining of adjacent lamellæ by transverse bars or **synapticulæ.** Thus the original segmental clefts eventually form a network, with rectangular meshes, on each side of the pharynx.

Skeleton.—The **notochord,** or supporting rod, is a cylindrical one, pointed at both ends, lying in the median dorsal line, and extending to both extremities of the body. It lies immediately above the gut and between the right and left myomeres. The rod is composed of special **notochordal tissue,** in which the cells are large and vacuolated, extending from side to side of the notochord. The nuclei lie to the dorsal or ventral side of the chord. The rigidity of the chorda dorsalis is due to the condition of turgescence produced in the cells by the fluid pressure in the vacuoles. The notochord is invested by a **notochordal sheath.**

The oral hood is supported by a number of T-shaped pieces, the top portions being innermost and joining to form a ring. The fins are strengthened by stiff connective tissue forming **fin rays.**

Cœlom.—The atrium has developed at the expense of a true body cavity. The cœlom is reduced to the following main spaces:

1. A pair of longitudinal cavities, one on either side of the dorsal region of the pharynx. These are connected to narrow canals in the primary lamellæ.

2. The bases of the cœlomic canals in the lamellæ join to form a median space below the endostyle.

3. Cœlom surrounds the intestine, but is reduced

on the right side owing to a posterior extension of the atrium.

4. A portion of the cœlom surrounds the "liver."

Blood System.—The blood passes forwards along a median **ventral aorta** embedded below the endostyle. Lateral branches—**afferent vessels**—supply the primary lamellæ. The secondary lamellæ receive their supply from the primary ones via the synapticulæ. After aeration the efferent vessels leave the gills, and join to form a **left** and **right** dorsal aorta, one on each

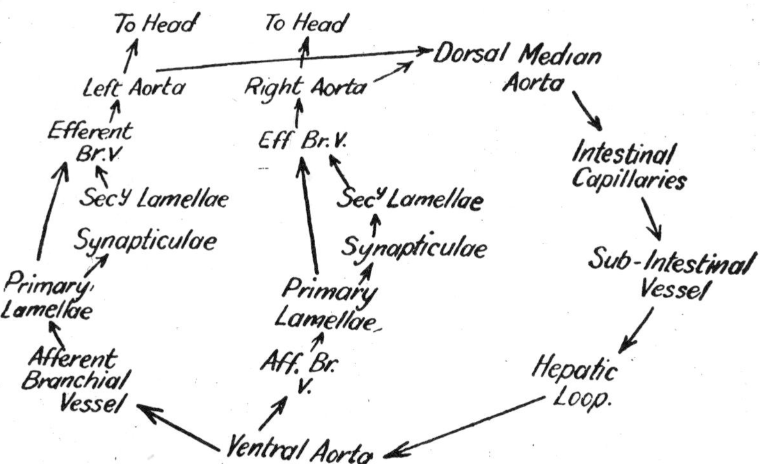

FIG. 28.—DIAGRAM OF BLOOD CIRCULATION IN *Amphioxus*.

side of the epipharyngeal groove. Just above the pharyngeal intestinal junction these lateral vessels unite and form the **median dorsal aorta.**

The intestine is supplied by branches and capillaries from this median vessel. After flowing over the intestine, in capillaries, the blood collects in a median **sub-intestinal** vessel, and passes from this vessel into the **hepatic portal system.** This system has the form of a forward loop in which the blood, however, flows through a **capillary system,** ramifying in the liver (instead of a single vessel to the loop). The bloodvessel leaves the liver near to where it enters, and curves forward as the ventral aorta. The hepatic portal system in the blood vascular circulation is eminently characteristic of the Vertebrata. The blood is colourless, contains a few red corpuscles, but no leucocytes (white corpuscles).

Excretory System.—There are between ninety and one hundred pairs of excretory organs. Each nephridium is situated at the dorsal extremity of a primary gill bar, and opens into a bay-like extension of the atrium. The main portion is in the form of a bent tube with a descending anterior and a horizontal posterior limb. On the dorsal side of the tube bunches of club-like **solenocytes** occur. Each solenocyte consists of a tubule ending in a protoplasmic knob containing the nucleus. From the nuclear region a long flagellum projects and sets up a current in the tubule (*cf.* flame cell and solenocyte).

Nervous System.—The central nervous system is a tubular structure, with thick walls, lying to the dorsal side of the notochord. Its cavity is the **neurocœle** and it is connected to the mid-dorsal region by a **dorsal fissure.** The neurocœle is dilated at the anterior end to form the **encephalocœle** or **cerebral ventricle.** The nerve cord is somewhat triangular in section. In the larva the cerebral ventricle is produced upwards to form the **olfactory pit.** The pit remains in the adult, although the connection vanishes. The first two pairs of nerves are known as **cerebral nerves,** and are sensory in function. The remaining nerves leave the cord alternately, left and right, a fact which is correlated with the alternation of the myomeres.

Reproductive Organs.—The sexes are separate, although there is no apparent secondary sex differentiation. Both kinds of gonad are built on the same plan. There are twenty-six pairs of metamerically arranged pouches on the body wall and projecting into the atrium. The gametes arise on the inner walls of these sacs. When the gametes are ripe the sac ruptures and the germ cells are freed, fertilization taking place in the water.

CHAPTER X

CRANIATA

Scyllium

In the vast majority of Chordates the notochord is replaced by the vertebral column of small bones, and the brain—swollen anterior end of nerve cord—is protected by a hard, usually bony, cranium. As examples of Vertebrates, the Dogfish, Frog, and Rabbit are usually taken. The student should compare the various organs in the three types.

The Craniata are divided into five classes:

1. **Pisces**—aquatic throughout life.
   (*a*) **Elasmobranchii.**—The skeleton is composed entirely of cartilage—*e.g.*, Dogfish, Sharks, Rays.
   (*b*) **Teleostei.**—The bony fishes; thin scales on the skin.

2. **Amphibia.**—Frogs, Toads, and Newts; spend their larval stages in water.
3. **Reptilia.**—Lizards, Snakes, Crocodiles, etc.
4. **Aves.**—Birds.
5. **Mammalia.**—Hair on the skin; young suckled by mother.

Scyllium canicula.

The Dogfish, or "Rough Hound," is one of the smaller sharks of British coastal waters.

External Features.—The body is elongated (2 feet) and fusiform, with the anterior broad and depressed, tapering to a more narrow and rounded posterior with an upward-tilted tail. The body is lighter in colour on the ventral side. In the skin are embedded **placoid scales,** which have backward-pointing spines. Each scale consists of a broad base of bone bearing a spine of dentine covered with enamel. The teeth of the Dogfish and its allies are also enlarged and modified placoid scales. A faint line along each side of the body marks the position of the **lateral line.** This is a tube running beneath the skin and opening to the surface at intervals by means of small pits. Groups of sensory cells (neuromast organs) lie at the base of the tube.

There are present typical fish fins of two kinds:

(*a*) **Unpaired Fins.**—(i.) Two **dorsal median** fins of triangular shape are placed towards the posterior of the body.

(ii.) A **ventral median** or **anal** fin is situated opposite the space between the two dorsal fins.

(iii.) The **caudal** or **tail fin** fringes the tail of the body. It has a narrow dorsal portion, continuous with a notched and larger ventral lobe. The posterior extremity of the vertebral column turns upwards into the dorsal lobe of the tail. Such a tail is of the **heterocercal** type.

(*b*) **Paired Lateral Fins.**—(i.) The anterior or **pectoral** fins are situated just behind the head of the dogfish and on the ventral side.

(ii.) A pair of smaller **pelvic** fins are placed close together on the ventral surface and on either side of the cloaca. In the males the pelvic fins bear on their inner sides a **clasper** each, used during copulation. A dorsal groove is present on each clasper.

All fins are supported by cartilaginous fin rays.

The mouth is set back on the ventral side of the head, and is a somewhat crescentic opening. Just anterior to the mouth are a pair of nasal openings, each of which is connected to the former by an **oronasal** (nasobuccal) groove. Behind each eye is a small round opening—the **spiracle.** There are five pairs of branchial or gill slits leading into the pharynx.

Between the pelvic fins is the **cloaca,** a median ventral opening into which the digestive, excretory, and reproductive systems open.

Skeleton.—The best and obvious way to study the skeletal structures is from an actual specimen. Here the more important points are summed up. The skeleton can be divided into two sets of elements:

1. **Axial**—backbone, skull, and gill arches.
2. **Appendicular**—limbs and their connections with 1.

Backbone.—The vertebræ (130) have solid regions (centra) pierced by the notochord. This structure still remains as biconical wedges between **biconcave** or **amphicœlous** vertebræ. The wedges are connected through the centra by a thin notochordal thread. The spinal cord is enclosed by the vertebral column in a neural canal formed by a neural arch of bones—neural and interneural plates, and neural spines. The anterior or trunk vertebræ have a pair of ventro-lateral transverse processes, but in the tail vertebræ these form ventral hæmal arches instead.

Skull.—The skull consists of a number of " boxes " fastened together. (Fig. 29.)

1. **Cranium,** central " box " protecting the brain.
2. **Pair of nasal capsules** in front of 1.
3. **Pair of auditory capsules** to the posterior lateral corners of 1.
4. Each lateral wall of the cranium is shaped like a saucer, so forming a pair of optic depressions in which the eyes lie. Supra- and sub-orbital ridges are clearly marked.

Numerous openings in the skull should be noted.

1. **Anterior fontanelle,** between cranium and nasal capsules.
2. Pair of foramina (openings) between the cranial and nasal cavities. The olfactory nerves pass through these openings.
3. The lateral cranial walls (between cranial cavity and optic recess) have numerous openings for the passage of cranial nerves and bloodvessels.
4. Grooves along which the carotid arteries pass run along the under side of the cranium.
5. **Foramen magnum,** at the posterior end of skull for the passage of spinal cord to the brain.

Visceral Arches (Fig. 29).—A series of seven arches are formed primarily in the pharyngeal wall. The first two arches have been modified. These arches are:

1. **Mandibular arch,** which forms upper and lower jaws. Each side of the upper jaw is a **palato-pterygo-quadrate** bar. The jaws fuse in the anterior median line. This upper bar is joined to the cranium by two ligaments on each side—an anterior **ethmopalatine** and a posterior **post-spiracular.** Each half of the

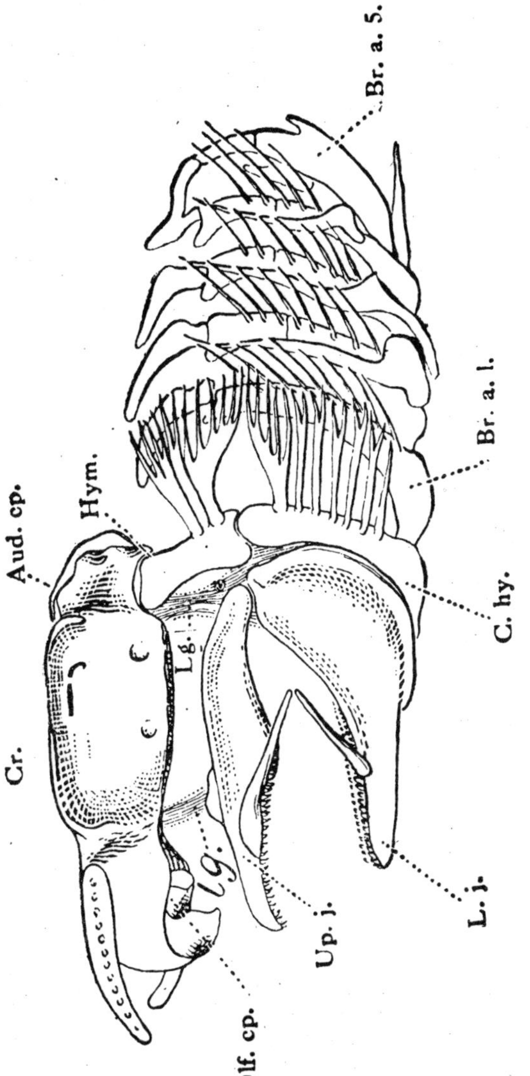

FIG. 29.—SKULL AND VISCERAL ARCHES OF THE DOGFISH (*Scyllium*) AS SEEN FROM THE LEFT SIDE. (AFTER W. K. PARKER.)

(From Gilchrist and Von Bonde.)

Aud. cp., Auditory capsule; Br. a. 1 and 5, branchial arches 1 to 5; C. hy., ceratohyal; Cr., cranium; L.j. and Up.j., lower and upper jaws; Lg., ligament; Olf. cp., olfactory capsule.

lower jaw is made of the lower portion of the arch—**Meckel's cartilage.** The two jaws articulate posteriorly by a movable joint.

2. The **hyoid arch** consists of two cartilages on each side and a median one below. The upper portion, **hyomandibular,** articulates with the otic region of the skull and with the ends of the palato-pterygo-quadrate and Meckel's cartilage. The lower lateral bar is the **ceratohyal,** articulating with the median **basihyal.**

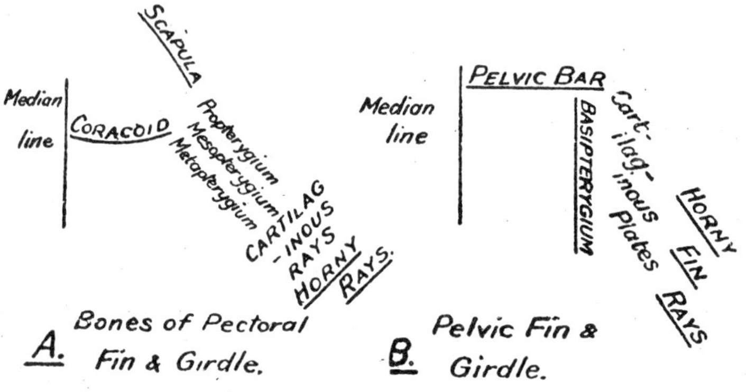

FIG. 30.—A, PECTORAL GIRDLE AND LIMB OF SCYLLIUM; B, PELVIC GIRDLE AND LIMB OF SCYLLIUM.

3 to 7 (inclusive). **Branchial Arches.** These consist of a number of elements, some of which bear backward-pointing **branchial rays** which support the gills.

Limbs.—The fins are supported by numerous cartilaginous rays. Each pair of fins is attached to a girdle embedded in the body (Fig. 28).

The **cœlom** is divided into an anterior **pericardium,** surrounding the heart, and a posterior **pleuro-peritoneal cavity** containing the viscera.

Enteric Canal.—The mouth opens into a wide pharynx into which open the gill clefts and spiracle. A short wide œsophagus passes into a U-shaped stomach having a longer left limb. The **pylorus** is a constricted muscular region between the stomach and intestine. The first portion (about 1 to 2 inches) of the intestine is the **duodenum** or small intestine. This is followed by a longer and wider **large intestine.** The first portion of this region, the **colon,** is very wide and contains within a **spiral valve** of membrane for the retardation of food and increase of absorptive surface. The last portion of the large intestine is the **rectum,** a narrow tube opening by the anus to the cloaca.

There are also a number of organs which are connected with the gut:

1. **Liver.**—A large bilobed organ attached to the anterior wall of the peritoneal cavity by the **falciform** or **suspensory ligament.** The rounded **gall bladder** is embedded at the anterior end of the left hepatic (liver) lobe. The hepatic secretions pass to the intestine by means of a **bile duct.**

2. **Pancreas.**—A light-coloured, elongated gland lying between the right limb of the stomach and the intestine. The **pancreatic duct** opens into the ventral side of the intestine.

3. **Rectal Gland.**—A small, elongated, oval gland ($\frac{3}{4}$ inch) entering the dorsal side of the rectum.

4. **Spleen.**—This is not strictly a part of the digestive system, but it is attached to the convexity of the U-shaped stomach.

Respiratory Organs.—These are in the form of gills situated in the five pairs of gill pouches. These pouches open internally to the pharynx and are compressed clefts between the branchial bars or arches which support them. Each hemibranch (half-gill) is a closely and deeply corrugated portion of highly

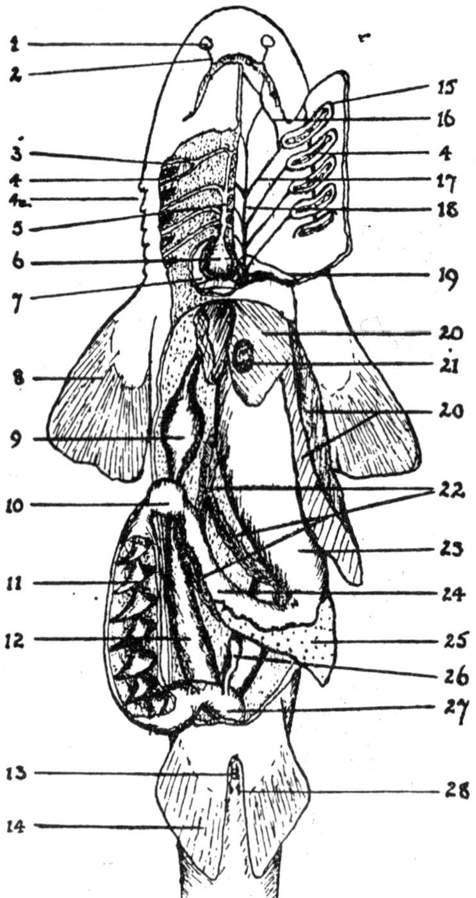

FIG. 31.—GENERAL DISSECTION OF FEMALE DOGFISH.

The right lobe of the liver has been removed; the left side of the floor of the mouth has been turned back to show the dissected roof of the mouth cavity.

1, Olfactory opening; 2, oronasal groove; 3, afferent branchial artery; 4, gills; 4*a*, external opening of gills; 5, ventral aorta; 6, heart (ventricle); 7, pericardium; 8, pectoral fin; 9, shell gland of oviduct; 10, pyloric sphincter; 11, spiral valve in intestine; 12, oviduct; 13, urinary papilla; 14, pelvic fin; 15, efferent branchial artery; 16, carotid artery; 17, epibranchial artery; 18, dorsal aorta; 19, subclavian artery from between epibranchials 3 and 4; 20, liver; 21, gall bladder; 22, pancreas; 23, cardiac and, 24, pyloric portions of stomach; 25, spleen; 26, rectal gland; 27, rectum; 28, abdominal pore.

vascular mucous membrane. The anterior **hemi-branch** is on the posterior surface of the hyoid arch, while the last pouch has only an anterior hemibranch. A few small ridges on the anterior wall of the spiracle form a vestigial gill—the **spiracular gill** or **pseudo-branch.**

Blood System.—*Scyllium* has a closed blood vascular system.

HEART.—The heart lies in the pericardium (cœlom) just to the front of the pectoral girdle. The heart has the form of an S-shaped tube of four chambers (blood flows through in order given):

1. *Sinus venosus*, a thin-walled, triangular chamber which receives the blood from the great veins at its basal angles. The apex opens into the—

2. *Auricle*, by the **sinu-auricular** aperture. This is a large, somewhat rounded chamber situated anterior to the sinus venosus, but on the dorsal limb of the heart "S." The auricle opens into the next chamber by means of an aperture guarded by two valves.

3. *Ventricle.*—This thick-walled chamber lies to the ventral side of the auricle. It is the pumping region of the heart.

4. From the anterior end of the ventricle a median stout tube, the **conus arteriosus,** runs forward to the pericardial wall. Beyond this the tube narrows and continues as the **ventral aorta.**

This ventral aorta sends off **afferent branchial arteries** to the gill arches two, three, and four on each side. The anterior end of the median vessel divides into two branches, and each of these immediately divides, so giving two vessels to each side, supplying the hyoid and first branchial arch. The blood then passes through the branchial capillary system, where oxygenation takes place. It is then gathered by **efferent branchials** which encircle the branchial clefts. From each efferent a single **epibranchial artery** runs backwards above the roof of the mouth. The epibranchials join to form a median dorsal aorta. From the first branchial cleft two vessels, **dorsal** and **ventral carotid arteries,** pass forward on each side to the head. (Fig. 30.)

The dorsal aorta runs backwards through the whole length of the body and ends as the **caudal** artery,

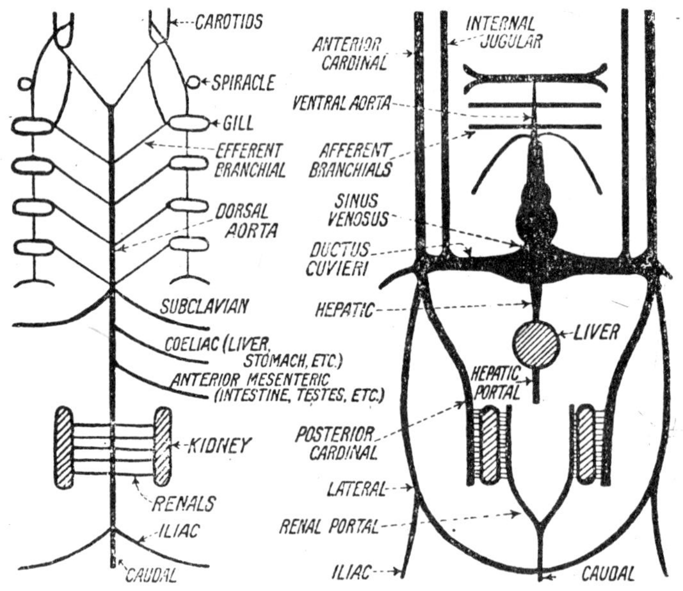

FIG. 32.—THE BLOOD SYSTEM OF THE DOGFISH.

Arteries shown on the left and veins on the right. The ventral aorta and afferent vessels, which are arteries, are shown, however, in the diagram of veins. Minor vessels are omitted.

(From "Aids to Biology.")

running through the hæmal arches of the caudal vertebræ.

ARTERIAL BRANCHES FROM DORSAL AORTA.—1. *Subclavian arteries* (paired), to the pectoral fins; given off between epibranchials 3 and 4.

2. *Cœliac artery* (unpaired), runs in the mesenteries,

and divides to supply stomach, liver, pancreas, and first part of intestine.

3. *Anterior mesenteric artery* (unpaired), supplies remainder of intestine and gives branches to gonads.

4. *Lienogastric artery* (unpaired), to part of stomach, the spleen, and part of pancreas.

5. *Posterior mesenteric artery* (unpaired), mainly to rectal gland.

6. Several *renal arteries* (paired), to the kidneys.

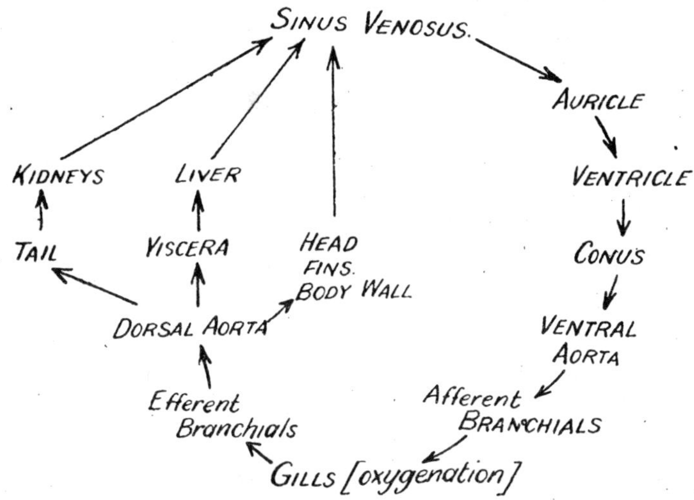

FIG. 33.—DIAGRAM OF BLOOD CIRCULATION IN *Scyllium*.

7. *Iliac arteries* (paired), to the pelvic fins.

8. *Parietal arteries* (paired), numerous small vessels supplying the body wall, given off throughout the length of the aorta.

The deoxygenated blood returns to the sinus venosus by means of large dilated veins (called sinuses, but not in the sense used in dealing with Invertebrates). The blood is collected from the various parts of the body by what may be termed "drainage systems":

1. *From the Head.*—By **anterior cardinal sinus, inferior jugular sinus** below throat to a transverse **ductus Cuvieri** on each side.

2. *From Fins and Body Wall.*—By **subclavian** sinus (pectoral fin), **iliac** sinus (pelvic fin), and **deep lateral** sinus on each side to ductus Cuvieri.

3. *From Tail and Posterior Region of Body.*—By a **caudal** vein, which bifurcates to form a pair of **renal portal** veins, which break up into a capillary system in the kidneys. These capillaries rejoin to empty into the **posterior cardinal sinuses,** which commence on the inner side of each kidney and empty into the ductus Cuvieri. These sinuses are much dilated anteriorly. This system, in which blood undergoes treatment by a renal capillary system, is known as the **renal portal system.**

4. *From the Intestine.*—The blood is collected into the **hepatic portal vein** from the alimentary canal and spleen. This vein breaks into a capillary system in the liver, from whence it empties by the **hepatic** sinus straight into the sinus venosus. This forms the **hepatic portal system.**

Nervous System.—The nervous system of the Vertebrates can be divided into two main portions—the **spinal cord** and the **brain.**

(*a*) Spinal Cord.—The cord is tubular, but owing to the enormous growth of the walls the lumen is comparatively small. There is also a narrow cleft running along the dorsal median line and one in the median ventral line. These are the dorsal and ventral fissures. The cord is composed of a more central mass of **grey matter** (nerve cells) and an investing layer of **white matter** (nerve fibres, each bound in a sheath of white material).

The spinal nerves to the body, etc., arise in pairs, each by a dorsal and ventral root. These two roots join, and from the common junction a dorsal and ventral branch supply the body wall, etc., and a ramus communicans connects the cord to the sympathetic nervous system. This latter system works independently of the central system, and has control of the visceral activities.

(*b*) BRAIN AND CRANIAL NERVES.—The brain originates with three regions—fore-, mid-, and hind-brain portions (prosencephalon, mesencephalon, and metencephalon). Owing to the subsequent division of the former and latter portions, the adult brain is made up of five secondary segments—**telencephalon, diencephalon** or **thalamencephalon, mesencephalon, metencephalon,** and **myelencephalon.**

1. *Myelencephalon or Medulla Oblongata.*—This is the posterior region of the brain, arising from the spinal cord. The roof of this portion is very thin. Most of the paired **cranial nerves** (see table on page 142) are connected to the myelencephalon, some arising dorso-laterally, others ventrally.

X. This is the most posterior cranial nerve—the **vagus,** arising by a number of roots. Many of the cranial nerves carry both sensory messages (inwards) and motor impulses (outwards)—*i.e.*, mixed nerves. The vagus is of such a constitution. It supplies the following parts from its separate branches:

(*a*) **Branchial branch** to the gill arches 2, 3, 4, and 5.

(*b*) The branchial branch continues posteriorly as the **visceral** portion to the heart, stomach, etc.

(*c*) **Lateral line** branch, supplying the lateral line sense organs.

IX. Just anterior to the vagus is the ninth cranial or **glossopharyngeal** nerve (mixed). It supplies the **first** gill slit, palate, and tongue.

VIII. The eighth nerve is the **auditory,** a sensory nerve to the ear.

VII. The seventh or **facial** nerve (mixed) is extremely important, and gives off a number of branches:

1. **Ophthalmic branch,** which runs along with a similar branch from the fifth nerve to the snout (sensory).
2. **Buccal branch** (sensory) joins main branch of fifth nerve, and with it crosses the optic orbit. Supplies the side of the head.
3. **Palatine branch** to the roof of the mouth (sensory).
4. **Hyomandibular branch** (mixed) passes down hyoid arch, and divides to supply the lower jaw.

VI. The **Abducent,** or sixth nerve, is a small one, arising from the floor of the myelencephalon. It supplies the rectus externus eye muscle.

[*Note.*—There are six eye muscles—viz., external, internal, superior and inferior rectus muscles, lying approximately at right angles to one another; and a superior and inferior oblique muscle at the anterior corners of the eye. Dissect out the orbit carefully for eye muscles and nerves.]

V. **Trigeminal,** or fifth cranial nerve, arises from the anterior end of the myelencephalon. It splits into three main branches:

1. **Ophthalmic branch,** which passes through the dorsal side of the orbit, and is distributed to the snout and dorsal portion of the head.
2. **Maxillary branch** to the skin under the eye and to the upper jaw.
3. **Mandibular branch** to the skin and muscles of lower jaw, therefore a mixed nerve.

2. *Metencephalon.*—This is a very short portion of the brain, and ventrally seems continuous with the myelencephalon. Its dorsal surface, however, unlike

the thin roof of the medulla, is much thickened as the **cerebellum.** This is particularly so in *Scyllium* and its allies. From the dorsal anterior end of the metencephalon cranial nerve IV, the **patheticus,** arises, and supplies the superior oblique eye muscle.

3. *Mesencephalon.*—The walls of this region are thickened dorso-laterally to form a pair of lateral **optic lobes,** in which the optic fibres to the retina of the eye originate. From the ventral surface of the mesencephalon there arises cranial nerve III or **oculo-motor** nerve. It supplies the superior, inferior, and internal recti, and the inferior oblique eye muscles.

4. *Diencephalon or Thalamencephalon.*—This is a very narrow region. From the dorsal median portion an upward projection, the **pineal stalk** or **body,** arises. The lateral walls are thickened as the **optic thalami.** The optic tracts pass along these regions to the optic lobes. The floor bears a hollow, backwardly pointing outgrowth, the **infundibulum,** whose lateral walls are thickened as the **inferior lobes.** The anterior border of the diencephalon is marked by the origin of nerve II or **optic** nerve. This pair of nerves cross, and their fibres intermingle in the **optic chiasma.**

5. *Telencephalon.*—This anterior segment is divided longitudinally into two **cerebral lobes** or hemispheres. The anterior of each lobe is produced diagonally forwards as a slender neck, ending in a swollen **olfactory lobe.** The olfactory lobes are in contact with the **olfactory sacs** or capsules. Numerous nerve fibres pass from the olfactory lobe (nervous) to the sac (actual sensory organ), and these fibres together constitute cranial nerve I (**olfactory**).

A very careful dissection of the head, the brain and cranial nerves, the eye socket and ear and nasal capsules should be made.

SUMMARY OF THE CRANIAL NERVES OF SCYLLIUM.

Number.	*Name.*	*Origin.*	*Branches.*	*Components.*
I.	Olfactory.	Telencephalon.	—	Sensory—nose.
II.	Optic.	Diencephalon.	—	Sensory—eye.
III.	Oculo-motor.	Mesencephalon.	(*a*) Superior rectus muscle. (*b*) Inferior rectus muscle. (*c*) Internal rectus muscle. (*d*) Inferior oblique muscle.	Motor.
IV.	Patheticus.	Metencephalon.	Superior oblique muscle.	Motor.
V.	Trigeminal.	Myelencephalon.	(*a*) Ophthalmic. (*b*) Maxillary. (*c*) Mandibular.	Sensory. Sensory. Mixed.
VI.	Abducent.	Myelencephalon.	External rectus muscle.	Motor.
VII.	Facial.	Myelencephalon.	(*a*) Ophthalmic. (*b*) Buccal. (*c*) Palatine. (*d*) Hyomandibular.	Sensory. Sensory. Sensory. Mixed.
VIII.	Auditory.	Myelencephalon.	—	Sensory—ear.
IX.	Glosso-pharyngeal.	Myelencephalon.	First gill slit; palate and tongue.	Mixed.
X.	Vagus.	Myelencephalon.	(*a*) Branchial arches. (*b*) Lateral line. (*c*) Visceral.	Mixed. Sensory. Mixed.

Sense Organs.—The nasal sac is contained within the olfactory capsule. The sac is lined with sensory epithelium, which is thrown into a number of folds.

The eye and ear are typically of the well-developed vertebrate type to be described later.

There are, however, a set of sensory organs peculiar to the fishes. These **neuromast organs,** as they are called, lie in the bottom of tubes which contain mucus, and which ramify over the body surface. The most important of these epidermal tubes is the lateral line. The neuromast organs are supplied by a special set of nerve fibres which enter the brain by means of the ophthalmic branch of the seventh, and the lateral line branch of the tenth, cranial nerves. The neuromast organs perform an accessory auditory function, as they can perceive low-frequency vibrations which are undetected by the ear.

Urinogenital Organs.—The excretory and reproductive organs of the Vertebrates are usually very closely connected.

Female.—1. **Ovary.** This is a single, soft lobulated organ lying just to the right of the middle line and attached by a peritoneal fold—the **mesoarium**—to the body wall. Ova in various stages of maturation can be discerned through the outer epithelium.

2. *Oviducts,* two in number and unconnected with the ovary, run the whole length of the body cavity. They unite anteriorly to open into the cœlom by a common median aperture. A swollen portion—the **shell gland**—is found about one-third of the tube's length from the anterior. A posterior enlargement of the oviduct forms a uterine chamber. The two oviducts then unite and open into the cloaca behind the anal aperture.

The kidneys lie above the dorsal wall of the peritoneum, which must be dissected away first. Each kidney consists of a narrow anterior and a wider posterior portion. The ducts from the former portions run over the ventral surface, dilating posteriorly as **urinary sinuses** which unite and open into the cloaca by a median urinary papilla. The ducts from the posterior region are four to six pairs of **ureters** which open into the urinary sinuses.

Male.—**Testes,** a pair of elongated soft bodies attached to the body wall by a peritoneal fold—the **mesorchium.** Fine tubules—**vasa efferentia**—pass from the testis of each side to a long body which corresponds to the anterior narrow kidney in the female. The **vas deferens** runs the entire length of this non-renal portion in a series of coils, and the whole structure is known as the **epididymis.** The posterior end of the tube widens to form a **vesicula seminalis.** This opens into the base of a large, thin-walled, blind-ended (anteriorly) **sperm sac.** The left and right sperm sacs combine to form the urinogenital sinus, a median portion which opens into the cloaca.

The posterior portion of the kidney resembles that of the female. The five ureters, often fusing, open into the urinogenital sinus. The anterior portions of the oviducts remain as vestigial structures just anterior to the liver in the male.

The ripe ova escape from the ovary into the abdominal cavity and then pass into the oviducts by the common median opening. Fertilization then occurs, following copulation, and the zygote is enclosed in a chitinous case secreted by the shell gland.

CHAPTER XI

AMPHIBIA

RANA

THE majority of Amphibians spend their young or larval stages in water, when they breathe by means of gills. Some forms retain the gills throughout life, although lungs are usually present in adult forms. The forms which remain in the water throughout life have median fins. These, however, differ from those of the fishes in that the amphibian fin is devoid of fin rays. The very important difference and advance in the Amphibia is in the paired appendages. The paired fins are replaced by **pentadactyle** limbs—*i.e.*, typically one upper and two lower limb bones, and five jointed digits.

The skin is devoid of any exoskeletal structures as a rule. It is damp and cold, and is used as an organ of respiration accessory to lungs or gills.

The class includes:

1. **Urodela.**—Tail retained throughout life and limbs of approximately equal size.

   (*a*) **Perennibranchiata.**—Retain gills throughout life—*e.g.*, *Necturus* and *Siren* of America, and the blind *Proteus* from certain Dalmatian caves.

   (*b*) **Derotremata.**—Gills lost in adult, but one gill cleft usually persists—*e.g.*, Giant Salamander of Japan and China (*Megalobatrachus*).

   (*c*) **Myctodera.**—Gills and gill clefts lost in the adults—*e.g.*, Newts and Salamanders.

2. **Anura.**—Frogs and Toads. No tail in adults. The trunk is short and broad, whilst the fore limbs

are much shorter than the hind limbs. Lungs are adult respiratory organs.

3. **Gymnophiona (Apoda).**—Snake-like, have neither limbs nor tail. Dermal scales are present. The group includes the Cæcilians.

As an example of the group the Common Frog, *Rana temporaria,* may be taken.

RANA TEMPORARIA

The common frog is found in and around ponds and damp situations all over the country.

External Features.—1. **Trunk** is short and broad, rather squat, and continues anteriorly—there is no neck—into a broad flattened **head.**

2. Anteriorly placed is a wide gaping **mouth,** which, when open, discloses the short muscular tongue (attached to the anterior of the lower jaw) with a bifid tip. It can be easily flicked forwards.

3. The external nares are a pair of small openings just above the mouth.

4. The eyes are prominent and bulging. Each has an upper eyelid and a **nictitating membrane.** The latter is a membraneous fold arising from the lower margin of the eye. It can be drawn over the eye.

5. Behind each eye is a circular patch of tightly stretched skin. This is a part of the ear, and is known as the **tympanic membrane.**

6. In the resting position a distinct hump marks the position of the sacral vertebræ.

Skeleton: 1. **Axial Portion.**—(*a*) The vertebral column is extremely short, made up of nine vertebræ and a posterior slender rod, the **urostyle.** The neural canal is large. Articulating projections protrude from the anterior and posterior dorsal portion of the neural arches. These are **zygapophyses.** The lateral walls of the neural arch give off a **transverse process** on each side (*cf.* Scyllium). The centra are **procœlous**—*i.e.*, concave anterior and a convex posterior face.

The first or **cervical** vertebra has a small centrum, no transverse processes or anterior zygapophyses. At the junction of neural arch and centrum there occurs a large oval facet on each side for articulation to the condyles of the skull (*vide infra*).

The centrum of the eighth vertebra is amphicœlous. The ninth or **sacral** vertebra is convex anteriorly, and has a double convexity posteriorly for articulation to the urostyle. The latter is regarded as a continuation of the vertebral column, which, however, has not become segmented in this region.

(*b*) *Skull* (Figs. 34-36).—The tadpole (larva) of the frog has a cartilaginous skull, which resembles that of the adult *Scyllium*. During the change from larval to adult life this cartilaginous skull becomes ossified—*i.e.*, bony—by deposition of lime salts, etc., in the cartilage. Also at this time other bones are formed in the membranes investing the skull. Thus the skull bones of the adult frog are of two kinds, according to their origin:

(1) **Cartilage bones,** those which are preformed in cartilage.

(2) **Membrane bones** are those which have been laid down in a membrane. These bones always lie to the outer side of cartilage bones.

The skull consists of cranium, nasal capsules, auditory capsules, and the altered first two visceral arches (mandibular and hyoid). The eye socket is very large, and lies between the cranium and upper jaw, which is firmly fused to the cranium.

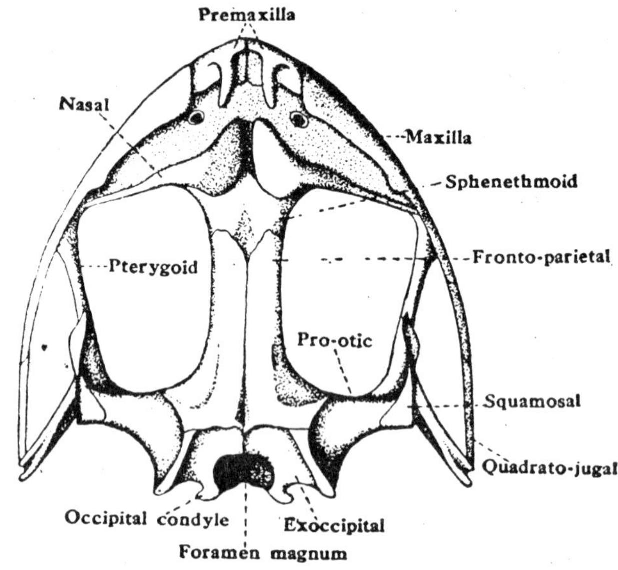

Fig. 34.—Dorsal View of Skull of Rana.

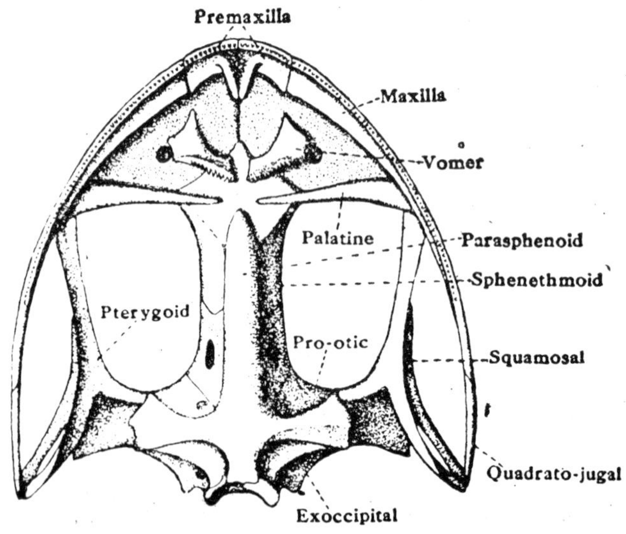

Fig. 35.—Ventral View of Skull of Rana.
(From Gilchrist and Von Bonde.)

The skull bones may be summarized thus:

Cartilage Bones.	*Membrane Bones.*
Exoccipitals.	Fronto-parietals.
Sphenethmoid.	Parasphenoid.
Mesethmoid.	Nasals.
Pro-otics.	Vomers.
*Palatines.	Squamosals.
*Pterygoids.	Premaxillæ.
Mento-Meckelians.	Maxillæ.
Posterior cornua.	Quadrato-jugals.
	Angulo-splenials.
	Dentaries.

The position and relation of these bones should be made out from an actual specimen.

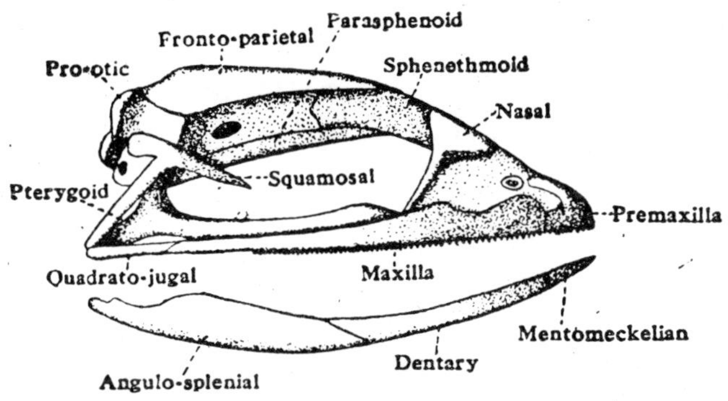

FIG. 36.—SIDE VIEW OF SKULL OF RANA.
(From Gilchrist and Von Bonde.)

2. **Appendicular Portion:** (*a*) *Pectoral Girdle and Limb* (Fig. 37, A).—The pectoral girdle is embedded in the body wall, and forms almost a circle. In this space between the dorsal ends of the girdle the vertebral column passes, but the two structures do

* The palatine and pterygoid are cartilage bones in most animals. In the frog incomplete ossification of the original cartilage results in the ossifying cartilage being replaced by membrane bones. Thus the palatine and pterygoid may be included with the membrane bones.

not articulate. Thus the girdle might be termed "floating." The top end of the upper arm bone fits into a depression in the girdle—the **glenoid cavity**—between the **scapula** and **coracoid.**

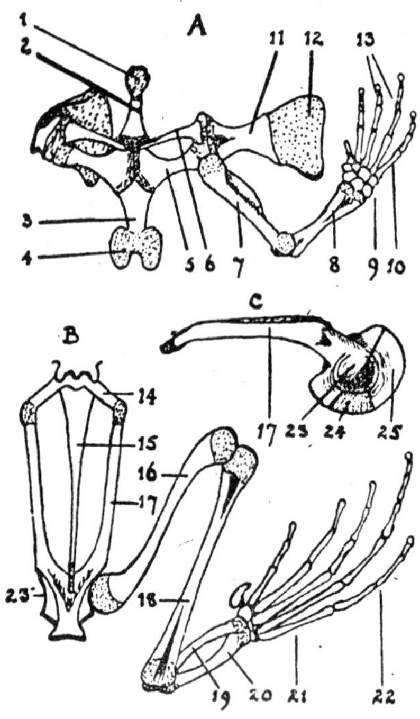

FIG. 37.—APPENDICULAR SKELETON OF RANA.

A, Pectoral girdle and limb; B, Pelvic girdle and limb; C, side view of pelvic girdle.

1, Episternum; 2, omosternum; 3, mesosternum; 4, xiphisternum; 5, coracoid; 6, clavicle; 7, humerus; 8, radio-ulna; 9, carpals; 10, metacarpals; 11, scapula; 12, suprascapula; 13, phalanges of hand; 14, sacral vertebra; 15, urostyle; 16, femur; 17, ilium; 18, tibio-fibula; 19, astragalus; 20, calcaneum; 21, metatarsals; 22, phalanges of foot; 23, acetabulum; 24, pubis; 25, ischium.

(*b*) *Pelvic Girdle and Limb* (Fig. 37, B).—The pelvic girdle is shaped like a long narrow **V.** Anteriorly the free ends articulate with the transverse processes of the sacral vertebra. The angle of the **V** is thickened and somewhat circular from the lateral aspect. There is a lateral depression—the **acetabulum**—in each side of this basal enlargement, for the articulation of the limb.

The ankle bones—tarsals—are not aggregated like the carpals (wrist bones). Two of the tarsals—the **astragalus** and **calcaneum**—are extremely elongated, thus giving the hind limbs an extra joint.

Digestive Organs.—The buccal cavity contains:

(*a*) **Internal nares** on the roof of the mouth.

(*b*) Downward bulges of the eyes.

(*c*) Openings of a pair of **Eustachian tubes** (*vide infra*) at the back part of the roof.

(*d*) Tongue on floor; free bifid tip points inwards when at rest.

(*e*) **Glottis**—the opening of the respiratory system—is found behind the tongue towards the back of the mouth cavity.

(*f*) **Teeth,** in a single row on maxillæ and premaxillæ of upper jaw only. Teeth also occur on the vomers just posterior to the internal nares. The teeth are not used for biting and chewing food, as they are only fused to the jaw bone, and not embedded in sockets as in higher animals. In the frog they prevent food from slipping out of the mouth.

From the posterior side of the buccal cavity the **pharynx** arises, and leads by a short **gullet** into the **stomach.** The latter has a wider anterior portion, and narrows off to the pyloric region, which passes into the **intestine.** The first portion of the intestine —the **duodenum**—loops forward parallel with the stomach. This is followed by a coiled region of intestine—the **ileum**—which widens to form the large intestine or **rectum** opening into the cloaca.

Accessory Digestive Organs.—1. **Liver,** a bilobed reddish gland attached to the anterior wall of the body cavity.

2. **Gall bladder** lies between left and right hepatic lobes. Ducts from the liver and gall bladder (hepatic and gall ducts) unite to form a common bile duct opening into the first portion of the duodenum.

3. **Pancreas,** an irregular glandular mass surrounding the bile duct, into which it sends its secretions. It lies in between the loop of the stomach and duodenum.

4. **Spleen,** a small rounded red body attached near to the anterior end of rectum.

Respiratory Organs.—By means of the glottis a small chamber—the **laryngo-tracheal** chamber—communicates with the pharynx. A pair of membraneous folds are present in this chamber. These are the vocal chords, whose vibrations produce the croak of the frog. From the posterior corners of the chamber two openings lead into a pair of **lungs.** These are elastic sacs lying in the antero-lateral portion of the cœlom. They vary in size according to their state of distension at death. Each lung is a thin-walled sac, whose walls, however, are folded to form numerous ridges. These ridges are richly supplied with blood capillaries.

The frog breathes with its mouth closed. Then by depressing the floor of the mouth air is drawn into the buccal cavity through the nostrils. The nostrils have valves controlled by muscles. As the mouth floor is raised the nasal valves close, and air is pumped through the glottis to the lungs. The air is exhaled by the aid of abdominal muscles and the elastic collapse of the lungs, as nasal valves open.

The skin of the frog is also an accessory respiratory organ. It is richly supplied with blood, which exchanges gases through the moist skin.

Blood System.—The circulatory system of *Rana* has advanced in many respects upon the type found in *Scyllium.*

A. HEART.—The heart lies in the **pericardium**—a fold of membrane. The heart has become more complex here than in *Scyllium*, and the **S**-shape has been lost, to a large extent, as the various chambers now form a more compact mass. There are five chambers to the heart (*i.e.*, the part within the pericardium).

1. The **sinus venosus** lies on the dorsal surface of the heart mass, and is triangular in shape. It opens by a sinu-auricular aperture into—

2. The **right auricle.** Owing to the air-breathing habit of the Vertebrates above the Fishes, the single auricle or atrium of the Pisces is replaced by a **right and left auricle.** The right auricle is larger than the left.

3. The **left auricle** receives the oxygenated blood from the lungs. At the base of the septum which divides the two auricles there is a common auriculo-ventricular opening guarded by valves.

4. The **ventricle** is the median posterior chamber of the heart mass. It receives the blood from the left and right auricles. The wall is very muscular, and the inner surface is deeply corrugated.

5. From the right ventral surface of the ventricle there arises the tubular **truncus arteriosus.** Valves (three) guard the opening between the truncus and ventricle. The truncus is divided into two passages by a longitudinally running spiral valve. The more distal portion of the truncus stem is known as the **bulbus aortæ.** This branches into a left and right trunk, each of which is divided by two longitudinal partitions into

(*a*) An anterior **carotid** trunk.
(*b*) A median **systemic** or **aortic** portion.
(*c*) A posterior **pulmo-cutaneous** arch.

The pulmo-cutaneous trunks open separately lower down the bulbus than the other two pairs of arches. These three trunks on each side eventually separate.

B. Arterial System.—An artery is a vessel which carries blood away from the heart. Such blood is usually pure and oxygenated, except the pulmonary artery, which carries blood away from the heart to the lungs for aeration.

The tadpole has four gill arches arising from the heart and passing through the gills to form the dorsal aorta. At the metamorphosis of the larva to the air-breathing adult, these arches alter as the gills disappear. The first pair of arches lose their connections with the aorta and turn forward as the pair of carotid trunks to the head. The second pair remain and enlarge as the systemic or aortic arches of the adult, whilst the third pair disappear altogether. The fourth pair lose their aortic connections, and send branches to the lungs and skin as the pulmocutaneous trunks.

Each of these arterial trunks supplies special portions of the body (Fig. 38).

1. *Carotid System.*—The carotid arch on each side sends off a **lingual** artery to the tongue. Just beyond this point of branching the arch has a swollen spongy portion—the **carotid labyrinth.** From beyond the labyrinth the arch bifurcates to form an **internal** and **external carotid artery.**

2. *Systemic or Aortic System.*—The right and left portions of the systemic arch loop dorsal to the heart and join to form a median **dorsal aorta.** This is the main artery of the body. It gives off the following branches (from before backwards):

(1) A pair of **subclavian arteries,** from each side of the systemic loop, pass to the arm. (These arteries arise from the median aorta in the Urodeles.)

(2) A median unpaired **cœliaco-mesenteric** artery divides into—

(*a*) Cœliac branch to the liver and stomach.

(*b*) Mesenteric branch to the mesenteries, intestine, and spleen.

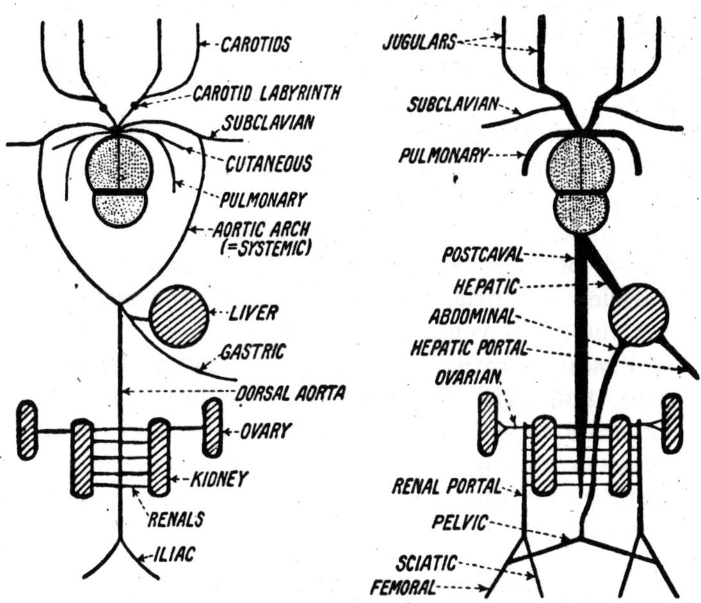

FIG. 38.—THE BLOOD SYSTEM OF THE FROG.

Arteries shown on the left and veins on the right. Minor vessels are omitted. Both diagrams are drawn from the ventral side, consequently the *ventral* abdominal vein is drawn aside to display the *dorsal* postcaval vein. The gastric artery does not run sideways, but straight downwards to the gut.

(From " Aids to Biology.")

(3) Paired **renal** and **gonadic** arteries supply the kidneys and gonads respectively.

(4) The posterior end of the aorta bifurcates into a **common iliac** artery in each leg.

3. *Pulmo-cutaneous Arch.*—This takes deoxygenated blood to the lungs and skin for purification. The

main arch divides, therefore, into **pulmonary** and **cutaneous** branches.

The arteries end in capillary systems. Each of these forms a network of minute vessels which come into intimate contact with the various tissues of the body. The vessels in each capillary field rejoin and give rise to the smaller veins. The blood then passes towards the heart by means of the venous system.

C. Venous System.—The veins are those vessels which collect the blood from the various parts of the body and take it to the heart. All veins except the pulmonary veins carry impure blood. The pure blood of the pulmonary veins passes to the left auricle. All other veins empty into the right auricle via the sinus venosus. (Fig. 38.)

Venous Drainage Systems.—1 and 2. **From head, arm, and skin on each side.** A left and a right **superior vena cava** (precaval) vein enters the sinus venosus on each side. Each anterior vena cava is formed by the union of three smaller drainage systems. (Fig. 39, A.)

(i.) **External jugular vein,** which is formed by the union of a **lingual** and **mandibular** branch draining the head.

(ii.) **Innominate vein,** formed by the **internal jugular** and **subscapular** branches from the head and shoulder region.

(iii.) **Subclavian vein,** the result of the union of the **brachial** vein from the arm and the **musculo-cutaneous** vein draining the skin and muscles of the side of the body wall.

3. **From the legs, viscera, and posterior of body.** The blood in this system passes through either the hepatic or renal portal system.

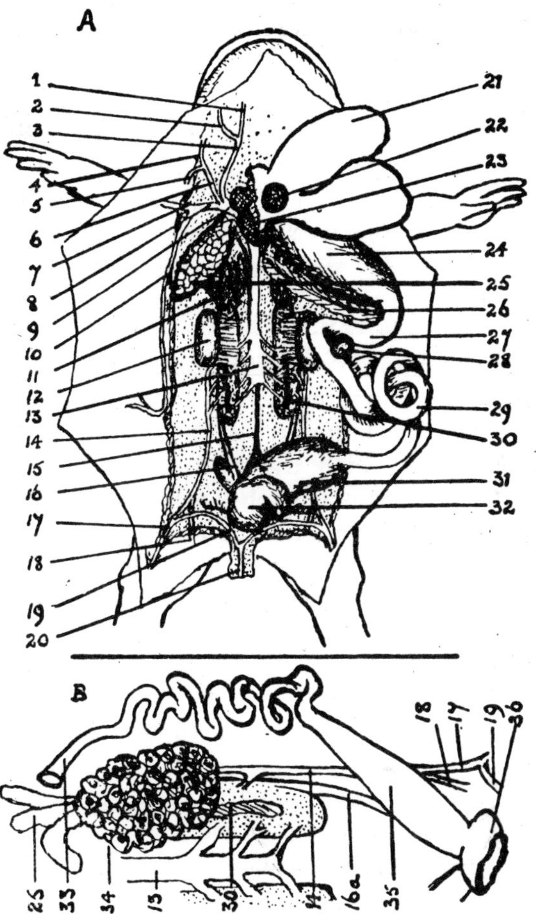

FIG. 39.—A, GENERAL DISSECTION OF MALE FROG; B, REPRODUCTIVE ORGANS OF FEMALE.

1, Lingual vein; 2, mandibular vein; 3, external jugular vein; 4, internal jugular vein; 5, subscapular vein; 6, innominate vein; 7, brachial vein; 8, subclavian vein; 9, right superior vena cava; 10, musculo-cutaneous vein; 11, fat bodies; 12, testis; 13, renal veins forming inferior vena cava; 14, renal portal vein; 15, aorta; 16, ureter with vesicula seminalis; 17, femoral vein; 18, sciatic vein; 19, pelvic vein; 20, anterior abdominal vein (turned back after being severed); 21, liver (right lobe removed); 22, gall bladder; 23, heart; 24, stomach; 25, lung; 26, pancreas and duct; 27, duodenum; 28, spleen; 29, ileum; 30, suprarenal body on ventral face of kidney; 31, rectum; 32, bladder; 33, top of oviduct; 34, ovary; 35, uterus; 36, cloaca.

Blood is collected from each leg by two veins:

(*a*) The **sciatic vein** to the inner side. This passes anteriorly into the **renal portal vein,** which sends the blood through the renal capillary system. The blood passes from the kidney by small renal veins to a median **posterior vena cava** (postcaval), which runs anteriorly to open into the sinus venosus.

(*b*) The **femoral** vein to the outside of the leg also joins the renal portal vein. Just posterior to the junction of the sciatic and renal portal veins the two femoral veins send off a branch each—**pelvic** veins—towards the middle line. These two pelvic veins join and run forwards in the ventral body-wall as the **anterior abdominal** vein. At the posterior level of the liver this latter vein bifurcates, and each branch turns upwards into a lobe of the liver. The blood thus brought then passes into the hepatic capillary system, and out by two short, broad hepatic veins into the post-caval vein just posterior to its entry into the sinus venosus.

The blood from the stomach, intestine, pancreas, and spleen is gathered up by a large **hepatic portal vein** which empties into the liver.

Thus it is clear that, although the impure or venous blood and the pure oxygenated blood are kept separate in the right and left auricles respectively, there being only one ventricle, the blood in it will be of a more or less mixed nature. As soon as the ventricle receives the blood from the auricles—oxygenated in left and impure in right portions—it contracts. The two types of blood are kept somewhat separate, partly in the muscular cavities of the ventricle, and partly by immediate contraction—not allowing the blood to mix to any great extent. Since the truncus arises from the right side of the ventricle, it will receive at first only venous blood from that side. The blood has three possible routes before it—along carotid, systemic, or pulmo-cutaneous arches. The carotid and systemic trunks, however, offer a great resistance to the blood flow, as they both have extensive capillary systems. Thus the path of least resistance is taken, the pulmo-cutaneous arches to the lungs receiving, therefore, a supply of mainly impure blood for aeration. This process is assisted by the fact that the pulmo-cutaneous arches open below the spiral valve of the truncus arteriosus.

Within a fraction of a second, however, the pulmo-cutaneous system fills up, and the carotid and systemic systems have their pressure reduced owing to the blood flowing into their capillary systems. Thus continued pressure exerted by the ventricle forces the blood past the spiral valve into the bulbus aortæ. Again the path of least resistance is taken. The carotid labyrinths retard the passage of blood, so that the systemic arches receive the " middle portion of blood "—*i.e.*, the slightly mixed venous and arterial blood. Thus the systemic arches fill up—*i.e.*, giving a higher resistance—and so the last portion of blood squeezed out by the final ventricular contraction will be mainly pure blood. As the pulmo-cutaneous and systemic trunks are now full, therefore having a big resistance, this pure blood passes through the carotid arches to the head, brain, etc.

Nervous System.—The nervous system is made up of wo main portions

1. **Cerebro-spinal system** of brain, spinal cord, and their nerves.
2. **Sympathetic system** of ganglia and nerves.

Spinal Cord.—The nerve cord which runs in the neural canals of the vertebræ is somewhat circular in section. It ends in the **filum terminale,** a fine thread of nervous tissue in the urostyle. The cord contains the neurocœle or canal. The inner mass of grey matter surrounding the canal lumen gives off a dorsal and ventral horn on each side.

Ten pairs of spinal nerves arise from the cord. Each nerve has a dorsal root and ganglion thereon, and a ventral root. The two roots join just outside the backbone, the common portion giving a dorsal and ventral branch to various parts of the body and a ramus communicans to the sympathetic system. The dorsal roots carry sensory or afferent impulses, and the ventral roots send out motor responsive orders.

The first spinal nerve is the **hypoglossal,** which curves forward to the tongue. A branch of the first nerve, together with the second and third spinal nerves, join to form the **brachial plexus,** from which the **brachial** nerve supplies the arm. Nerves 4, 5, and 6 are small and separate. The leg is supplied by the **sciatic nerve,** which arises from the sciatic plexus formed by the junction of spinal nerves 7 to 10 inclusive.

Brain.—The parts of the brain are essentially the same as those of *Scyllium,* although the proportion varies. The brain has a small cerebellum, large optic lobes and diencephalon, and large cerebral hemispheres and olfactory bulbs. The latter pair of bulbs are fused in the middle line. The other portions of the brain resemble those found in *Scyllium.* The brain of *Rana,* like all vertebrate brains, contains cavities which are really the swollen anterior end of the spinal cord lumen. The cerebral hemispheres each have a **lateral ventricle** or space. Each connects by a **foramen** of **Munro** with the **third ventricle,** a deep but narrow cavity in the thalamencephalon. The **fourth ventricle** is that of the medulla oblongata. It is connected to the third ventricle by a narrow passage, the **iter** or **aqueduct,** which gives off a cavity into each optic lobe.

The cranial nerve distribution is the same as that of *Scyllium* in all essentials.

Sympathetic Nervous System.—This system consists of a chain of ganglia on each side of the backbone. Each ganglion is connected to the central nervous system by a ramus communicans. The cord connecting the ganglia is single except between ganglia one and two, where it is double, forming a loop (ansa subclavia) through which the subclavian artery passes. The anterior end of the sympathetic cord is connected with the cranial nerves (five and ten). The sympathetic nerves supply the viscera by means of plexuses.

The structure of the organs of special sense will be referred to in a later chapter.

Urinogenital Organs : *Kidneys.*—These are a pair of elongated, oval, dark-red bodies lying on the dorsal side of the posterior part of the body cavity. An elongated yellow **adrenal body** lies on the ventral surface of each kidney. A **ureter** passes from the posterior lateral wall of each kidney to open into the dorsal side of the cloaca. Opening on the ventral side of the cloaca is a bilobed thin-walled sac, the **urinary bladder,** into which the urine, excreted by the kidneys, passes by gravitation.

Male Organs.—Testes, a pair of white ovoid bodies, lie below the anterior end of the kidneys, to which they are attached by a thin fold of peritoneum. The spermatozoa pass by a number of **vasa efferentia** to the kidney above the testes. The spermatic fluid then passes to the exterior by way of the urinary tubules and ureters. The latter are therefore urinogenital ducts in the male frog. A vesicula seminalis is attached to the outer side of each ureter by numerous fine tubules. Bright yellow **fat bodies** are attached to the testes.

Female Organs.—The **ovaries** are large and studded with the black and white eggs. A fat body is attached to each ovary. The **oviducts** are a pair of much convoluted tubes. The narrower anterior end of each oviduct opens by an oviducal aperture near the base of the lung. The posterior portion of each tube is wide and thin-walled (uterus), and opens into the cloaca. The ova when mature break away from the ovary and pass into the oviduct, whose walls secrete an albuminous substance which swells when in contact with water. The eggs, with their coverings, are accumulated in the uteri for deposition in the breeding season.

CHAPTER XII

REPTILIA—AVES

REPTILIA

The Reptiles resemble the Amphibians in being lung-breathing, cold-blooded Vertebrates with pentadactyle limbs. They differ from the Amphibians in that the body has an exoskeleton of horny scales, often reinforced by bony plates. Twelve cranial nerves are present in most Reptiles. The Reptiles lay eggs with chalky shells. The young develop within the shell, the embryos having an amnion and allantois. These two structures, **fœtal membranes,** are characteristically present in the Reptiles, Birds, and Mammals during embryonic development (*vide infra,* Development of Chick).

The heart shows a stage in evolution between the amphibian, and the avian and mammalian hearts. In most Reptiles the heart has two auricles and a ventricle, which is incompletely divided into a right and left chamber by a septum. In the Crocodiles, however, the division is complete, so that two auricles and two ventricles are present, as in the avian and mammalian heart. There is no conus arteriosus, the arches opening into the ventricles separately. The right portion of the aortic arch is well developed, and carries the greater amount of blood. The renal portal system persists in the Reptiles.

The Reptilia includes:

1. **Lacertilia.**—The limbs are usually present and adapted for walking. The mouth opens only to a moderate extent, while the rami of the mandible (lower jaw) are fused to one another at the front. Movable eyelids are usually present, *e.g.*, Lizards, such as Skinks, Geckos, Monitors, Iguanas and Chameleons.
2. **Ophidia.**—Reptiles with a long, narrow body, but without limbs. The mouth can be opened to give a wide gap, as the maxillæ, palatines, and pterygoids are not fixed, and the rami of the mandible are not fused, but connected to each other by elastic fibres. Movable eyelids are absent. The snakes crawl by means of movement of the ribs. Each pair of ribs is attached to a large ventral scute (typical of snakes) which can thus be moved along the ground, *e.g.*, Vipers, Grass Snakes, Sea and Fresh-water Snakes, Pythons and Boas.
3. **Chelonia.**—Tortoises and Turtles have a bony external box—carapace dorsally and plastron ventrally—of dermal bones fused with

portions of the endoskeleton. The skull is box-like and toothless.

4. **Crocodilia.**—Crocodiles, Alligators, and Gavials. The horny scales are reinforced by bony dermal plates.
5. **Rhynchocephalia.**—This is the most ancient group of Reptiles, of which there is only one living representative, the Tuatara (*Sphenodon*) of New Zealand. No bony armour is present. The most interesting feature is found in the pineal organ. In Sphenodon the apex of this organ shows a very striking resemblance in structure to an eye. Moreover, the "pineal eye" comes to lie just under the skin of the dorsal surface of the head, owing to the presence of a mid-dorsal foramen between the parietal bones. This condition is possibly a relic of an ancient reptilian type having three eyes.

The existing Reptiles are remnants of the big class which reached its maximum in number and size in the Mesozoic period. The decline of the Reptilia in the Tertiary period coincided with the rise of the Birds and the Mammals.

The extinct forms included such reptiles as Plesiosaurus and Ichthyosaurus (marine forms); Diplodocus, Stegosaurus and Triceratops (quadrupedal forms); Megalosaurus, Iguanodon (bipedal forms); and various Pterodactyls (flying forms).

AVES

The Aves are Craniata, in which the exoskeleton is in the form of feathers covering the greater part of the body. The body is supported by the two hind limbs, the fore pair being modified as wings. These latter are usually provided with large feathers (quills) to enable the wing movements to sustain the bird in the air. The legs are covered by overlapping horny scales.

The bones are very light, yet strong, and contain ramifications of the air cavities which arise from the lungs. The beak replaces toothed jaws. (N.B.—Ancestral birds did possess teeth.) The right portion of the aortic arch persists, the left part having been lost. The right ovary and oviduct have been lost also. The olfactory organs are poor, the eyes, however, being extremely well developed.

The Birds are oviparous—*i.e.*, lay eggs—the actual fertilized ovum having yolk and albumen added and encased in a calcareous shell. The embryo has an amnion and allantois. The young may be able to run, find food, etc., as soon as hatched, their bodies being covered with downy feathers (*e.g.*, chicken). The young of many other birds hatch in a naked helpless state (*e.g.*, blackbird).

CHAPTER XIII

MAMMALIA

THE Mammalia are the highest group of Vertebrates. Mammals are **warm-blooded** and breathe by means of lungs. The body is covered with **hair,** and the young are suckled by the mother from the **mammary glands.** The skull has **two condyles** for connection with the vertebral column, while the lower jaw consists of a **single bone** on each side. Mammals have **two sets of teeth**—milk, and permanent sets. Each tooth is set in a separate socket in the jaw. In addition the teeth are as a rule of different shapes (heterodont), being divisible into cutting **incisors,** gripping **canines** (dog teeth), and chewing cheek teeth of **premolars** and **molars.** The basic number of teeth is forty-four, although modifications occur in many Mammals. The number and arrangement of the teeth is expressed by a **dental formula** giving the arrangement of a half upper over a half lower jaw and reading from the middle line of the mouth. Thus the common formula for all mammals is:

$$\text{i.}\ \frac{3}{3},\ \text{c.}\ \frac{1}{1},\ \text{p.}\ \frac{4}{4},\ \text{m.}\ \frac{3}{3}.$$

Or more simply:

$$\frac{3 \cdot 1 \cdot 4 \cdot 3}{3 \cdot 1 \cdot 4 \cdot 3} = 44 \text{ in all.}$$

The cœlom is divided by a muscular **diaphragm** into an anterior thoracic cavity containing the heart and lungs, and a posterior space containing the

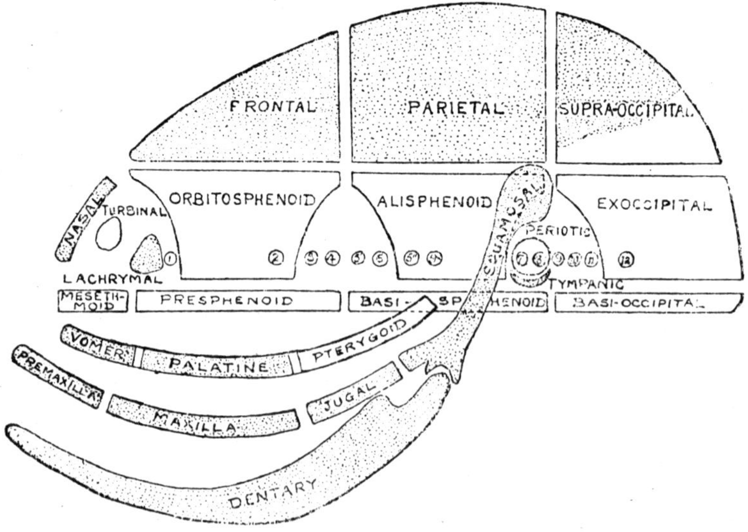

FIG. 40.—DIAGRAM TO ILLUSTRATE THE RELATIONSHIP BETWEEN THE BONES OF THE MAMMALIAN SKULL. (AFTER FLOWER.)

Membrane bones shaded; cartilage bones clear. Small circles and inserted numbers indicate position of openings through which pass the cranial nerves.

viscera. The heart is completely divided into right and left halves, there being one auricle and one ventricle on each side. The **left** half only of the aortic arches persists. The hæmoglobin of the red blood is contained in corpuscles, which are usually round and non-nucleated.

In the brain the two cerebral hemispheres are connected by transverse fibres—the **corpus callosum**—not found in lower Vertebrates. Subdivision of the optic lobes has produced four parts—the **corpora quadrigemina.** An external ear and three auditory ossicles in each middle ear are typical.

With the exception of the Monotremes (*vide infra*) all Mammals are viviparous, the young being born in an advanced state of development.

The group includes a large number of the more "common" animals. The Rabbit (*Lepus caniculus*) may be taken as an example before dealing with the more specialized characters of the mammalian orders.

Lepus caniculus.

The external features of the rabbit may be summed up thus:

1. Quadrupedal animal, with complete covering of hair (fur) over the body.
2. Mouth bounded by fleshy lips, the upper one being divided by a longitudinal cleft running to the nostrils. This exposes chisel-shaped incisor teeth. A pair of obliquely slit nostrils above the mouth.
3. Pair of large lateral eyes with three eyelids, upper and lower ones hairy, and an anterior hairless **nictitating membrane.**
4. **Vibrissæ,** long stiff tactile hairs, are present on the head.
5. External ears, **pinnæ,** crown the head, their

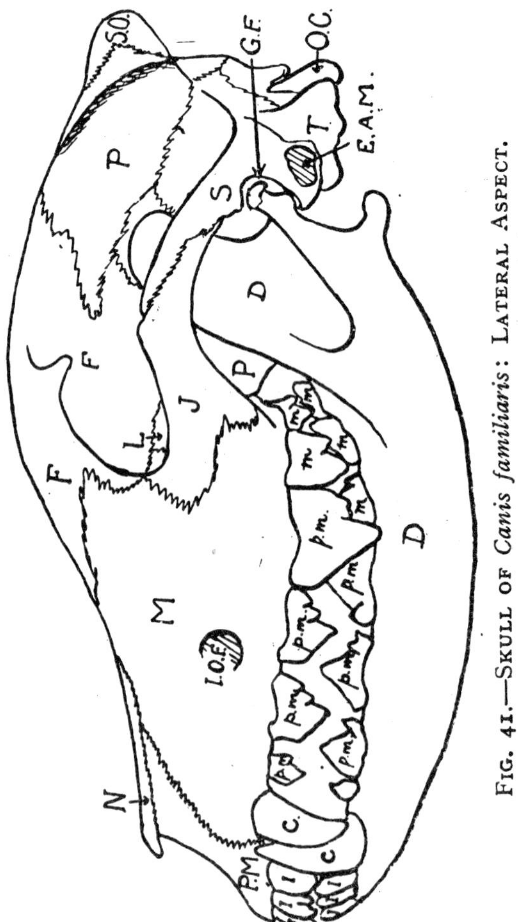

FIG. 41.—SKULL OF *Canis familiaris*: LATERAL ASPECT.

Description of Figs. 41 *and* 42.

A.S., Ali-sphenoid; B.O., basi-occipital; B.S., basi-sphenoid; C., canine; D., dentary; E.A.M., external auditory meatus; E.O., exoccipital; F., frontal; F.M., foramen magnum; G.F., glenoid fossa; I., incisor; I.O.F., infra-orbital foramen; J., jugal; L., lacrimal; M., maxilla; m., molar; N., nasal; O.C., occipital condyle; P., parietal; Pa., palatine; P.M., premaxilla; p.m. premolar; P.S., presphenoid; Pt., pterygoid; S.O., supraoccipital; S., squamosal; T., tympanic; V., vomer; Z.A., zygomatic arch.

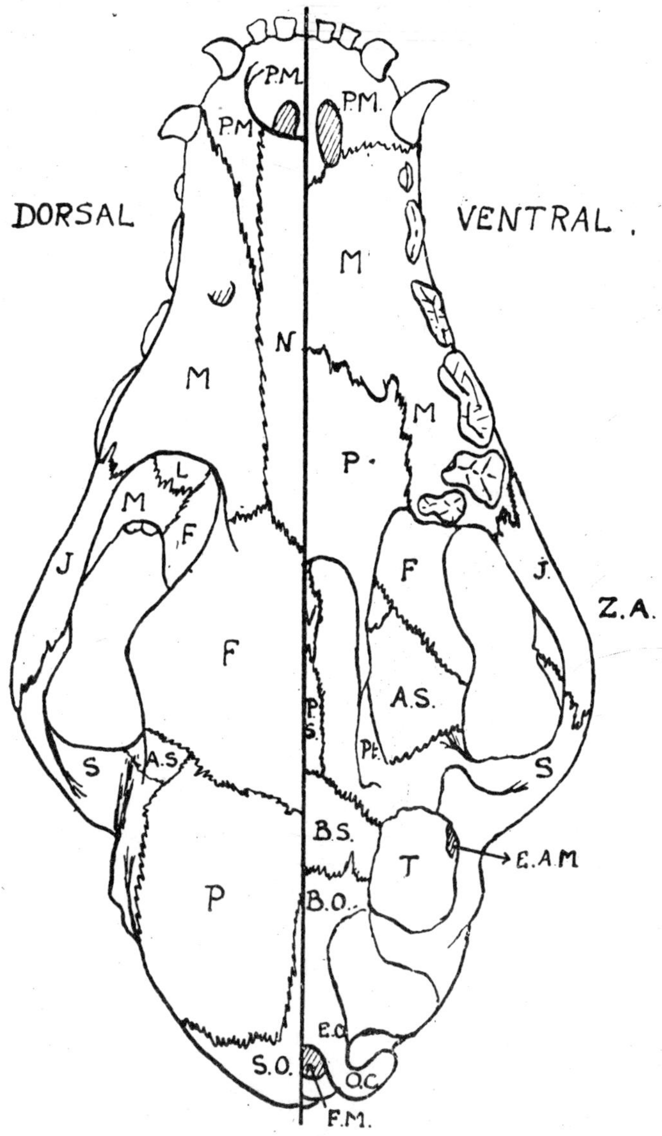

FIG. 42.—SKULL OF *Canis familiaris:* COMBINED DORSAL AND VENTRAL VIEWS.

openings pointing laterally and slightly forward.

6. A distinct, though short, **neck** is present. The trunk consists of thorax and abdomen; the latter in the female has four or five pairs of teats.
7. The **anus** lies below the root of the tail. In the male the **penis,** with the urinogenital aperture, lies just anterior to the anus. A pair of **scrotal sacs,** containing the testes, lie one on each side of the penis. In the female the urinogenital opening is a small slit-like **vulva.** Lying in the vicinity of the anus and genital organs are two bare areas into which open the **perinæal glands,** which secrete a strong characteristic odour.
8. The fore limbs are much shorter than the hind ones. The five digits of each fore limb and the four of each hind leg are clawed.

Skeleton: (1) **Axial Portion**—(*a*) *Vertebral Column.*—This portion consists of five regions—cervical, thoracic, lumbar, sacral, and caudal—each having vertebræ of a characteristic type. The number of vertebræ in each region is usually constant: seven cervical, twelve or thirteen thoracic, seven or six lumbar, four sacral, and fifteen caudal vertebræ. Between the centra are tough cartilaginous **intervertebral discs.**

There are twelve pairs of ribs: seven "true" ribs attached to the **sternum,** or breast bone, and five false or floating ribs. All the ribs, except the last four pairs, bear two articulating facets: the **capitulum,** at the vertebral extremity, which connects with the centrum; and the **tubercle,** an elevation below the head of the rib, which connects with the transverse process.

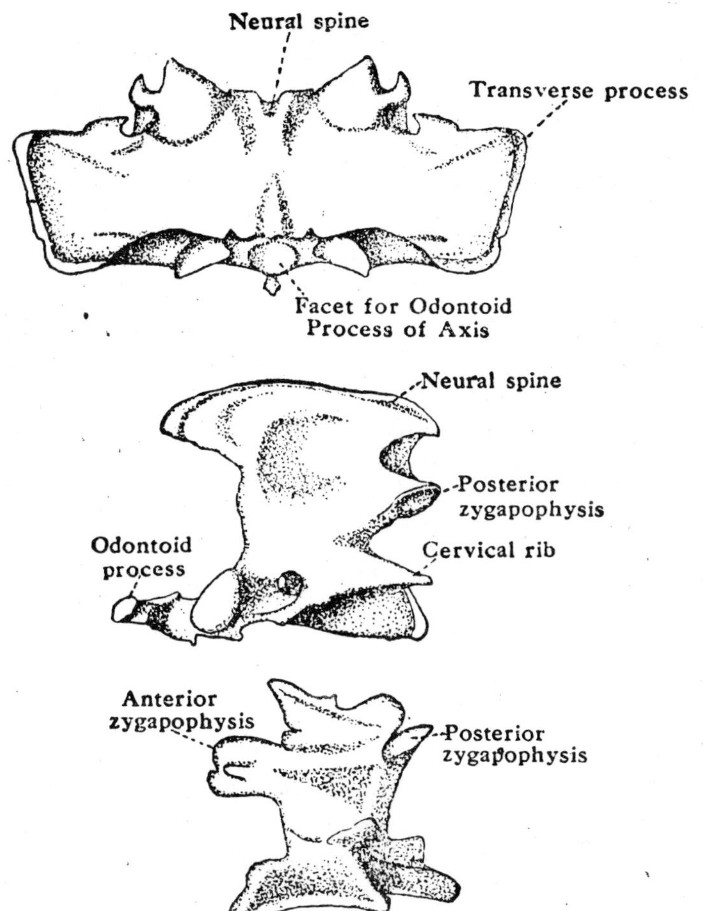

FIG. 43.—A, DORSAL VIEW OF THE ATLAS VERTEBRA OF THE RABBIT; B, LEFT-SIDE VIEW OF THE AXIS VERTEBRA OF THE RABBIT; C, LEFT-SIDE VIEW OF THE SIXTH CERVICAL VERTEBRA OF THE RABBIT.

(From Gilchrist and Von Bonde.)

The **sternum,** or breast bone, is made up of six segments, of which the first is the largest. The last segment is connected with a rounded cartilaginous plate, the **xiphisternum.**

(*b*) *The Skull* of the Rabbit is rather specialized and very often the skull of the dog is studied instead (see diagrams at end of book). The main points of interest in the rabbit's skull may be summarized thus:

1. The skull is long and rather narrow, with an elongated snout region.

2. The arrangement of the teeth is typical of the rodent dentition. The premaxilla of each side of the skull carries two incisors, the second lying behind the first and not side by side, as in most animals. (*Note.*—Many Rodents have only one incisor in each maxilla.) Behind the incisors is a large gap (diastema) and there are **no canines** present. The three premolars and three molars on each side of the upper jaw are similar in shape and are used for grinding. The arrangement of teeth on the mandible is somewhat similar to that of the upper jaw, there being, however, only one incisor on each mandible, followed by a diastema and two premolars and three molars.

It must be noted that the incisors—as in all Rodents—grow throughout life from persistent pulps. The front incisors have a thick layer of enamel on the outer convex surface. The incisors lying immediately behind are smaller and have a thicker layer of enamel on their inner or concave side. The incisors of the lower jaw become bevelled off (owing to having thicker enamel on their anterior surface), and work in the Λ-shaped groove arising by unequal wear of the upper incisors. Thus a very efficient cutting edge is formed.

The dental formula of the Rabbit is: $\frac{2.0.3.3}{1.0.2.3}$.

(2) **Appendicular Portion:** (*a*) *Pectoral Girdle and Limb.*—The girdle is composed of a large dorso-laterally placed **scapular** portion and a small slender **clavicle.** The scapula is a triangular, thin, flattened bone with a distal extension of cartilage, the **supra-**

scapula. Along the central outer portion of the scapula runs a **spine** ending in a forked region. The

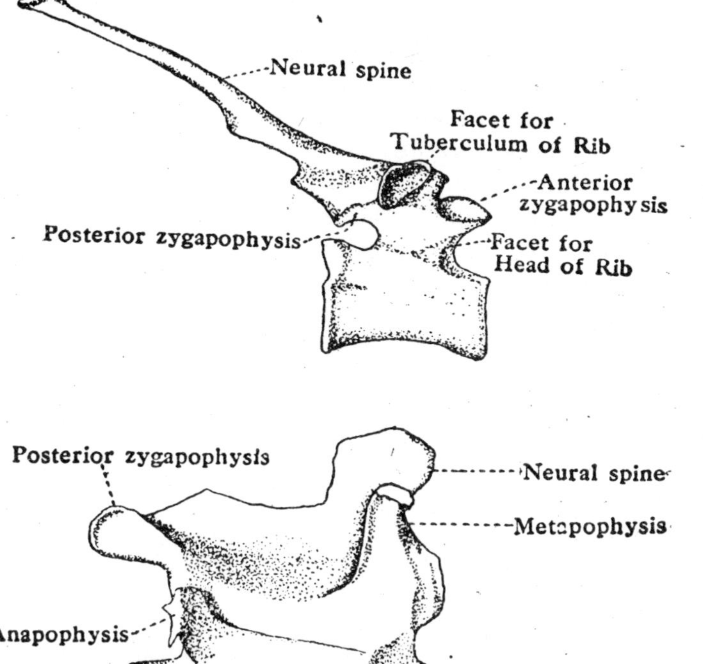

Fig. 44.—A, Right-side View of the Fifth Thoracic Vertebra of the Rabbit; B, Right-side View of the Second Lumbar Vertebra of the Rabbit.

(From Gilchrist and Von Bonde.)

lateral projection is the **metacromion,** the ventral one the **acromion.** The lower end or apex of the scapula is thick, and terminates in a concave surface, the **glenoid cavity,** which receives the head of the humerus. The anterior rim of the glenoid cavity is thickened to form the **coracoid process.**

The upper arm bone, the **humerus,** has a large **head** which fits into the glenoid cavity. Just below the head is a **greater tuberosity** (external), separated from the **lesser tuberosity** (internal) by the **bicipital groove.** Upon the anterior surface of the shaft is the **deltoid ridge.** The distal end of the humerus has a large pulley-like **trochlea** for articulation to the ulna, and a smaller **capitellum** surface for the radius. The two lower arm bones, **radius** and **ulna,** are fixed together firmly. The upper end of the ulna forms a knob-like **olecranon** process. The radius is shorter than the ulna, and between the former and the olecranon process is a somewhat circular notch, the **sigmoid cavity,** into which the trochlea of the humerus fits.

The wrist bones, **carpals,** are arranged in two rows of four, with a single bone, the **centrale,** between the two. The proximal carpals (inside outwards) are **scaphoid, lunar, cuneiform,** and **pisiform,** the distal carpals being **trapezium, trapezoid, magnum, unciform.**

Five **metacarpals,** slender, elongated, palm bones, follow, and each digit then has three **phalanges,** except the first, which has two.

(*b*) *Pelvic Girdle and Limb.*—The three pelvic bones of each side have fused to form an **os innominatum.** These two fuse dorsally to the sacrum and ventrally to each other by a pubic symphysis or junction. The girdle is shaped thus: **bd.** The **ilium** forms the free anterior portion, and the posterior of the upright is the **ischium.** The **pubic** bone (pubis) is somewhat U-shaped and joins the anterior and posterior points only of the ischium. Thus a space, the **obturator foramen,** is formed. The **acetabulum** is a depression on the outer side of the os innominatum just where the ilium and ischium fuse; this takes the head of the femur.

The **femur** has a prominent head, external to which is the **greater trochanter.** Below this is the **third trochanter,** and on the inner side and below the head is the **lesser trochanter.** The distal end of the femur has two articulating surfaces; the **patella,** or knee cap, is an ossification in front of the femur-tibiafibular joint. The two lower leg bones, the **tibia** and **fibula,** have fused, the latter being merely a spine-like process upon the former. The tibia has a ridge-like projection upon it, the **cnemial crest.** The tarsals (ankle bones) are in two rows—proximally astragalus and calcaneum, and distally **meso-cuneiform, ecto-cuneiform,** and **cuboid** —with the **navicular** intercalated between them. There are four **metatarsals,** and each digit has three phalanges.

The cœlom of the rabbit is divided into thorax (with heart, lungs, etc.) and abdomen (viscera, kidneys, genital organs, etc.) by a thin muscular partition, the **diaphragm,** which runs in a transverse direction.

Digestive Organs.—The buccal cavity has on its floor the tongue, a muscular organ covered with epithelium in which are scattered taste buds. The roof of the mouth is separated from the nasal cavity by the **hard palate,** which is continued backwards as the **soft palate,** ending in front of the internal nares. Opening into the mouth are the ducts of four pairs of salivary glands—the **parotids, infraorbitals, submaxillaries,** and **sublinguals.**

The pharynx is not clearly marked off from the mouth, but starts at about the level of the end of the hard palate. The nares open into the upper or nasal division of the pharynx, which is divided from the buccal pharynx by the soft palate. A pair of **Eustachian tubes** open into the upper portion. From

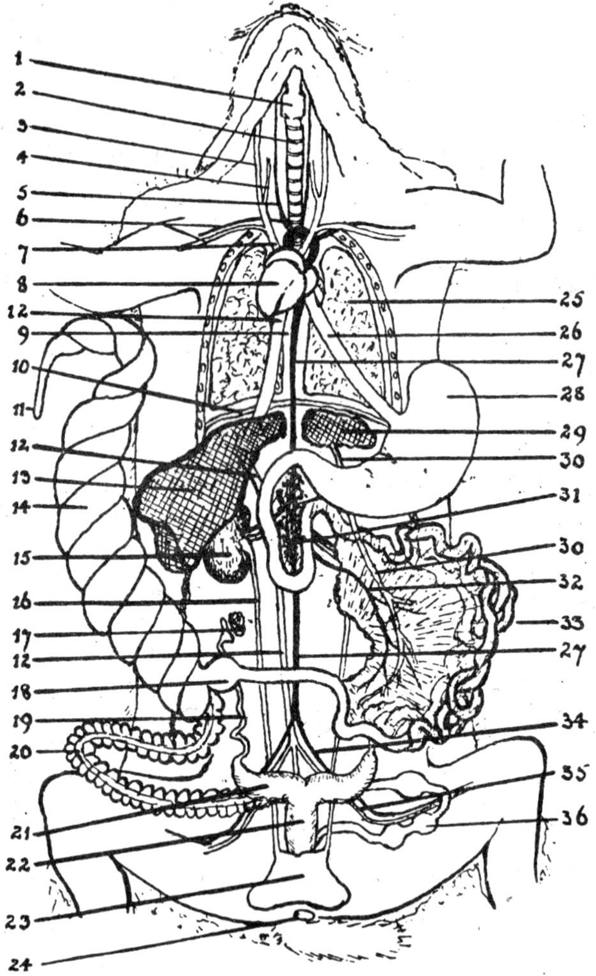

FIG. 45.—GENERAL DISSECTION OF FEMALE RABBIT.

1, Larynx; 2, trachea; 3, external jugular vein; 4, internal jugular vein; 5, carotid artery; 6, subclavian artery (black) and vein; 7, precaval vein; 8, heart (displaced towards right); 9, thoracic cavity; 10, diaphragm; 11, appendix; 12, postcaval vein (displaced towards right); 13, right lobe of liver; 14, cæcum; 15, kidney; 16, ureter; 17, ovary; 18, sacculus rotundus; 19, fallopian tube; 20, colon; 21, uterus; 22,

(*Continued at foot of facing page.*)

the ventral part of the buccal pharynx the slit-like **glottis,** protected by a flap-like **epiglottis,** leads to the respiratory system. The pharynx leads into the **œsophagus** or **gullet,** which runs down the neck and thorax, passing through the diaphragm, to open into the **stomach.**

The stomach is **U**-shaped, and the œsophagus enters between the two limbs. The **cardiac** portion—blind-ended—is wide, whilst the narrower **pyloric** portion gives rise to the greatly coiled **intestine.** The first portion is the **duodenum,** which forms a loop. The remainder of the small intestine is the **ileum,** and its posterior end is marked by a rounded enlargement —the **sacculus rotundus.** The large intestine consists of an anterior **colon** with sacculated walls, continuing as a narrow, smooth-walled, posterior **rectum** to the anus. From the junction of ileum and colon a wide blind tube is given off. It has a narrow spiral valve within. This tube is the **cæcum,** and it ends in a small fleshy **vermiform appendix.**

The **liver** is five-lobed and attached to the diaphragm. A thin-walled **gall bladder** is attached to the liver. The gall or cystic duct joins the hepatic ducts to form a common bile duct opening into the pyloric end of the duodenum. The **pancreas** and its duct lie in the duodenal loop. The **spleen** is bound to the stomach region by a membraneous fold.

---

vagina; 23, bladder; 24, anus; 25, lung; 26, œsophagus; 27, aorta; 28, stomach; 29, left lobe of liver, dissected away from right lobe and cut away (the two lobes send blood to the postcaval vein by means of hepatic veins); 30, hepatic portal vein from alimentary canal and shown entering separated and dissected left hepatic lobe; 31, pancreas in duodenal loop; 32, anterior mesenteric artery; 33, ileum (coiled and bound by mesentery); 34, common iliac artery; 35, external iliac vein; 36, rectum with pellets of fæces (the renal arteries (black) and veins (double lines) are shown between the kidneys and duodenal loop).

Respiratory System.—Just below the glottis is the **larynx,** a chamber with cartilaginous walls. Across this chamber the membraneous shelf-like **vocal cords** are stretched. Passing from the larynx is the **trachea,** or wind-pipe, which bifurcates in the thorax to give two **bronchi,** one to each lung. Trachea and bronchi are supported by cartilaginous rings in their walls.

Each **lung** is enclosed in a **pleural sac.** The bronchus enters the root of the lung and forms a ramifying system of **bronchioles.** Each bronchiole supplies a **lobule** of the lung. A lobule consists of the tissue around a bronchiole, and is supplied by the latter with **terminal bronchioles.** Each of these ends in a small chamber (infundibulum), from which numerous thin-walled **alveoli** open.

Circulatory System: 1. Heart.—The heart is situated in the thorax, slightly to the left of the median line, and between the two pleural sacs. It lies within the **pericardium,** a double peritoneal fold. The heart apex is directed backwards and to the left. It consists of two auricles and two ventricles, their cavities being separate. Valves guard the opening between the left auricle and left ventricle, and the right auricle and right ventricle. Each " sail " valve is a flap of tissue whose movement is controlled by delicate fibres (chordæ tendineæ). When the ventricle contracts, the edges of these valves meet and prevent the blood from returning to the auricle. The left auricle-ventricle opening is guarded by **two** such flaps, and is known as the **bicuspid** or **mitral** valve, whilst that on the right side of the heart is of **three** flaps and forms the **tricuspid** valve.

2. Arterial System.—The aorta leaves the left ventricle and curves to the left and then downwards. This is the remains of the aortic or systemic arches of the frog. It gives off all the arteries to the body. These are as follows, in order down the aorta:

1. **Right subclavian artery,** which supplies the fore limb as the **brachial artery,** having first given a **vertebral** artery, and an **internal mammary** artery to the chest.
2. **Right common carotid artery,** which divides at the angle of the jaw to give an **internal** and **external carotid** artery.
3. **Left common carotid artery,** with distribution similar to 2.
4. **Left subclavian artery** arises separately, but is distributed as in 1.

[*Note.*—The arrangement detailed above is found in some rabbits. There is, however, considerable variation in the points of origin of these four vessels from the curve of the left aorta. Very often two or three of these vessels do not arise directly from the aorta, but arise from a short **innominate artery.** The arrangement of these first four arteries, with regard to the innominate artery and aortic arch, may vary. This variation is shown below, using the numbers 1 to 4 to indicate the arteries (above) and [ ] to show those arising together from the innominate artery.

(*a*) 1.2.3.4. (*b*) [1.2.]3.4. (*c*) 1.[2.3.]4.
(*d*) [1.2.][3.4.] (*e*) [1.2.3.]4. (*f*) 1.[2.3.4.]
(*g*) [1.2.3.4.] (*h*) 1.2.[3.4.]

Variation (*e*) occurs more frequently than the others.]

5. **Paired intercostal arteries** arise from the aorta in its passage through the thorax.
6. **Cœliac artery** (unpaired), the first abdominal vessel, passes to liver, stomach, and spleen.
7. **Anterior mesenteric artery** (unpaired) supplies the intestine and pancreas.
8. A pair of **renal** arteries supply the kidneys, but that on the right leaves the aorta anterior to the left one.

9. **Genital arteries** (paired) take blood to the gonads.
10. **Posterior mesenteric artery** (unpaired) to rectum.
11. The posterior end of the aorta forks to form two **common iliac arteries.**
12. A small **caudal** artery arises just above the aortic bifurcation.

The impure blood returns from the various parts of the body by one of three main drainage systems:

1. *Left Precaval Venous System (or Left Superior Vena Cava).*—This **precaval** vein, which opens into the right auricle, is formed by the junction of an **internal** and **external jugular** vein and the left **sub-clavian** vein.

2. *Right Precaval Venous System.*—This system is similar to that of the left, but in addition it receives the **azygos** vein from the ribs.

3. *Posterior Venous System.*—The **postcaval** vein receives the blood from the posterior part of the body. It is formed at the posterior end of the body by an **internal iliac** vein from each leg. Just anterior to this junction a pair of **external iliac** or **femoral** veins empty into the postcaval vein. In front of these a pair of **ilio-lumbar** and then a pair of **genital** veins drain the lumbar regions and gonads. A **renal** vein drains each kidney.

The alimentary canal is drained by numerous veins which empty into the liver by way of a large **portal vein.** The blood, after passing through the hepatic capillary system, enters the postcaval trunk by a wide, short, **hepatic vein.** Thus there is a **hepatic portal system,** but no renal portal system.

The blood supply to and from the lungs is by means of pulmonary vessels. The venous or impure blood passes to the lungs by the **pulmonary artery** from the right ventricle. The blood after aeration returns to the left auricle by means of the **pulmonary veins.** Thus there are two blood circles—one to and from the lungs, the other to and from the body.

Nervous System.—The most striking advances in the nervous system of mammals have taken place in the brain.

Brain.—The **cerebrum,** or **cerebral hemispheres** (telencephalon), form the most conspicuous portion

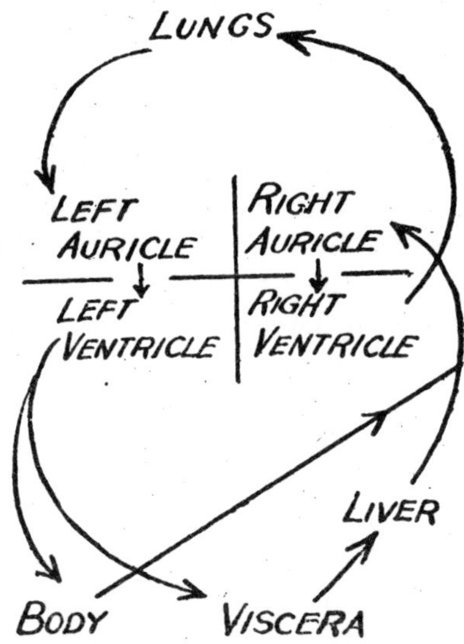

FIG. 46.—DIAGRAM OF THE BLOOD CIRCULATION OF *Lepus.*

of the brain. The hemispheres are separated by a **median fissure,** but they communicate with one another by a ridge of transversely running fibres forming the **corpus callosum.** The surface of the hemispheres is marked by several shallow grooves, the forerunners of the numerous grooves or sulci of the apes and man. One of these grooves is the **Sylvian fissure** at about the middle of each side of each hemisphere. This divides an outer **temporal lobe** off from the rest of each mass. A pair of small

olfactory lobes are joined to the cerebrum by two short olfactory tracts.

The thalamencephalon is overhung by the posterior regions of the cerebrum. Its side walls are thickened as the **optic thalami.** The pineal stalk and body project upwards between the hemispheres, whilst the floor of the thalamencephalon gives the **infundibulum** and attached **pituitary body.**

The mesencephalon is also covered by the cerebrum. The two optic lobes have become divided transversely to form four **corpora quadrigemina.**

The hind brain has a prominent cerebellum which is divided into five smaller corrugated lobes—a median **vermis,** two small outer **flocculi,** and between each flocculus and the vermis a **lateral lobe** on each side. The **pyramids** are the thickened borders of the **ventral fissure** of the medulla oblongata.

Cranial Nerves.—There are twelve pairs of cranial nerves. The first ten pairs resemble those of *Scyllium* and *Rana* in origin and function, but the seventh nerve has no ophthalmic branch.

The eleventh or **accessory** nerve arises from the medulla region by many roots—from the region of the fifth nerve to just behind the vagus roots. This nerve supplies certain cervical muscles. The twelfth or **hypoglossal** nerve, which supplies the tongue and neck, arises from the ventral side of the medulla and corresponds to the first spinal nerve in *Rana.*

Urinogenital Organs: *Kidneys.*—Each kidney is of the typical " kidney shape," the inner side being slightly concave and forming the **hilus.** They are attached to the dorsal wall of the cœlom, the left one being slightly posterior to the right kidney. An adrenal (or suprarenal) body lies to the anterior of each kidney. In section the kidney is seen to have a central portion or **medulla** surrounded by a peripheral **cortex.**

The kidney tubules converge towards the hilus and open into the dilated end of the **ureter,** a chamber known as the **pelvis.** The ureter runs backwards and opens directly into the **urinary bladder.** In the male the ureters open nearer the neck of the bladder than those of the female.

Male Organs.--The pair of oval **testes** occupy a

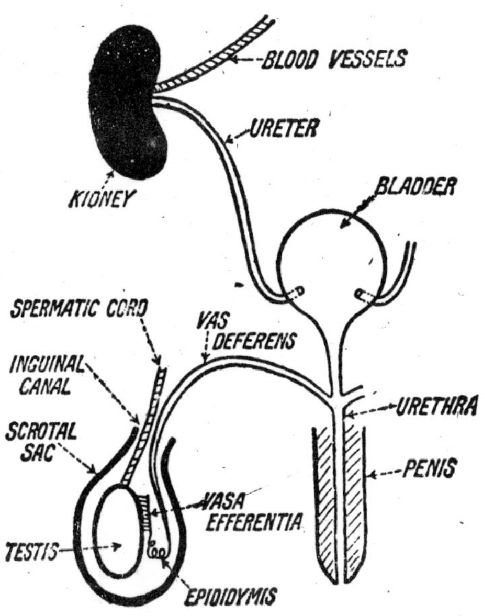

FIG. 47.—DIAGRAM OF THE MALE GENITO-URINARY ORGANS OF THE RABBIT.

(From " Aids to Biology.")

position in the general body cavity in the young male rabbit. However, on reaching maturity the testes descend into a pair of **scrotal sacs.** The cavities of these sacs are put into communication with the body cavity by **inguinal canals.** Each testis is connected to its original position by a **spermatic cord** of connective tissue, which contains the spermatic artery and vein. The old mesonephric region of the embryo also passes back with the testis, to which it adheres as the **epididymis.** This is divided into an anterior **caput epididymis** and a posterior **cauda epididymis** connected by the **gubernaculum.** Each epididymis is a mass of coiled tube, which leaves the scrotal sac as the **vas deferens.** The vasa deferentia open into a small median sac—the **uterus masculinus**—lying

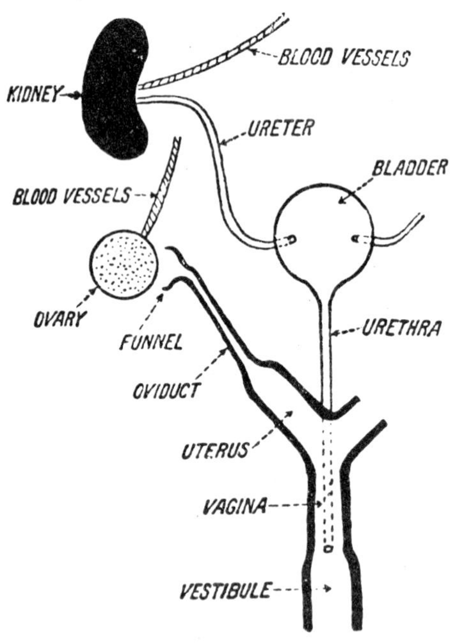

FIG. 48.—DIAGRAM OF THE FEMALE GENITO-URINARY ORGANS OF THE RABBIT.
(From " Aids to Biology.")

below the neck of the bladder. The latter and the uterus masculinus join to form the urino-genital canal or **urethra,** which opens at the end of the penis. The **prostate** and **Cowper's glands** are accessory reproductive organs surrounding the urethral region.

Female Organs.—The pair of small oval **ovaries** are attached to the dorsal wall of the body cavity just behind the kidneys. Their surface is covered with small knob-like projections—the **Graafian follicles**—each containing a very small ovum. The oviducts open by fimbriated or fringed apertures which receive the ripe ova. The first portion of each tube is narrow and sinuous, and called the **Fallopian tube.** This tube then widens to form a **uterus.** The two uteri unite in the middle line as the **vagina,** which is joined by the neck of the bladder, so forming the urino-genital canal or **vestibule** opening at the vulva. The latter is bounded by a pair of folds, the **labia majora.**

Fertilization is accomplished in the upper ends of the oviducts. The ova then pass to the uterus, to which they are attached by a **placenta.** The young are born in an advanced condition.

THE COMMONER MAMMALIAN ORDERS

Lepus caniculus belongs to the mammalian order known as the **Rodentia,** one of a number of groups.

The group Mammalia is divided into three sub-classes and a number of orders.

Sub-Class I.: PROTOTHERIA

This sub-class is composed of one order—the **Monotremata**—containing only two species. The mammary glands are devoid of teats, the milk oozing on to the surface of the abdomen. The eggs are yolked and laid enclosed by a tough shell. The young when hatched are suckled by the mother. The oviducts are distinct throughout their entire length.

The two examples are the Platypus or Duck-mole (*Ornithorhynchus*) and the Spiny Anteater (*Echidna*) of Australasia.

Sub-Class II.: METATHERIA (MARSUPIALIA)

The young are born alive, but in a comparatively rudimentary condition. They are transferred to the **marsupium** or pouch, and there attach themselves to a mammary nipple. When development is completed the young still use the pouch for some time.

This sub-class includes the Opossums (*Didelphyidæ*), the Bandicoots (*Peramelidæ*), the Wombats (*Phascalomyidæ*), and the Kangaroos (*Macropodidæ*).

Sub-Class III.: EUTHERIA

Here there is no marsupium and the young are nourished *in utero* until born in a well-developed condition. The majority of the more well-known mammals belong to one of the orders of this sub-class.

Order I.: Edentata.

The teeth are usually absent in the adult state; if present, are very imperfect and devoid of enamel. This order comprises the Sloths (*Bradypodiæ*), the American Ant-eaters (*Myrmecophagidæ*), the Armadillos (*Dasypodidæ*), the Scaly Ant-eaters (*Manidæ*), and the Cape Ant-eaters (*Orycteropodidæ*).

Order II.: Cetacea.

Aquatic mammals with large head and fish-like body outline. The pelvic limbs are absent, whilst the pectoral ones have become paddle-like flippers. A **horizontal** caudal fin, devoid of fin rays, is present. The nostrils open together on the dorsal side of the elongated head. Teeth may be present or replaced by **baleen**—*i.e.*, whalebone. This order includes the Whalebone Whales (*Balænidæ*), the Sperm Whales (*Physeter*), the Killers (*Orca*), the Porpoises (*Phocæna*), and the Dolphins (*Delphinu*).

Order III.: Ungulata.

This comprises the "hoofed" animals of various kinds (herbivorous).

Section A: Ungulata vera.

The weight of the body is taken by the tips of the digits (digitigrade or unguligrade), of which there are never more than four on each limb.

Sub-order (a): Perissodactyla.

The axis of the limb runs down the median plane of the third digit. The other digits show a tendency to be reduced. The stomach is simple and the cæcum large. Here are placed the Horses, Asses, Zebras, Tapirs, and Rhinoceroses.

Sub-order (b): Artiodactyla.

The limb axis runs between the third and fourth digits, which form a symmetrical pair. The others may be small or absent. The stomach is complex, being composed usually of four parts, while the cæcum is small. Here are included the **Ruminants**—Camels, Oxen, Sheep, Goats, Antelopes, Deer, and Giraffes; and the non-ruminant types—Pigs, Peccaries, and Hippopotami.

Section B: Subungulata.

The feet are plantigrade—*i.e.*, digits lie flat—and there may be five functional digits. This group includes the Coney (*Hyrax*), the Elephant (*Elephas*).

Order IV.: Carnivora.

Flesh-eating mammals with clawed digits. The stomach is simple and the cæcum small or absent. The cerebral hemispheres are large and convoluted.

Sub-order (a): Carnivora vera (or C. fissipedia).

Limbs separate and adapted to terrestrial existence. Digits with claws. The last premolar in the upper jaw and the first molar in the lower bite across one another like scissors. These are called **carnassial** teeth. The sub-order includes the Cats (*Felidæ*), Hyænas (*Hyænidæ*), Dogs (*Canidæ*), Bears (*Ursidæ*), Weasels (*Mustelidæ*), and Otters (*Lutridæ*).

Sub-order (b): Carnivora pinnipedia.

The limbs are adapted to aquatic life, being webbed between the digits, and the hind limbs being bound together to form a false tail-like projection. The Eared Seals or Sea-lions (*Otaridiæ*), the Earless Seals (*Phocidæ*), and the Walruses (*Trichechidæ*) are examples of this sub-order.

Order V.: Rodentia.

Herbivorous mammals, usually of small size, clawed digits, and plantigrade locomotion. No canine teeth are present, and the incisors grow persistently. The cæcum is large. A large order, including Mice and Rats (*Muridæ*), Rabbits and Hares (*Leporidæ*), Squirrels (*Sciuridæ*), Beavers (*Castoridæ*), and Porcupines (*Hystricidæ*).

Order VI.: Insectivora.

Small insect-eating mammals with clawed plantigrade limbs. Small pincer-shaped incisors and sharply pointed molars—*e.g.*, Moles (*Talpidæ*), Shrews (*Soricidæ*), and Hedgehogs (*Erinaceidæ*).

Order VII.: Chiroptera.

Flying types, in which the fore limbs, especially the second to fifth digits, are modified to support a membraneous wing between the arm and leg. These are the Bats.

Order VIII.: Primates.

The most advanced of the Eutheria adapted to arboreal life, with thumb and/or big toe opposable to the other digits, which have flat nails. Here are placed the Lemurs, Marmosets, Howling Monkeys, Spider Monkeys, Baboons, Gibbons, Orangs, Chimpanzees, Gorillas, and Man (*Homo sapiens*).

CHAPTER XIV

GENERAL PHYSIOLOGY AND HISTOLOGY

ALL organisms, whether plant or animal, are built of protoplasm and its derivatives. Organisms are constantly changing due to growth, to repair of worn parts, and to reproduction. All work done in the body of an organism requires the expenditure of energy. The work varies in quality and quantity in different organisms and in the same organism at different times. The oxidation of elaborated foods produces the energy required by the organism.

The main classes of food materials are **Carbohydrates, Fats** and **Proteins.** The essential difference between the Plant and the Animal lies in the fact that the former is able to **build up these foods from simpler substances,** while the latter can use only the **complex materials** already made by the bodies of other organisms. The animal **breaks down** these substances and **selects** the **materials** it requires for its own use, and eliminates unwanted material. It is obvious that Animals depend on Plants, for the latter are the ultimate source of all food materials.

The Plant is able to build up (synthesize) its materials by virtue of possessing **chlorophyll,** which traps **sunlight energy.** The energy thus obtained builds **carbon dioxide** and **water** into **glucose,** which is a simple carbohydrate. (*Note.*—Intermediate steps have been left out and only general ideas are given here.) The sun's energy is, of course, trapped in the

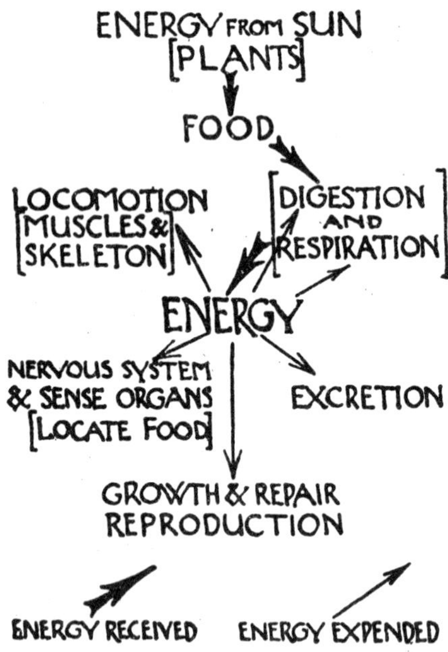

FIG. 49.—DIAGRAM TO ILLUSTRATE "ENERGY RELATIONSHIPS" IN THE ANIMAL BODY.

glucose molecules as potential energy. The oxidation of glucose (or other carbohydrates) releases the potential energy, which becomes available for work in the body of the organism. The glucose molecule is thus split and carbon dioxide and water molecules freed. Thus organisms depend upon the sun as the ultimate source of their energy. These processes may be summarized by the following equations (they not exact chemical equations):

(i.) *Synthesis by Plant :*

$$CO_2 + H_2O + \text{Energy} \longrightarrow (C_6H_{12}O_6.\text{Potential Energy}) + O_2.$$

(ii.) *Oxidation by Plant or Animal:*

$$(\underset{\text{Glucose}}{C_6H_{12}O_6}.\text{Potential Energy}) + O_2 \longrightarrow CO_2 + H_2O + \text{Energy for use in the Organism.}$$

The whole of the animal's body is organized to make use of the energy it requires. Certain parts sort out the food materials, and others are concerned, either directly or indirectly, with the transformation and use of that energy.

Nutrition.

The raw food materials consist of substances containing Carbohydrates, Fats and Proteins in varying proportions. These substances are usually in forms which are too complex for the animal to absorb into its tissues as they are. Hence the process of digestion acts upon such materials, which are broken down into simpler forms ; the usable substances are absorbed and the waste material eliminated.

Carbohydrates.—Carbohydrates are compounds of Carbon, Hydrogen and Oxygen, and the last two are always present in the same relative proportions as they appear in water. The simplest carbohydrates (**Monosaccharides**) include **glucose** (grape sugar) and **fructose** (fruit sugar). Both have the same formula $C_6H_{12}O_6$ (but differ in internal molecular structure) and are often called **hexose** sugars (six carbon atoms in each molecule).

The **Disaccharides** may be regarded as originating

from two molecules of a monosaccharide with the elimination of a water molecule, thus:

$$C_6H_{12}O_6 + C_6H_{12}O_6 \longrightarrow C_{12}H_{22}O_{11} + H_2O$$
$$\text{Glucose} + \text{Fructose} \longrightarrow \text{Sucrose} + \text{Water.}$$

Conversely, the addition of a water molecule (hydrolysis) to a disaccharide (*e.g.*, sucrose or cane sugar, and maltose or malt sugar) may result in two monosaccharide molecules, thus:

$$C_{12}H_{22}O_{11} + H_2O \longrightarrow 2C_6H_{12}O_6$$

Finally, the complex carbohydrates known as **polysaccharides** may be regarded as being formed by the union of a number of monosaccharide molecules with the elimination of a certain number of water molecules. Examples of this type are **glycogen, starch,** and **cellulose,** and they all have the formula $(C_6H_{10}O_5)_n$. When hydrolysed the molecule splits into n molecules of monosaccharide sugar:

$$(C_6H_{10}O_5)_n + nH_2O \longrightarrow nC_6H_{12}O_6.$$

The splitting up of the complex carbohydrates into simpler forms like glucose can be performed experimentally (see other textbooks). It must be realized that a similar process occurs in the digestion of food in the animal body (*vide infra*).

Fats and Oils.—These substances are composed of Carbon, Hydrogen and Oxygen, the last substance being present in relatively small amounts. Fats and oils may be regarded as the " salts " of certain fatty acids and glycerine (*e.g.*, Palmitic acid, Stearic acid, and Oleic acid, forming with glycerine the fats known as Palmitin, Stearin, and Olein respectively. They vary in hardness, the latter being very soft).

Fats and oils may be emulsified when shaken up in water. (This occurs during digestion.) In this state the tiny droplets of fat may be more easily attacked by digestive enzymes.

Fats and oils, having less oxygen (and therefore more available Carbon and Hydrogen) than Carbohydrates, are better fuels. The value of a fuel depends upon the number of atoms in the compound which are still capable of being oxidized. Thus a fat, weight for weight, produces over twice as much energy as does a carbohydrate or protein. In the animal body fats are used in particular for the production of heat energy.

Proteins.—Proteins are very complex colloidal substances intimately associated with living things. They form part of the structure of all organisms and form protoplasm itself. Eggs, cheese and the lean flesh of all animals are common examples of protein material. It has been found that protein molecules when split chemically resolve, among other things, into a number of simpler substances known as **amino-acids.** There are some twenty-odd amino-acids, and a protein molecule varies according to the number and arrangement of the amino-acid molecules it contains. Thus it is evident that there will be considerable variation in the number of proteins, each one differing from others in the finer molecular structure.

All proteins contain Carbon, Hydrogen, Oxygen, Nitrogen, Sulphur, and usually Phosphorus. The proteins vary in complexity from the highly organized **nucleo-proteins,** through the less complex **globulins** and **albumins** to the simple **peptones.** The work of digestion is to reduce the more complex proteins to simpler forms from which the body may select the material with which to build up its own special proteins.

VITAMINS

On certain occasions in the past, it has been noted that restrictions in diet have led to symptoms of certain diseases in man. The case of the disease known as "scurvy" is well known, the disease being associated with the era of sailing ships, when the sailors' diet consisted mainly of salted, pickled and dried foods. The addition of fresh vegetables, when available, led to the curing of this condition. This case is typical of the group of substances known as **vitamins,** in that their absence from a diet induces certain " deficiency diseases." It is usual, therefore, to define vitamins only in such negative terms as—" substances present in natural foodstuffs in small amounts, but not forming part of the main classes of foodstuffs, and whose absence from the diet is followed by disease, and often death." More recently, the term " vitamin " has come to include any substance which the body cannot make for itself, and which must therefore be supplied in the animal's diet.

Early work on vitamins indicated that some of these substances seemed to be present in fats, whilst others were soluble in the watery portion of foods. Thus four main vitamins were early recognized—fat-soluble A and D, and water-soluble B and C. Since the end of the first decade of this century, however, a considerable and growing volume of research work has been done on vitamins and other food factors. This has shown that some of the " original " vitamins could be broken down further, the essential substances isolated, and that the principles could be synthesised. Here only the more important vitamin can be outlined as they exist in the present state our knowledge.

Vitamin A—Axerophthol—$C_{20}H_{29}OH$.

This is a fat-soluble vitamin first recognized in 1913-14, isolated in a pure state in 1937 and synthesized in 1945-47. It can be formed by the hydrolysis of **carotin** thus:

$$C_{40}H_{56} + 2H_2O \longrightarrow 2C_{20}H_{29}OH.$$

It appears to be related to the dark purple chromoprotein called **rhodopsin,** which is present in the retinal rod cells and known as " visual purple." The absence of vitamin A leads to disturbances of eyes and vision; retardation of growth in young; and to digestive disorders; impairment of epithelial surfaces resulting in diminished resistance to infection; " toad skin "; and defective tooth development.

This vitamin is found with the carotin associated with chlorophyll pigments in all green vegetables. It is concentrated in animal fats and is abundant in butter, cream, cod- and halibut-liver oils

Vitamin B Complex.

The original material, first designated vitamin B (the anti-beri-beri vitamin), was for some time considered to be a single substance, but in 1926 it was shown to contain at least two factors—vitamins B_1 and B_2. Later vitamin B_2 itself was shown to be made up of several further factors, so that the original vitamin B is now usually referred to as Vitamin B Complex, although its main constituents are known by their own specific names, such as B_1,B_2,B_6,Biotin (vitamin H), Folic acid, B_{12} and B_{13}.

Vitamin B_1—Aneurin(e) [Thiamin(e) U.S.A.]— $C_{12}H_{17}ON_4SCl.HCl$.

Recognized first in 1911 it was isolated pure in 1926 and synthesized in 1936-37. It is a water-soluble substance necessary in the internal respiration of cells and carbohydrate metabolism. Its deficiency leads to fatigue, loss of weight and beri-beri in man, together with polyneuritis (demyelinization of the myelin sheaths of peripheral nerves). This latter condition is particularly marked in birds. Paralysis of the heart may result as well as disease of the kidneys. Beri-beri is more marked in hot climates, due no doubt to increased tissue respiration.

This vitamin is found especially in the germ oil of cereals—*e.g.*, wheat germ, rice bran, all cereals, and in yeast, pork, liver, nuts, eggs and legumes. It is destroyed if alkaline sodium bicarbonate is added to such foods during cooking. It is excreted rapidly by the body and must therefore be replaced daily in the diet.

Vitamin B_2—Riboflavin(e), [formerly Lactoflavin: Vitamin G]—$C_{17}H_{20}N_4O_6$.

Recognized in 1917, isolated pure in 1933, synthesized in 1935, it is a water-soluble yellow pigment, also essential in cell respiration. Its deficiency leads to skin inflammations, nerve sheath degeneration and corneal opacity. It is found in milk, yeast, liver, wheat germ, meat, eggs, cheese, peas and green vegetables.

Nicotinic Acid—$C_6H_5O_2N$.

This substance is associated with Riboflavin in vitamin B_2. Deficiency leads to Pellagra, a disease in which the characteristic symptoms are dermatitis, diarrhœa and dementia. Nicotinic acid is present in liver, kidney meat, wheat germ, yeast, cereals, cheese and eggs.

Vitamin B_{12}—$C_{61\text{-}64}H_{86\text{-}92}O_{13}N_{14}PCo$.

This was recognized in 1926 as a liver factor and isolated pure in 1948. Its absence from diet causes

Pernicious Anæmia. Its best food sources are liver, milk powder and beef extract. This is the only vitamin known to contain a trace element—cobalt.

Vitamin C—Ascorbic Acid—$C_6H_8O_6$.

Although the result of the absence of this vitamin (scurvy) has been known for very many years it was only in 1918 that it was recognized, isolated pure in 1928 and synthesized in 1933. It promotes growth and the formation of antibodies in the blood. Its absence leads to:

(*a*) Redness, tenderness and bleeding of gums; which later thicken and retract to expose the base of the teeth: teeth may fall out.
(*b*) Easy bruising of flesh due to capillary fragility.
(*c*) Prostration and collapse.

Thus it is essential for the formation of intercellular material and formative cells, healing of wounds and fractures, and capillary resistance.

Vitamin C is found in abundance in fresh fruits, especially blackcurrants, citrus fruits, tomatoes and raw green vegetables. During cooking or drying of foods, oxidation easily destroys it. Hence sterilized milk supplied to infants, without additional vitamin C, soon induces scurvy.

Vitamin D [D_2 and D_3]—Calciferol—$C_{28}H_{44}O$.

Recognized in 1919 and isolated pure in 1931-32 this fat soluble-vitamin is essential for calcium phosphorus metabolism—*i.e.*, formation of bone and teeth. It can be synthesized by the irradiation of dehydrocholesterol in ultra-violet light, when "natural" vitamin D is formed [$C_{27}H_{44}O$]. Thus it is formed in the human skin fat during sunbathing.

Deficiency of vitamin D causes deformity of the

skeleton, bowed legs, malformation of the chest, teeth defects, enlargement of joints and bulging forehead—*i.e.*, rickets in children and osteomalacia in adults.

The best sources of this vitamin are in fish-liver oils, animal fats, butter, cream, eggs and liver.

Vitamin E—alpha-Tocopherol—$C_{29}H_{50}O_2$.

A fat-soluble vitamin first recognized in 1922 and isolated in 1936, it was synthesized in 1936. It appears to be essential for fertility and reproduction in certain animals, probably by maintenance of the secretion of the hormones of the anterior lobe of the pituitary gland. It also appears to exert a synergistic action on vitamin A.

Its deficiency leads to habitual abortion in the female and loss of fertility in the male, due, in both cases, to degenerative changes in the tissues of the reproductive system. Vitamin E is found in wheat germ oil, green vegetables, lettuce, eggs and liver.

The vitamins form part of a group of substances sometimes called "essential metabolites." Such substances form necessary links in the innumerable chains of complex reactions, which make up the activities of living organisms. Modern research is slowly sorting out these reactions and establishing the inter-relationships of some of these substances, their reactions with one another, and their place in the body metabolism.

Digestive Processes (Mainly Mammalian).

When food has been captured it is often broken up by teeth (*e.g.*, mammals) or other such structures near the mouth (*e.g.*, mandibles of crayfish and cockroach). When of suitable size the food passes down the digestive tract and is acted upon by digestive juices containing **enzymes.** An enzyme may be defined as an organic catalyst. An enzyme thus controls the speed of the chemical reactions in either direction and is not itself changed in the process. The direction of the chemical change is determined by other conditions occurring in the organ concerned. Each enzyme is specific—*i.e.*, it acts on one particular substance—the substrate, and thus enzymes may be classified into **proteases** (protein splitters), **amylases** (starch splitters) and **lipases** (fat splitters). Many individual enzymes have been isolated and named—*e.g.*, pepsin and ptyalin (note that *-in* usually denotes a specific enzyme and not an enzyme type or class).

Mouth.—Digestion commences in the mouth as the **saliva,** containing **mucin** and **ptyalin,** is mixed with the food. The mucin when mixed with the food facilitates swallowing. The ptyalin, which only works in neutral or alkaline solution, immediately converts starch into maltose (disaccharide). The food is then collected as a **bolus** at the back of the pharynx, the nasal pharynx is closed by the soft palate, and the epiglottis shuts the respiratory opening, and so the bolus is tipped into the œsophagus. From this point the subsequent movement of food in the alimentary canal passes from voluntary control until the waste reaches the anus. The food bolus passes slowly down the alimentary canal driven by muscular movements. This process is known as **peristalsis.** It consists essentially of a wave of muscular expansion followed closely by a wave of muscular contraction which forces the bolus into the expanded portion. (The process may be illustrated by pushing a small orange through a stocking by means of a small metal ring on the outside.)

Stomach.—When the food enters the stomach the latter is stimulated to produce **gastric juice.** The juice contains **pepsin, rennin,** and **hydrochloric acid** (0·5 per cent.). Thus the alkaline reaction started in the mouth is gradually stopped. The pepsin, which only works in an acid medium, breaks some of the proteins down to **peptones.** The rennin curdles the milk and the "curd," containing the protein called **casein,** is attacked by the pepsin. The carbohydrates and fats undergo no digestive changes in the stomach. The food is constantly mixed with the gastric juice by the peristaltic action of the stomach. When the food material is broken up sufficiently to form a thick creamy **chyme,** then the pyloric sphincter muscle allows small quantities of the chyme to pass into the intestine. This process of emptying the stomach may start soon after the food has been received and the material passes on as it is made ready. In this way a normal meal has left the stomach in about four hours.

Intestine.—The anterior portion of the small intestine receives digestive and other juices from three sources and the whole medium is alkaline again.

(*a*) *Liver.*—Besides certain **excretions** which colour the fæces, the **bile** from the liver contains **bile salts.** These salts assist in the complete emulsification of the melted fats in the food.

(*b*) *Pancreas.*—There are four important substances produced here and passed to the intestine by the pancreatic duct. They are given out under the influence of **secretin,** a hormone which is produced by the duodenal wall when the chyme passes into it.

(i.) *Sodium carbonate,* which gives the alkalinity to the duodenal contents, and combines with the fatty acids (when produced) to form soluble and diffusible soaps.

(ii.) *Steapsin*—a lipase, splitting the fats into fatty acids and glycerine.

(iii.) *Amylopsin*—an amylase which acts upon any unchanged starch and reduces it to maltose.

(iv.) *Trypsinogen*—an inactive form of the enzyme **trypsin.** This enzyme is so powerful that if it were present in the pancreas this organ would be digested! The trypsinogen is activated by an intestinal secretion (enterokinase) in the intestine itself. Trypsin reduces unchanged proteins to amino-acids (by way of peptones).

(*c*) *Intestinal Wall.*—The intestinal juice called the **succus entericus** contains four important secretions:

(i.) *Enterokinase,* which as mentioned above activates trypsinogen into active trypsin.

(ii.) *Erepsin,* which converts peptones into amino-acids.

(iii.) *A maltase,* which converts such disaccharide sugars as maltose and sucrose into monosaccharide hexose sugars like glucose.

(iv.) *Secretin.*—This belongs to the class of organic substances known as **hormones.** They are liberated into the blood stream and have a profound effect upon various organs of the body. Secretin is produced by certain duodenal glands (stimulated by the entrance of food from the stomach) and passed by way of the blood stream to the pancreas, which is thus stimulated to secrete its digestive juices.

By this time all of the food materials, except cellulose, have been reduced to simple forms. Cellulose is so complex that the amylases make little or no impression upon it. Cellulose breaks down under the influence of bacteria in the large intestine and resultant sugars, etc., are then absorbed. For this reason herbivorous animals have longer intestines and cæca in proportion to their body size than do carnivores.

The changes brought about in the food by digestion are summarized on the opposite page.

Absorption.

The inner surface of the intestine is covered by a large number of small conical projections known as **villi.** Each villus is covered by an absorptive epithelium and supplied by a small artery which breaks up into capillaries. These rejoin and the blood goes out by way of a small vein. In addition, each villus has a large blind-ended **lacteal** vessel connected to the **lymphatic** vessels in the intestinal wall. The villi increase the absorptive area of the intestine.

The amino-acids and monosaccharide sugars pass through the walls of the villi and enter the blood capillaries, and so by way of the smaller veins to the hepatic portal vein, which carries the absorbed material to the liver. The fatty acids (in the form of soap) and the glycerine diffuse through into the lacteals, where they recombine into oil globules. The globules are then removed by the lymphatics to a place of storage.

Unusable material left in the intestine has excess water removed, and finally passes out of the anus as **fæces.** The fate of the absorbed food will be discussed later.

Respiration.

The food absorbed as a result of the digestive processes is required to give energy (movement, heat, chemical action, etc.) to the body. Hence Oxygen is necessary, and this is obtained from the air by most animals (**aerobic** respiration). Certain animals (parasites) and certain plants do not use atmospheric oxygen and are said to show **anaerobic**

FOOD MATERIAL AND ENZYME ACTION

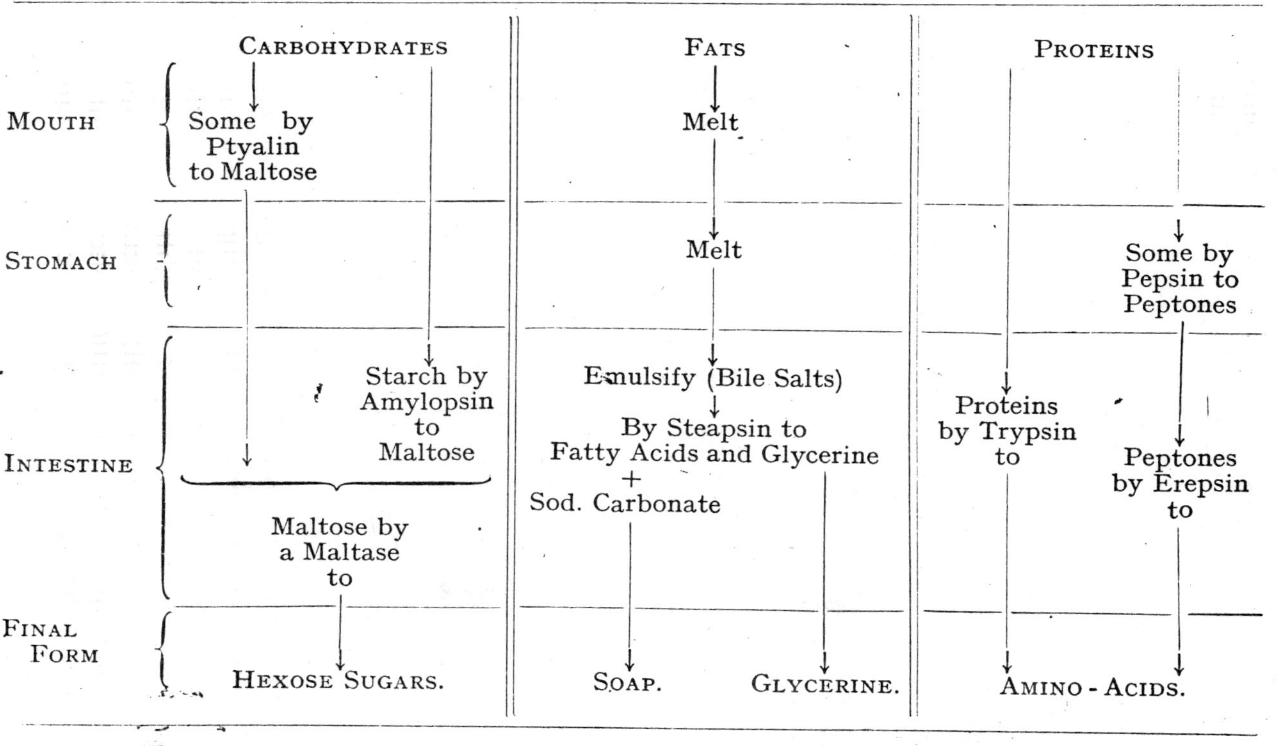

respiration. Such organisms obtain their energy by releasing it from a complex molecule—*e.g.*, sugar.

$$C_6H_{12}O_6 \ldots \longrightarrow \underset{\text{(Alcohol)}}{2C_2H_5OH} + 2CO_2 + \text{Energy.}$$

In aerobic organisms the sugar's stored energy is used up, thus:

$$C_6H_{12}O_6 + 6O_2 \longrightarrow 6CO_2 + 6H_2O + \text{Energy.}$$

Actually the process is not quite so simple as this, but the above gives a general idea of what happens.

The word "respiration" is often confused with breathing, and hence to clarify this it is convenient to divide the processes involved into two groups. Before the food fuel can be oxidized the Oxygen has to be brought into the body, and after oxidation waste substances (CO_2 and some H_2O) must be removed. Thus these processes, often termed breathing, may be called **external respiration.** The exchange of gases is achieved with the help of respiratory organs, such as gills or lungs. In small animals these gaseous exchanges often take place by means of the general body surface. Insects take the air direct to all parts of the body by means of their tracheal system. In most of the other animals the respiratory organs are linked to the tissues by the blood system. The actual process of oxidation which concerns the cells of various body organs may be termed **internal** or **tissue respiration.**

The essential feature of respiratory organs is the possession of a large damp surface area for the diffusion of gases. The respiratory area bears a definite relationship to body volume. As the body of the organism enlarged, the respiratory area—*i.e.*, surface of body—became too small for the satisfactory exchange of gases. Thus respiratory organs developed to give a big surface area in as small a space as possible. This was accomplished by folding the surface as seen in the respiratory filaments of the gills of the Crayfish and Fish, and in the sacculated wall of the Frog lung, and finally in the spongy lung of the higher Vertebrates.

In gills the blood runs through capillaries which lie underneath the thin surface membrane covering the gill filaments or platelets. As fresh water streams over the gills the Oxygen diffuses into the blood and the Carbon dioxide out into the water. External respiration in the frog has been dealt with on a previous page. An outline of the structure of the mammalian lung is given under "Rabbit."

The breathing of the mammal is due to the setting up of a variable negative pressure in the thorax. This portion is cut off from the rest of the cœlom by the muscular diaphragm, which when relaxed is dome-shaped. The chest walls are supported by ribs. Each is set on the backbone on a movable pivot (head of the rib) and at an angle so that the distal end (breastbone end) points downwards. The lungs lie in this cavity, and any change of pressure is only possible by air passing to or from the lungs themselves. If air enters the chest (after a wound) the lung (or lungs) automatically collapses. **Inspiration** of air into the lungs is due to the enlargement of the thoracic cavity. This is accomplished first by a lowering of the convexity of the diaphragm (by muscular contraction), thus increasing the anterio-posterior size of the thoracic cavity. Secondly, the **intercostal** muscle sheet (with ribs attached) is fastened to the vertebral column in the neck region by way of the neck muscles to the shoulders. Contraction of the intercostal muscles (which run obliquely from rib to rib) causes the distal part of the ribs to rise, thus increasing the chest circumference. These two sets of movements will therefore result in an increase in the volume of the chest and a consequent diminution of pressure to below that of the outside air. Hence air rushes down the trachea to equalize pressure and causes the lungs to expand, as the air itself cannot reach the thoracic cavity. Thus the bigger the chest expansion the deeper is the breath. When the diaphragm and intercostal muscles relax the thoracic volume decreases, and so pressure increases and consequently equalization is attained by the forcing out of air from the lungs (**expiration**). Breathing, therefore, in the mammal is an automatic action in which the lungs themselves take no part. (It must be remembered, however, that the percentage of CO_2 content of the lungs has a bearing upon the rate of breathing.) The tissue respiration is intimately connected with the blood system, and will be dealt with under that heading.

Transport System.

The blood system links up all parts of the body and has three main kinds of function:

1. **Transport.**—It carries foods in solution from the alimentary canal through the liver to all parts of the body. Oxygen is also transported from the respiratory organs to the tissues. Waste substances given off by the tissues are carried to the eliminating organs—the lungs (CO_2 and H_2O), the kidneys (nitrogenous wastes, excess salts and water) and the skin (water, salts).
2. **Regulation.**—The blood carries the hormones secreted by the endocrine or ductless glands. These substances exert a profound influence on the growth and development of the body, but they reach these parts through the "postal system" of the blood circulation. In warm-blooded animals, the blood is used

for heat distribution in the mechanism of heat regulation.

3. **Protection.**—When the skin is pierced the blood by its power of clotting prevents excessive loss of blood, and invasion by disease organisms. The production of antitoxins in the blood is the body's main protection against disease and harmful organisms which may have gained entry to the body.

The blood is kept circulating by the action of the heart, and thus vessels leaving the heart (**arteries**) must be able to withstand the pressure surges of the heart and yet pass the blood on with little diminution of pressure. Hence, arteries have thick muscular and elastic walls which do not collapse when cut. When the smaller arterial branches reach their distribution area of the body they divide up into very minute branches which form an anastomosing field of **capillaries** in the tissues. The blood is forced through the capillaries, which rejoin and leave the tissue as a small **vein.** As pressure is low, the veins are wide, thin-walled, valved vessels which collapse when cut. It must be remembered that the names artery and vein refer to the relationship of a vessel with the heart, and not to the type of blood flowing in it. In the Mammals it is true that all arteries (except the pulmonary) contain pure blood and all veins impure blood except the pulmonary veins. In the Fishes, however, some arterial vessels contain impure blood.

The type of blood system referred to above where the blood runs in a system of tubes is known as a **closed** blood system. In the cockroach and crayfish the arteries have open ends, and the blood escapes from them to bathe the various tissues. The flow in these spaces is slow, but moves towards the pericardial sinus and so back to the heart. This type of circulation is known as an **open or hæmocœlic** blood system.

Blood consists of a fluid portion (**plasma**) and a compound which readily combines with oxygen. In many animals this compound is red **hæmoglobin**—*e.g.*, Man, Frog, Earthworm. (Hæmoglobin is a compound of a protein—**globin**—and an iron-containing pigment—**hæmatin**.) In many Invertebrates the hæmoglobin is replaced by **hæmocyanin,** which contains a copper pigment, but the whole functions in the same way as red blood. The compound may be dissolved in the blood fluid, as in the Earthworm or the Crayfish; or it may be contained in definite **corpuscles,** as in the Vertebrates.

The blood plasma is 90 per cent. water, contains certain dissolved proteins (*e.g.*, **fibrinogen**), and numerous corpuscles. These latter may be of different kinds.

1. **Erythrocytes** or red corpuscles. In animals below the Mammalia (*e.g.*, Frog) they are flattened, oval, nucleated discs. In Mammals they are biconcave (end view), non-nucleated and circular in outline (top view). They contain hæmoglobin, and are therefore absent when this pigment is in solution in the plasma (Earthworm). Their numbers vary (often inversely with their size), as the following figures show:

Number of Red Corpuscles per Cubic Millimetre.

Frog, 400,000. Pigeon, 4,000,000.
Cat, 8,000,000. Dog, 6,500,000.
Man, 5,000,000.

The red corpuscles arise in the giant cells (erythroblasts) of the red bone-marrow.

2. **Blood platelets.** These are groups of minute cells which assist in the clotting of blood. It is obvious that the capacity of blood to clot over a wound

saves enormous wastage of body material. The platelets aggregate near the wound and so start the clot. They then produce **thrombokinase,** which turns the **prothrombin** in the blood to **thrombin.** This, acting on the **fibrinogen,** turns it to the insoluble and fibrous **fibrin,** which traps the corpuscles and so produces a clot.

3. **Leucocytes** or white corpuscles. They are larger but much less numerous than the red corpuscles (Man, 6-8,000; Frog, 5,000; Dog, 10,000; Cat, 15,000; Pigeon, 15-30,000 per cubic millimetre). They are amœboid and uni- or poly-nucleated cells. They are able to migrate through the walls of the capillaries into the tissues and lymph spaces. They ingest invading bacteria (phagocytosis), aid in the absorption of fats, help to keep the blood plasma constant in constitution, and in some animals (*e.g.*, Cockle and Crayfish) assist in blood clotting.

Hæmoglobin is a bluish red in colour. When exposed to oxygen (*e.g.*, in the lung or gill) it readily combines with it to form a bright red **oxyhæmoglobin** (oxygenated blood). This "purified" blood reaches the capillaries, and, the surrounding tissues having a great "attraction" for the oxygen, it leaves the hæmoglobin, which assumes the dull red colour of deoxygenated or impure blood. Thus the oxygen is carried in large quantities by hæmoglobin, which after giving it up can recombine continually with fresh oxygen. (*Note.*—Carbon monoxide goes into permanent combination with hæmoglobin, hence its poisonous nature.)

Carbon dioxide from the tissues is carried to the lungs partly in the red corpuscles (but with constituents **other than** hæmoglobin) and partly in the blood plasma. The full details are not known for certain as yet, but it seems that the CO_2 in the plasma is partly in solution and partly as carbonates or bicarbonates. The CO_2 content of the blood is related directly to the work of the tissues (increased activity increasing the CO_2 output). This content affects the respiratory centre in the medulla of the brain and an increase or decrease (as the case may be) in the respiratory rate results. Thus the administration of a mixture of CO_2 and O_2 to suffocated persons often revives them, as the CO_2 stimulates the respiratory centre and restarts normal respiratory movements.

The plasma transports the dissolved food to the tissues. The concentration of these substances is controlled by the liver. The glucose is converted to insoluble glycogen by, and is stored in, the liver. " Between meals " this is used as required, being first turned to glucose and then liberated by the liver into the blood. Excess carbohydrates have oxygen removed, and are then stored as fats along with any other excess fats which have not been used. Fat may be stored in any part of the body and used when required. The waste nitrogenous materials which are produced in the liver are conveyed by the blood to the kidney for elimination from the body.

The capillaries cannot come into intimate contact with all of the cells in their immediate region. Through the capillary walls there passes blood plasma and leucocytes to form **lymph.** The lymph with its dissolved food materials bathes the cells, and so brings them into intimate contact with the food they require. The lymph is drained away into a lymphatic system of ducts and eventually empties into one the larger veins before it enters the heart.

Skeleton, Supporting Tissues and Muscles.

The skeleton performs two chief functions—to give shape and support to the body, and to give attachment to the muscles. The Invertebrates have an exoskeleton with the muscles working inside (speaking generally). The skeleton is very often made by the deposition of lime salts by the outer cuticular layer—*e.g.*, Crayfish, various worms which build tubes, and the molluscs. Certain exoskeletal structures are present in the Vertebrates. These include scales, feathers, hair, horns, teeth, and various types of nail (hoof, claw, etc.).

In the Vertebrates the main skeleton is within the body and is known as an endoskeleton. Its general plan has been presented in the various types already studied. Besides bone, the skeleton may be of cartilage (Dogfish), and in either case certain other **connective tissues** which assist in body support may be included here. Covering tissues (epithelia) will also be dealt with.

Epithelium.

This tissue lines all external and internal surface (endothelium) of the body (*e.g.*, skin, peritoneal membrane). They are large cells which differ in shape according to their work.

(*a*) **Cubical:** cells shaped like cubes.

(*b*) **Columnar:** greatest measurement at right angles to surface.

(*c*) **Squamous** or **pavement:** thin and flat; greatest length parallel to surface; used for covering large areas—*e.g.*, body cavity walls.

(*d*) **Ciliated columnar:** cilia at free end. This is used where currents are needed in the fluid in tubes, etc.—*e.g.*, pharynx of Frog, respiratory and reproductive ducts, gills of Mussel. (*a*) to (*d*) are **simple** epithelia.

(*e*) **Stratified columnar** or **squamous:** where there are several layers of cells—*e.g.*, epidermis of the body.

The epithelium may grow in from the surface to

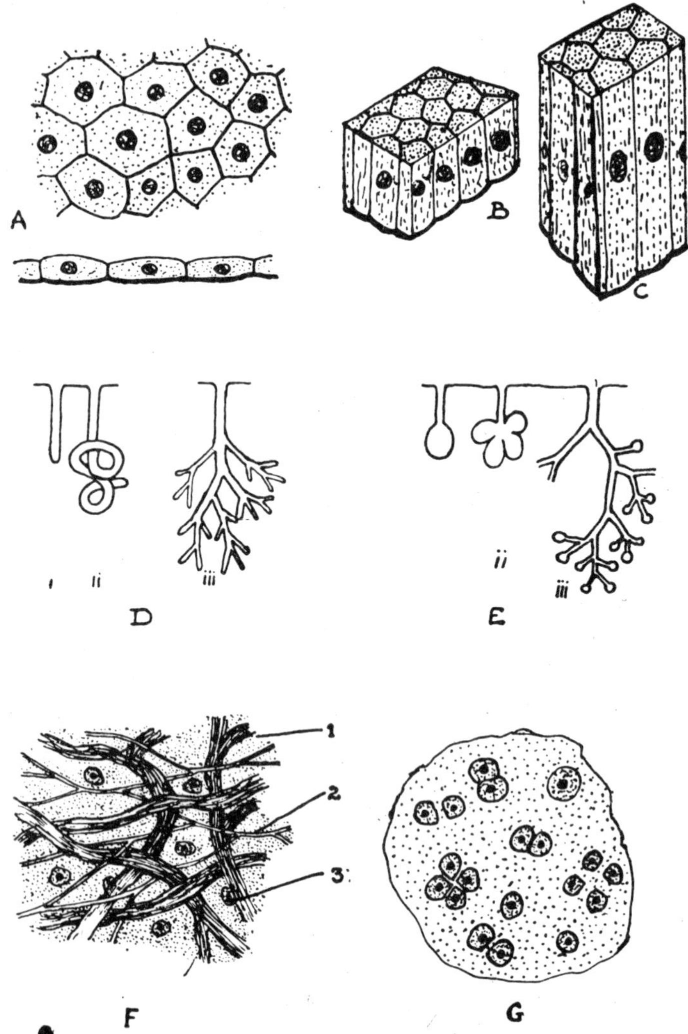

FIG. 50.—DIAGRAMS SHOWING TYPES OF TISSUES.

A, Squamous epithelium (surface and side view); B, cubical epithelium; C, columnar epithelium; D, tubular glands (i and ii, simple; iii, compound); E, alveolar glands (i and ii, simple; iii, compound); F, areolar tissue (1, white fibres; 2, yellow fibres; 3, cells in general matrix); G, cartilage showing cells (chondroblasts) in matrix.

form single or branched diverticula. This gives rise to **glandular** tissue. The glands may be of a simple or branched **tubular** type, as in the sweat gland; or they may be simple or branched **alveolar** glands (in which the distal portions are swollen), as in the skin of the frog (simple) or in the mammalian sebaceous or oil glands (compound).

Connective Tissues.

Mesodermal in origin, they are distinguished by the large amount of intercellular substance produced by the cells themselves. This substance, the **matrix,** varies in character, and so determines the type of connective tissue.

(*a*) Adipose or Fat Tissue.

Fatty material is stored in the cells; very little matrix present.

(*b*) Fibrous Tissues.

The cells are branched or spindle-shaped, and the matrix contains two kinds of fibres. Firstly, there are sinuous bundles of **white fibres** of collogen. The bundles branch but do not rejoin again. Secondly, there is a reticulate mass of single **yellow** fibres of elastin. The proportion of these two kinds of fibres determines the type of connective tissue. Thus **areolar** tissue contains approximately equal amounts of white and yellow fibres in a general matrix. It is used as packing tissue between other tissues (*e.g.*, below the skin). **Dense fibrous** tissue is made up of groups of white fibres running together to form large bundles. It does not stretch, and so is used for strong membranes and tendons. **Elastic** tissue is composed almost entirely of yellow elastic fibres with little ground substance—*e.g.*, neck ligament of ox and horse.

(c) Cartilage.

There is abundant matrix of chondrin, containing cell nests. It is found in connection with the skeleton of lower Vertebrates, and forms the embryonic and early skeleton of the higher Vertebrates.

Hyaline cartilage is nearly pure chondrin, milky in appearance, and has no fibres. It covers ends of bones at joints and ribs; also found in the nose, ear, and larynx of higher Vertebrates.

In **fibrous cartilage** the matrix is invaded by fibres.

The cells, embedded in the matrix, grow and divide in the normal way. Externally the cartilage is bounded by an envelope of connective tissue (**perichondrium**) bearing bloodvessels.

(d) Bone.

Bone may arise directly from connective or fibrous tissue (membrane bone) or by the ossification of cartilage (cartilage bone). The result is a matrix of calcium phosphate and carbonate in a ground substance of organic ossein. The bone is pierced by numerous fine tubules which are grouped in a definite manner in the long bones. Each group is called an **Haversian** system, and is composed of:

1. **Haversian canal,** with bloodvessels, etc. running in the direction of the long axis of the bone.
2. Arranged in several concentric rings around each Haversian canal are the **lacunæ,** spaces occupied by the bone-forming cells. From each lacuna minute **canaliculi** radiate into the matrix.
3. The bony matrix alternates with the lacunal rings, so that bone **lamellæ** are formed.

All bones in the skeleton arise separately. In some cases adjacent bones gradually fuse together at maturity, while others become closely interlocked by "jig-saw" joints (*e.g.*, bones in the skull). Other bones remain free from one another and assist in movement. An **imperfect joint** is formed when adjacent bones are so tightly bound together by ligaments that little movement can occur (*e.g.*, human vertebræ). **Perfect** joints allow of greater freedom of movement and the adjacent ends of bone are smooth. The **ball and socket** joint allows of considerable freedom of movement (*e.g.*, shoulder and hip joints). The **hinge** joint limits movement to one plane (*e.g.*, elbow and knee). The joint is "tied" by strong ligaments and there may also be bony projections to counteract the possibility of too much movement, which would injure the joint. Each joint is enclosed in a capsule and lubricated with **synovial fluid.** This lubricant is actually the result of the decomposition of the worn hyaline cartilage over the ends of the bones.

The bones, in conjunction with the muscles, perform definite movements, resulting in strength or speed of movement. They are, in fact, the "crank pins" or levers of the animate machine. The head forms a first order lever; the ankle and foot a second order lever; and the elbow joint (forearm) a third order lever.

Muscular System.

True muscles originate in the mesoderm. Their structure varies as does their capacity for speed, strength, and endurance. Muscles control the internal movement and the external movements (locomotion) of all animals. In the Insects muscles may contract several hundred times per second (flying). The typical contraction of muscle cells is due to the possession of internal **myofibrillæ.**

The muscles of the body are arranged in reciprocal pairs. This is necessary in order that all movements

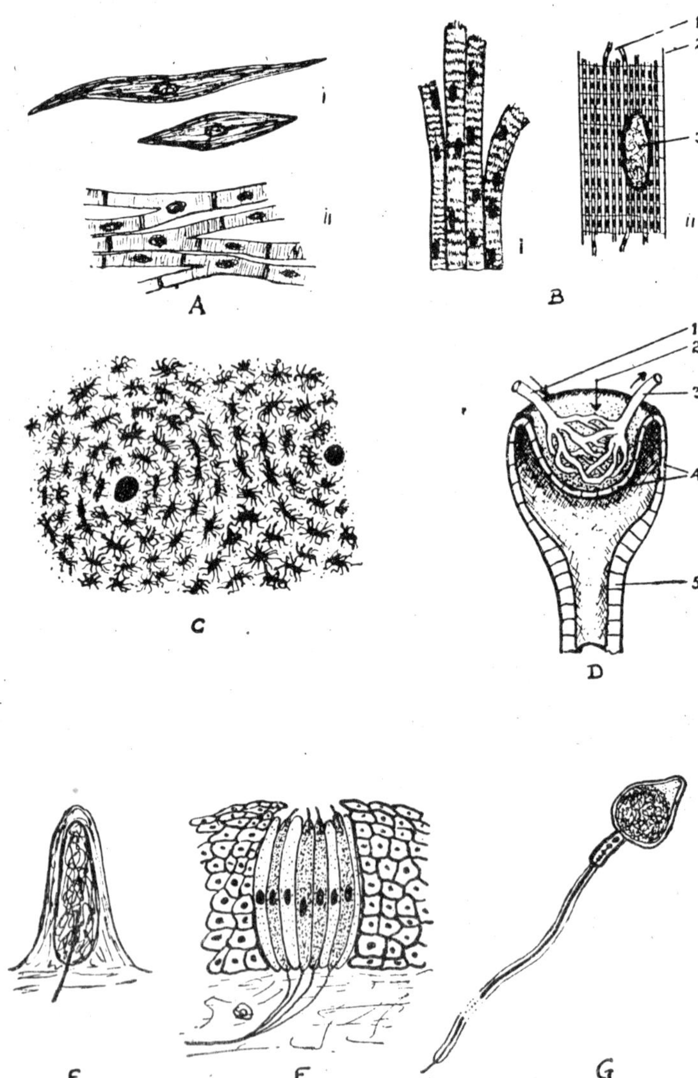

FIG. 51.—DIAGRAMS A-G SHOWING TISSUES.

A, Unstriated muscle cell at rest and contracted. B, Striated muscle: i, several fibres; ii, details of single fibre; 1, fibril; 2, sarcolemma; 3, one nucleus of syncitium. C, Section of bone showing one Haversian system. D, Section of a

(*Continued at foot of facing page.*)

should be reversible. Thus, in general terms, each pair of reciprocal muscles consists of an extensor and a flexor muscle. The contraction of one is accompanied by the relaxation of the other, and *vice versa.*

In the Vertebrates there are two kinds of muscles.

(*a*) Smooth or Involuntary Muscles.

Long spindle-shaped cells, uninucleate, with numerous fine longitudinal myofibrillæ. In the Vertebrates smooth muscle is not under the control of the will; it contracts slowly. It forms the muscles of the viscera, walls of arteries and veins of the bladder, and the iris of the eye.

(*b*) Striped or Voluntary Muscles.

This type is under control of the will (except cardiac muscle tissue). It usually occurs in larger masses than smooth tissues, and is capable of rapid contraction. It is composed of numerous long cylindrical primitive fibres—really a long mass of protoplasm with scattered nuclei (such a type of organization is called a **syncitium**). The protoplasm of these elements contains many fibrillæ, each having alternate light and dark bands. As the bands of neighbouring fibrillæ correspond, the muscle gets a characteristic cross-banded appearance. Each muscle fibre is surrounded by a structureless envelope, the **sarcolemma.** Fibres are bound into bundles, and

---

malpighian body of the kidney: 1, afferent arteriole; 2, glomerulus; 3, efferent arteriole; 4, outer and inner walls of Bowman's capsule; 5, wall of kidney tubule. E, Touch corpuscle from mammalian skin. F, Taste bud showing gustatory cells with "taste hairs" and supporting cells. G, Mammalian spermatozoon showing head (mostly nucleus), middle piece (with centrosomes) and tail (with axial filament).

so into muscles, by a connective tissue (**perimysium**), carrying nerves and bloodvessels.

Heart or cardiac muscle is cross-banded, but not under the control of the will. The cells are short, usually uninucleate; they branch, and the branches connect adjacent muscle cells.

The muscles of the skeleton are attached across joints, so that on contraction the relative position of the bones is altered. During their movement energy is used as a result of the oxidation of food, and wastes are left behind to be removed by the blood. Glycogen is required by the muscles, but the energy is not derived by the simple oxidation of this substance. Recent investigations have shown that during muscular work lactic acid, phosphagen, creatine and phosphoric acid are produced, and the chemical energy released is converted to mechanical energy expressed by the shortening of the muscle.

The whole process can be simplified and summarized thus:

Blood Sugar—to muscles converted
to **Glycogen,** broken down
to **Lactic Acid** and **Energy** (released).

↙ ↘

Some Lactic Acid + O_2

gives CO_2 and H_2O and **Energy** + rest of **Lactic Acid**

↓

Glycogen.

The accumulation of lactic acid in the muscles causes fatigue. Thus rest is necessary, wherein oxidation can convert the acid into glycogen. Muscles, therefore, can work for some time under an "oxygen debt" which, when it becomes too great (fatigue), must be cancelled by rest (excess of oxidation over lactic acid production).

Excretion.

As a result of the internal work performed by the various parts of the body certain waste products are formed. These are harmful to the tissues and must be eliminated. Some of them pass out with the expired air (CO_2 and H_2O), and others pass out through the skin, but the nitrogenous wastes in particular leave by means of the excretory organs. Proper functioning of the excretory system is obviously an essential of healthy animal life.

It seems that the waste material collected originally in the cœlom. In the lower animals the waste still passes from the cœlom to the outside by means of tubes (nephridia), open internally to the cœlom and externally on the outside of the animal—*e.g.*, Earthworm, Crayfish. Later the blood, instead of depositing the waste in or near the cœlom, took the waste to the excretory organs. In the Insects the Malpighian tubules are bathed in blood. In the lower Vertebrates the first kidney or pronephric tubules resemble the nephridia of the worm. They open to the cœlom, and the tubules of each side of the body join a common duct to the exterior. Indeed, in certain lower Vertebrates the openings of these tubules and the tubules themselves enlarge to form the oviducts. The second kidney or mesonephric tubules of the Vertebrates are more intimately connected with the blood. Finally, the true kidneys (metanephros) of the Mammalia never open to the cœlom, but develop as outgrowths from the mesonephric duct into nephrogenous tissue.

The outer cortex of the mammalian kidney consists of the excretory capsules, while the medullary region is made up of the tubules which collect the fluid and pass it to the pelvis.

Each tubule is lined with columnar epithelium, and

ends in a **Malpighian capsule.** This is the widened end of the tubule, which is intucked to form a cup-like **depression.** A small artery enters the cup and breaks up into capillaries, which rejoin and leave as a vein. This network of capillaries is called a **glomerulus.** The kidneys excrete uric acid, water, dextrose, and certain salts (in man).

Urea is prepared in the liver. The amino-acids which are not used cannot be stored as such. The nitrogen is removed, leaving a residual fuel substance. The liver splits up the excess amino-acids (**deamination**) by extracting **ammonia** and leaving a **keto-acid.** The latter is then converted into glycogen, in which condition it is stored. The poisonous ammonia combines with CO_2 to form **ammonium carbonate** [$(NH_4)_2CO_3$], which is then dehydrated (water removed), and so converted to **urea** [$(NH_2)_2CO$]. The urea then dissolves in the blood, to be extracted by the kidneys.

The liver is very complicated in the Mammals. It is built of numerous **hepatic lobules.** Each lobule is made up of cells arranged in rows radiating from a central cavity. The branches from hepatic portal vein, artery, and bile duct run together in the same connective tissue to form Glisson's capsules. The hepatic portal vein branches to form interlobular veins running around each lobule. From these capillaries pass through to join in the central cavity of the lobule as an intralobular vein. These are collected by sublobular veins, which join together to form the hepatic vein. The bile capillaries penetrate into the tissue and then join to form perilobular ducts.

The skin possesses **sweat** glands which open on the surface of the body as "pores." They exude sweat on to the surface of the body. Sweat contains common salt and urea, so that the sweat glands are excretory in function. The evaporation of sweat assists in the cooling of the body.

Nervous System and Sense Organs.

The nervous system shows increasing complexity from the lower organisms to the higher animals. Its prime functions are to put the animal in touch with its environment and to control the internal activities of the body. The origin of the nervous system may be traced in the ectodermal nerve network of the Cœlenterata. Here, stimuli received by the sensory cells are spread by means of intercalated "ganglion" cells to all parts of the body, so that a general response may result.

The higher Invertebrates have developed a more compact nervous system. The main portion of the nervous system has become concentrated in the solid ventral nerve cord with its anterior ganglia and double cord with segmental ganglia (Earthworm, Crayfish, Insect).

In the Vertebrates the nervous system arises from the ectoderm as a hollow tube (see "Embryology"). The anterior of the tube (**spinal cord**) enlarges and forms the **brain,** the whole of the system lying to the dorsal side of the body.

The essential constituent of nervous tissue is the **nerve cell, ganglion cell,** or **neurone.** It consists of, in essentials, a cell mass, containing the nucleus, giving off numerous branches of varying length. Stimuli pass only in one direction, so that each neuron has afferent and efferent tracts. The number of cell processes varies, giving **uni-, bi-,** or **multi-polar** cells. The efferent process, often extremely long, is called the **axon.** It usually breaks up into numerous branching twigs or **telodendra.** There are usually several afferent processes, very short and with numerous branching **dendrites.**

The actual nerve cells and processes are grey in colour, but the latter are usually surrounded by a **medullary sheath** of **myelin,** a substance rich in fat. The sheath terminates at the base of the dendrites. The medullary sheath is not cellular, but is usually

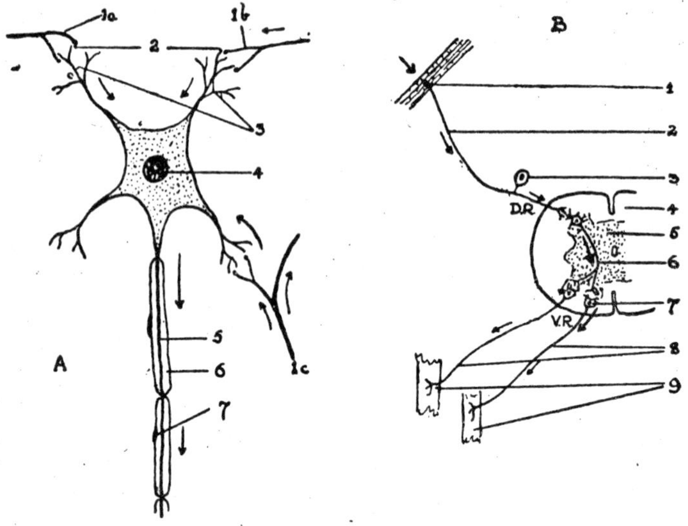

FIG. 52.

A. NEURONE.—Diagram to show its structure and function. 1a, 1b, 1c, ends of nerve fibres from other neurones; 2, synapses between telodendra of adjacent cells and dendrites of cell shown; 3, dendrites; 4, nucleus; 5, axon; 6, myelin sheath; 7, nucleus of sheath of Schwann.

B. REFLEX ARC.—1, Sensory end in skin; 2, sensory axon; 3, cell body of sensory neurone (in ganglion on dorsal root—D.R.); 4, white matter, and 5, grey matter of nerve chord; 6, intermediate neurone; 7, cell body of motor neurone; 8, motor neurone fibres [passing out by ventral root—V.R.] and stimulating reciprocal muscles (9).

surrounded by a **sheath of Schwann,** with scattered nuclei.

A nerve consists of numerous axons, bound together by a connective tissue sheath (**perineureum**). They are white, owing to the presence of myelin. In the brain and spinal cord are tracts of medullated fibres (**white matter**) and masses of the cell bodies (**grey matter**). Local aggregations of cell bodies in the course of a nerve form **ganglia.**

The neurones of the nervous system pass the impulses or messages from one to another, but there is no actual continuity between the dendrites of adjacent neurones, although the dendrites may touch. The impulses pass across these contact points, or **synapses** as they are called, and so travel on through the next neurone. Messages are received from the sensory structures, and pass to the central nervous system by the inward path of **Sensory or Afferent neurones.** These neurones have their cell bodies collected in a mass (ganglion) just outside of the central nervous system. The impulses received in the central system have to be transmitted to the appropriate structures, whose actions are suitable responses to the original stimuli (*e.g.*, muscular contraction, glandular activity). The outgoing path is by way of an **Efferent or Motor neurone.** The simplest reaction of the nervous system occurs when a given stimulus always brings about the same automatic reaction (*i.e.*, not under control of the will). Such a reaction is known as a **Simple Reflex Arc.** In the hypothetical case such an arc is concerned with one sensory and one motor neurone, with their synapse in the spinal cord. Actually the reflex actions which do occur are more complicated, althoug still not consciously controlled. Examples of such reflexes are the "knee-jerk"; or the involuntary eye-blink when a foreign object comes suddenly near to the eye. In such cases the stimulus may pass in by one afferent neurone, but on reaching the spinal cord the impulse passes to many neurones intercalated between the sensory and motor neurones. These extra neurones convey the impulse to many motor neurones, so that the response is made by

A

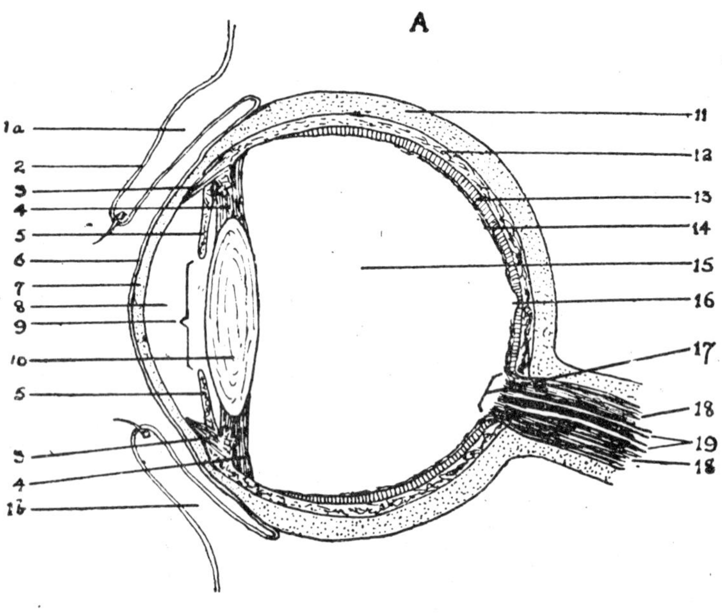

B

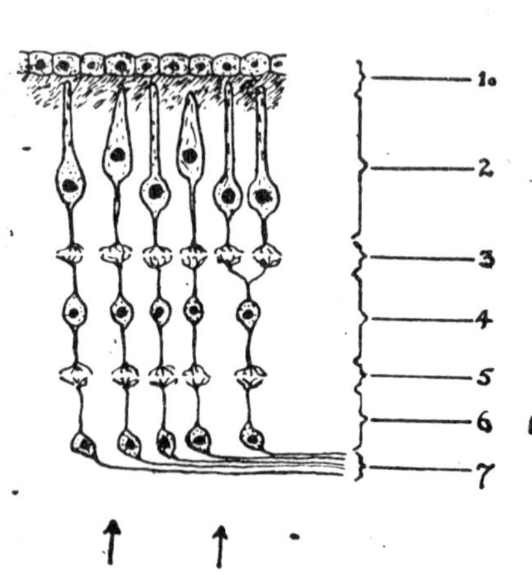

Fig. 53.

A. Diagram of Mammalian Eye.—1*a*, Upper eyelid; 1*b*, lower eyelid; 2, epidermis; 3, ciliary muscles; 4, suspensory liga-

(*Continued at foot of facing page.*)

larger portions of the body. Further complication is introduced by the fact that every movement is controlled by reciprocal muscles, hence there is **reciprocal innervation,** inhibiting one muscle and simultaneously stimulating the other to action.

In addition to the central nervous system the Vertebrates possess a **Sympathetic Nervous System** (*e.g.*, easily seen in the Frog). It consists of a sympathetic nerve cord on either side of the backbone, each arising anteriorly from the Gasserian ganglion of the fifth cranial nerve. Each cord is connected to the spinal nerves on its side of the body, and where each spinal nerve connection (ramus communicans) joins the cord there is a sympathetic ganglion. From these sympathetic ganglia nerves are distributed to the viscera (heart, intestines, etc.) not under voluntary control. These nerves—most of them without medullary sheaths—often form large **plexuses** on or near certain organs (*e.g.*, solar plexus).

Eye.

An outline of the development of the eye is given under the development of the chick (p. 224). The adult eye consists of four layers of cells:

(*a*) **Sclerotic Layer (Sclera).**—This forms the outer protective layer or sense capsule of the eye. It is usually white in colour. The sclera is continued over the "window" of the eye as the **cornea.** This portion of the outer box is perfectly transparent, so that light

---

ment; 5, iris (pigmented epithelium); 6, conjunctiva; 7, cornea; 8, aqueous humour; 9, pupil; 10, lens; 11, sclerotic layer; 12, choroid; 13, retina; 14, retinal capillaries; 15, vitreous humour; 16, fovea centralis; 17, "blind spot"; 18, optic nerve; 19, retinal artery and vein.

B. Structure of Retina.—1, Pigment layer; 2, rods and cones; 3, outer molecular layer; 4, link neurones (inner granular layer); 5, inner molecular layer; 6, ganglionic layer; 7, axons which collect together at blind spot to form optic nerve. Arrows indicate direction of light.

may pass into the eye. The cornea is covered externally by a thin transparent **conjunctiva,** which is continuous with, and a modified part of, the epidermis of the body. The sclerotic is made of fibrous tissue in the higher Vertebrates, but in the lower types is usually cartilaginous. **Sclerotic bones** are local ossifications of the sclera found in many birds and reptiles.

(*b*) **Tunica Vasculosa.**—This is the layer which lies just within the sclera. The main part of this envelope is the **choroid,** which is supplied by the ciliary arteries, and so is the chief source of nourishment for the sensory parts of the eye. This portion ends at the periphery of the eye "window" as a circular **ciliary process** (**ciliary muscles**). This process is connected to the eye lens by the **suspensory ligament,** and by means of muscular contractions, etc., the focal length of the eye is varied (accommodation) by change in the curvature of the lens.

Beyond the ciliary process the tunica vasculosa is continued as a curtain in front of the lens. This curtain or **iris** is circular in outline, with a central perforation, the **pupil,** for the passage through of light into the eye. The iris is pigmented with various colours. It is muscular, circular muscles (**sphincter pupillæ**) by contraction diminishing the size of pupil, radial muscles (**dilator pupillæ**) enlarging the pupil (*cf.* iris diaphragm on microscope and camera).

(*c*) **Pigmented Epithelium.**—A thin layer developing a large amount of black pigment. The actual sensory cells are eventually isolated by this pigment, so that each can be affected only by the light falling directly upon it.

(*d*) **Retina.**—The actual sensory portion of the eye is the innermost layer, ending just behind the ciliary process. It consists of several layers, the actual sensory elements being on the side of the retina farther away from the lens—*i.e.*, next to the pigment epithelium. Hence the light rays must pass through the thickness of the retina before reaching the sensory elements.

1. **Sensory layer.** Each sensory cell bears upon its outer (epithelial) end the actual percipient structures, either a **rod** or a **cone.** The rods and cones are embedded in a pigment layer. This layer prevents halation.
2. **Outer granular** (nuclear) **layer** is composed of the bodies, and their nuclei, of the sensory cells.
3. **Outer molecular** (reticular) **layer** lies within 2. It consists of the interlacing dendrites from the cell bodies of layers 2 and 4.
4. **Inner granular layer** of cell bodies whose processes form a link between the actual sensory cells and the ganglionic layer lining the retinal cup.
5. **Inner molecular layer** is composed of the interlacing dendrites of 4 and 6.
6. **Ganglionic layer** of cells which send out axons to run over the inner surface of the retinal cup. These axons collect together at one point, where they pierce the whole of the eye layers and run to the diencephalon as the **optic nerve.**

There are no sensory cells at the place where the optic nerve pierces the eye layers, there is formed a **blind spot.** Usually there is a point at the centre of the retina where vision is most distinct. Here the sensory cells are more crowded, while the retinal layers are thinner. This is called the **yellow spot, macula lutea,** or **fovea centralis.**

The lens and its suspensory ligament divide the space within the optic cup into two cavities. The

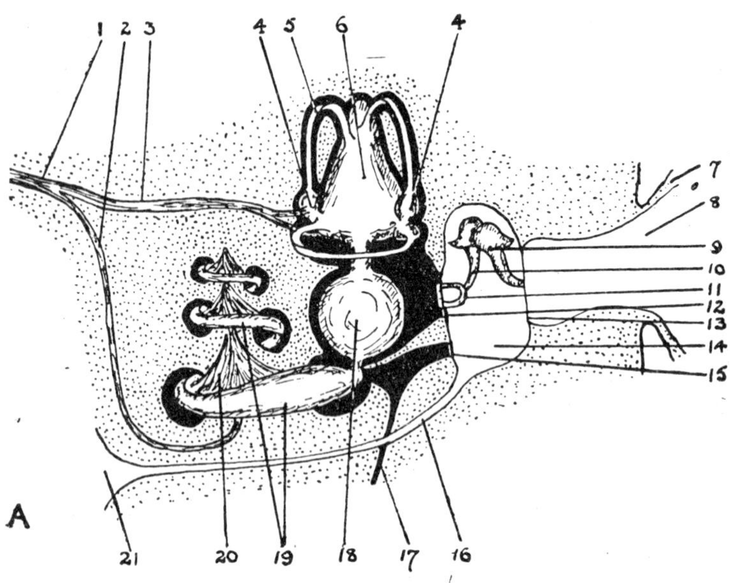

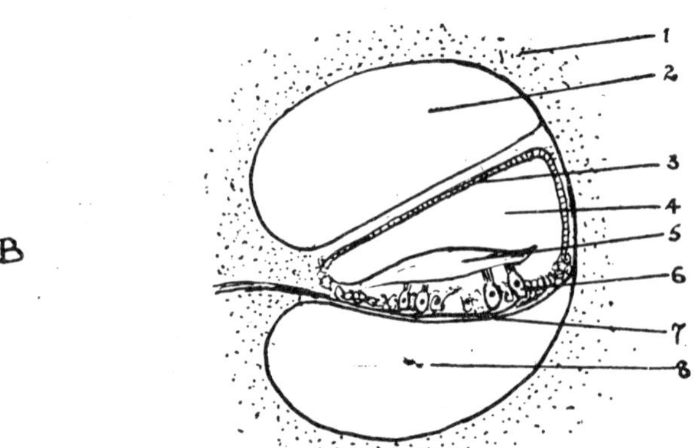

FIG. 54.

A. DIAGRAM OF MAMMALIAN EAR.—1, Auditory nerve; 2, cochlea nerve; 3, vestibular nerve; 4, ampullæ of semicircular canals; 5, semicircular canal; 6, utriculus; 7, external pinna; 8, external auditory meatus; 9, malleus; 10, incus; 11, stapes on fenestra ovale (12); 13, tympanic

(*Continued at foot of facing page.*)

space in front of the lens is filled with a refracting fluid, the **aqueous humour.** The cavity between the lens and retina is filled with a semi-solid **vitreous humour.**

The **lacrimal** (lachrymal) or **tear** gland is situated to the outer and upper part of the orbit. It secretes "tears," whose function is to clean and wash the eye. The fluid passes over the eyeball to be collected by the **lacrimal duct,** which passes from the inner angle of the eye to the cavity of the nose.

Ear.

The ear resembles the lateral line organs of fishes in many respects. The essential portion constitutes the **inner ear,** and is found in all Vertebrates. The **middle ear** first appears in the Amphibia, where it is marked externally by the tympanic membrane. The **outer ear** develops to a varying degree only in the Amniotes. The ear arises as an epiblastic invagination during development.

This auditory vesicle divides into two regions—an upper **utriculus** and a lower **sacculus.** The former produces **three semicircular canals,** one in each geometric plane. In one end of each canal is a patch of sensory epithelium around which the canal wall expands to form an **ampulla.** All the portions of the inner ear form the **membraneous labyrinth,** which is filled with fluid, the **endolymph,** in which float minute particles, the **otoliths.**

When the protecting otic capsule develops, the membraneous parts are enclosed and protected by a

---

membrane; 14, tympanic cavity (middle ear); 15, fenestra tympani; 16, Eustachian tube to pharynx (21); 17, perilymph duct; 18, sacculus; 19, spirals of scala media; 20, spiral ganglion. Note: black areas denote spaces filled with perilymph.

B. Transverse Section of Scala Media.—1, Periotic bone; 2, scala vestibuli; 3, Reissner's membrane; 4, scala media; 5, tectorial membrane; 6, sensory receptor cells; 7, basilar membrane; 8 scala tympani; 5, 6 7, organ of Corti.

skeletal or **bony labyrinth.** Between the bony and membraneous labyrinths there is a small space filled with a fluid, **perilymph.**

Where the middle ear is developed the lateral part of the skeletal wall has two openings into it from the inner ear. These openings are, however, closed by membrane. The upper one—**fenestra ovale** or **vestibuli**—has a membrane which supports a small bone. The lower one—**fenestra tympani** or **rotunda**—is smaller and only has a membrane.

In the lower Vertebrates (*e.g.*, *Rana*) there is a small blind outgrowth from the sacculus forming the **lagena.** In the Mammals the lagena becomes greatly elongated and spirally coiled. With the surrounding bony labyrinth it forms the spiral **cochlea.**

In cross-section the cochlea is seen to be divided by two longitudinally running membraneous partitions into three spiral tubes. The two outer ones—the upper **scala vestibuli** and the lower **scala tympani**—are formed between the membraneous and bony labyrinths, and contain perilymph. The central spiral tube is the enlarged lagena, and is now known as the **scala media** or **cochlear duct,** filled with endolymph. Enclosed in the scala media is the actual sensory region—the **organ of Corti.**

The middle ear, which first appears in the Amphibia, consists of a cavity (**cavum tympani**) connected to the pharynx by the **Eustachian tube.** The middle ear is separated from the outside by a thin **tympanic membrane.** The tympanic membrane and the fenestra ovale are connected across the cavity by slender bones or ossicula auditus. (*Note.*—Only one bone, the **columella,** is present in the middle ear of amphibians, reptiles and birds.) The **stapes** lies on the external surface of the membrane across the fenestra ovale. It is touched by the **incus,** which in turn is joined to the **malleus,** which rests upon the inner side of the tympanic membrane. These bones transmit the vibrations (caused by sound waves) of the tympanic membrane across to the inner ear.

The external ear is found in its simplest form (birds) as a pit, at the base of which lies the tympanic membrane. In the higher types a **conch** or **pinna** is formed, often with cartilage and muscles, for directing sound waves towards the tympanic membrane.

The ear is primarily an organ of orientation, the otoliths by their movement affecting the sensory patches in the semicircular canals. The perception of sound has developed later in evolution. The sound waves striking the tympanic membrane cause it to vibrate. This is facilitated by the fact that the air pressure in middle and outer ear is equalized through the medium of the Eustachian tubes. These vibrations are passed across to the fenestra ovale by the auditory ossicles. Thus the perilymph is set in motion, and so affects the sensory organs by means of the endolymph taking up the vibrations from the perilymph.

CHAPTER XV

EMBRYOLOGY

SEGMENTATION — AMPHIOXUS — RANA (METAMORPHOSIS) — CHICK (EARLY DEVELOPMENT) — FŒTAL MEMBRANES—MAMMALIAN DEVELOPMENT

SEGMENTATION

THE zygote gives rise to a new individual, in cellular animals, by increasing in size and dividing into numerous cells. The first few divisions of the zygote constitute the **segmentation** or **cleavage** of the fertilized ovum. The method and rapidity of cleavage

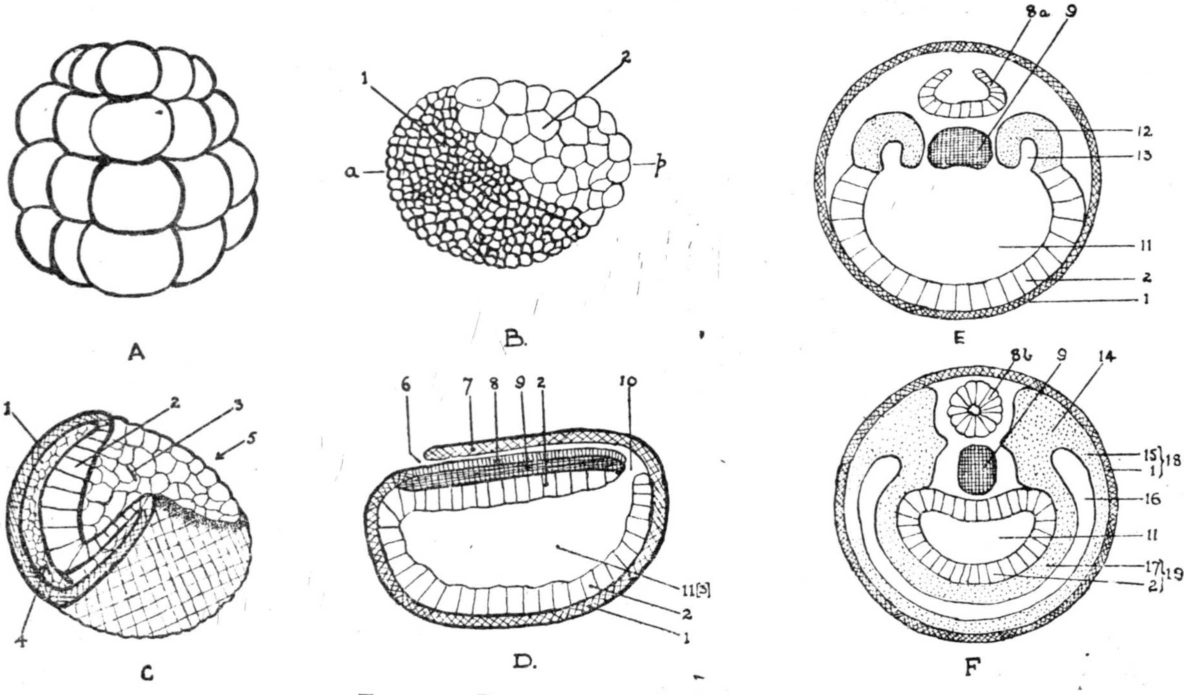

Fig. 55.—Development of Amphioxus.

divisions depend to a great extent upon the amount of reserve food which is stored in the cytoplasm. Where such inanimate reserves are plentiful there is considerable retardation of the mitotic divisions. The yolk usually lies towards the lower side of the ovum, so that an **animal pole** and a **vegetable pole** can often be distinguished. The segmentation at the latter pole is often much retarded, and even in some cases no cleavage occurs there. In such types —Birds—the cleavage is confined to a **germinal disc** area at the animal pole of the egg.

If segmentation occurs throughout the whole of the zygote it is said to be **complete** or **holoblastic.** Such cleavage may result in numerous cells of approximately the same size—**equal;** or in an upper cap of small animal cells and a lower region of larger vegetable cells—**unequal.** When an excessive amount of yolk prevents complete division, segmentation is **incomplete** or **meroblastic.**

AMPHIOXUS

As *Amphioxus* shows almost equal and holoblastic segmentation, the early development of the body or germ layers can be studied more readily.

The first two cleavages are vertical and at right angles to one another, so forming four **blastomeres.**

FIG. 55. —DEVELOPMENT OF AMPHIOXUS.

A, early blastula; B, late blastula; C, late gastrula; D, longitudinal section of post-gastrula stage; E, transverse section young larva; F, transverse section older larva showing triploblastic nature and cœlom.

1, Ectoderm; 2, endoderm; 3, archenteron; 4, blastocœl; 5, gastrula lip; 6, neuropore; 7, neural fold; 8, neural plate [7 and 8 are sections along neural tube formation]; 9, notochord; 10, neurenteric canal; 11, primitive gut; 12, mesodermal pouches; 13, cavity of mesodermal pouches; 14, mesoderm (segment); 15, somatic mesoderm; 16, cœlom; 17, splanchnic mesoderm; 18, somatopleure; 19, splanchnopleure.

The third is nearly equatorial, giving four upper and four lower (and slightly larger) cells. These two layers are then divided by cleavage lines between the equator and each pole, and by vertical ones, into numerous small cells, forming a sphere. As the blastomeres do not touch each other on their inner sides, a hollow sphere or **blastula** results, with a cavity—the **blastocœle**—whose wall is a single layer of cells.

One side of the blastula then becomes intucked (invaginated) into the blastocœle. Continued invagination allows one side of the blastula to approach the inside of the wall opposite. Thus the blastocœle is practically obliterated, and a deep two-layer cup, or **gastrula,** is formed. The outer layer of cells is the **ectoderm,** the inner is the **endoderm.** The gastrula opening is the **blastopore,** and leads into the hollow of the cup—the primitive gut, or **archenteron.**

The gastrula lengthens, so that eventually the blastopore becomes a small opening (due to the growth of the lips) at the future posterior dorsal end of the body. The dorsal surface flattens, and a central longitudinal row of cells becomes columnar and forms a deep strip known as the **neural** or **medullary plate.** The ectoderm at each side of this plate then grows over it and joins, so that the plate lies below the ectoderm. Between this plate and the ectoderm is a space into which the blastopore opens posteriorly, as the latter was also enclosed during the burying of the neural plate. The plate then folds its sides upwards and over until a tube is formed enclosing a **neural canal.** The blastopore, now known as the **neurenteric canal,** leads from the gut to the neural canal for a time, but it eventually closes. The anterior end of the neural canal remains open as the **neuropore,** and leads into the olfactory pit.

Whilst the above changes are taking place the endoderm also is undergoing certain alterations.

The endoderm below the neural plate gives rise to a longitudinal upward fold, which constricts off from the archenteron from before backwards. A rearrangement of these cells gives a rod-like vacuolated **notochord** between the gut and the nervous system.

Hollow outgrowths also appear to the dorso-lateral regions of the anterior end of the gut. Five such outgrowths appear: first an anterior median unpaired one, behind this a pair of smaller pouches, and then a pair of dorso-lateral grooves, one per side. From these grooves pouches are cut off anteriorly, while the groove extends backwards at the same time. Thus a number of paired dorso-lateral pouches arise, the first pair separately. These pouches are **mesodermal somites.** The somites eventually become constricted off from the archenteron, and grow in between the ectoderm and endoderm of the embryo. Thus the inner layer of the gastrula might be termed the **primitive** endoderm, as it gives rise to the true endoderm and to the mesoderm of the mesodermal somites. Small portions of the archenteron are enclosed in each somite, which grows down and around the gut. The outer mesodermal wall is applied to the ectoderm, the inner one to the endoderm proper. The space left between the outer and inner mesodermal layers is the **cœlom.** Thus the embryo has assumed its typical triploblastic nature with the three **germ layers**—ectoderm, mesoderm, and endoderm.

These three germ layers arise in all embryos of the Triploblastica. They form, by their further development, all the adult structures.

Fate of Germ Layers.

1. **Embryonic Ectoderm.**—It gives rise to the nervous system, and forms the **ectoderm** of the adult, and any ectodermal structures and modifications.

2. **Embryonic Mesoderm.**—This arises as mesodermal somites—pouches derived from the primitive endoderm. The outer or somatic mesoderm fuses with the ectoderm, to form the **somatopleure,** whilst the inner layer of mesoderm, applied to the endoderm, forms with it the **splanchnopleure.** The mesodermal derivatives include skeletal and muscular structures. The spaces of the somites extend and fuse to form the body cavity or **cœlom.**

3. **Embryonic Endoderm.**—The primitive endoderm gives rise to notochord, mesodermal somites, and embryonic or true endoderm. The latter lines the alimentary canal. The muscular layer of the gut is derived from the mesoderm.

It is unnecessary to go any further into the development of *Amphioxus* here.

RANA

The eggs of the frog are covered with a thin layer of albumen. As they are deposited by the female, the male, which is clasped tightly to her back, sheds spermatozoa over the eggs. Thus fertilization is external.

The fertilized egg of the frog has an upper, black-pigmented animal pole and a lower white yolky portion. The first cleavage divisions—segmentation is holoblastic but unequal—resemble those of *Amphioxus.* In subsequent divisions the vegetable pole lags, so that the blastula has a wall of uneven thickness—a roof of small pigmented cells and a floor of large yolky cells, the two kinds merging into one another at the sides. The wall of the blastula in the frog is composed of more than one layer of cells. Hindered considerably by yolk, the gastrulation differs from that of *Amphioxus.* The black cells are the future ectoderm, the yolky ones the future endoderm.

The black ectoderm grows downwards by the outer yolk cells dividing into two cells—an outer small cell which becomes a pigmented ectoderm cell, and an inner yolky cell, part of the true endoderm. Thus the ectoderm extends by the cutting off of a skin of ectodermal cells from the surface of the yolky ones. This process is known as **epiboly.** Ectoderm is not, however, formed over the whole of the yolk. To one side of the black area a crescentic lip appears with its convexity upwards. At this point growth of the convex side of the slit causes a lip to be formed. Between the under side of the lip and the yolk cells is a narrow, slit-like space—the **archenteron.** This overhanging lip has an outer ectodermal layer, but an inner layer of small endoderm cells forming the roof of the enteron. The crescentic lip gradually closes until a complete ring is formed, so giving the blastopore, which here is filled by a **yolk plug.** This plug is simply the exposed portion of yolk cells which have not been covered by epiblast. The blastopore's lateral walls then join to form the **primitive groove,** and the opening is narrowed to a very small size. The blastocœle has been obliterated by this time.

When gastrulation is complete, the enteron has a floor of numerous layers of large yolky cells merging laterally into a thin roof of small cells. The notochord is cut off along the dorsal median line. The mesoderm arises by the splitting off of an outer layer of endoderm, so forming a layer between the ectoderm and yolky endoderm. The mesoderm splits into somatic and splanchnic layers.

Meanwhile external changes are taking place. The dorsal surface flattens to form a plate whose edges thicken to form neural or medullary folds, continuous in front, enclosing the blastopore behind. These folds turn inwards, meet, and finally fuse. The outer walls of the fold become continuous as the outer body surface, whilst the inner walls of the folds form a tube—the neural canal. The blastopore becomes a temporary neurenteric canal.

The anus forms just below the blastopore's position. The tissue above the anus grows out to form the tadpole's tail. Two pairs of branchial arches and external gills protrude from the head of the young **tadpole.**

Soon after hatching (fourteen days) a third pair of external gills are formed. The mouth is provided with horny jaws. In a short while four pairs of gill clefts appear. The external gills wither and are replaced by new gills on the walls of the clefts. A fold of skin arises anteriorly to the clefts, and grows backwards, covering the gills and their clefts. This fold or **operculum** fuses to the body behind the clefts except at a point on the left side. This leaves an opening, common to both left and right opercular chambers, for the passing of the water outwards. The sucker which the tadpole possessed beneath the head as a means of attachment now degenerates.

The hind limbs appear at the base of the tail, first as a pair of small knobs, which later become jointed and produce toes. Although the fore limbs arise at the same time as the hind ones, they are not visible until later in development, as they develop at first within the opercular cavity.

Meanwhile the lungs have been developing, and they begin to function at the end of about eight weeks, while the gills degenerate. After another fortnight the tadpole completes its metamorphosis into a young frog. The horny jaws are cast, the mouth changes its shape and enlarges. The fore limbs appear through the operculum, the gill clefts close, and the tail shortens by being absorbed by the rest of the body.

EARLY DEVELOPMENT OF CHICK

I. **To the End of First Day.**—The extremely large amount of yolk in the eggs of birds results in meroblastic segmentation. Cleavage commences by the appearance of a furrow running across the germinal disc. This is crossed by another one, and then several furrows arise until the disc has an irregular mosaic appearance. Meanwhile a cleavage line under the surface, and parallel with it, cuts off this outer

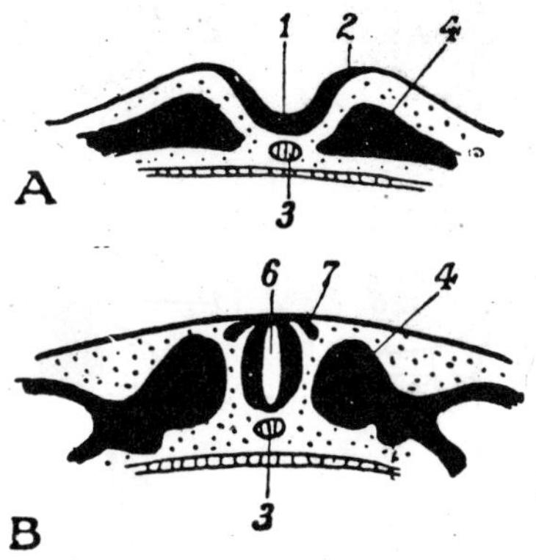

Fig. 56.—Two Stages in the Development of the Neural Tube.

1, Medullary plate; 2, medullary fold; 3, notochord; 4, mesodermal somite; 6, neural tube; 7, ganglionic crest.
(From "Aids to Embryology.")

mosaic area from the underlying yolk. Further horizontal cleavage planes give rise to a disc of two or more layers of cells in depth. Thus a cap of cells forming the **blastoderm** is already present when the **egg is laid.**

The blastoderm consists of an outer layer of ectoderm cells separated by a narrow **segmentation cavity** from a lower layer of cells—the endoderm. The lower layer of cells is separated off from the underlying yolk by a narrow cleft—the **sub-germinal cavity**—which is the first indication of the future enteron. Thus part of the blastoderm rests upon the edge of the yolk, while the central area has an underlying space. This in surface view gives rise to a peripheral **area opaca** and a central **area pellucida.**

At the commencement of incubation the blastoderm spreads, so that in twenty-four hours it is about

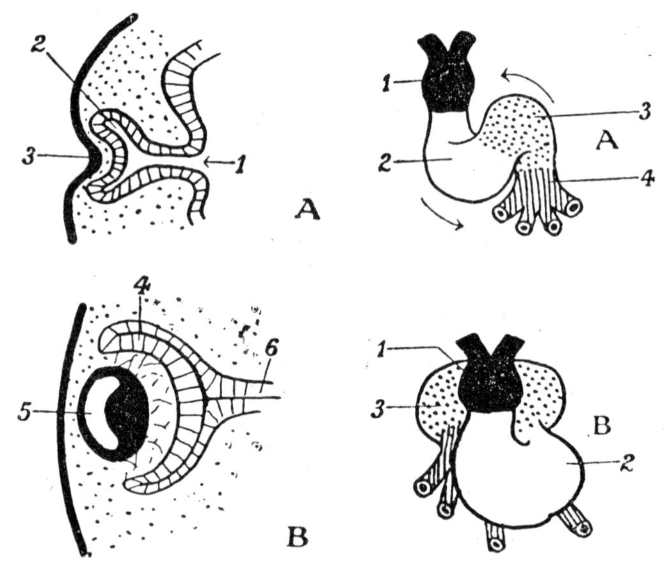

FIG. 57.—(1) THE DEVELOPMENT OF THE OPTIC CUP AND LENS VESICLE.

1, Optic evagination; 2, optic bulb; 3, lens plate; 4, optic stalk; 5, lens vesicle; 6, optic stalk.

FIG. 58.—(2) THE DEVELOPMENT OF THE HEART LOOP.

A, The V-shaped loop; B, the complete loop.

1, Bulbus cordis; 2, ventricular loop; 3, auricular loop; 4, sinus venosus.

(From " Aids to Embryology.")

20 mm. in diameter. Complete enclosure of the yolk, however, does not occur until about the seventeenth day.

Soon after incubation begins an elongated opaque band—the **primitive streak**—appears in the posterior part of the area pellucida. As this streak grows backwards the area pellucida also enlarges, so that the streak is always contained within the area, which assumes a pear-shaped outline. A narrow **primitive groove** then appears running down the centre of the primitive streak.

A transverse section through this streak shows that

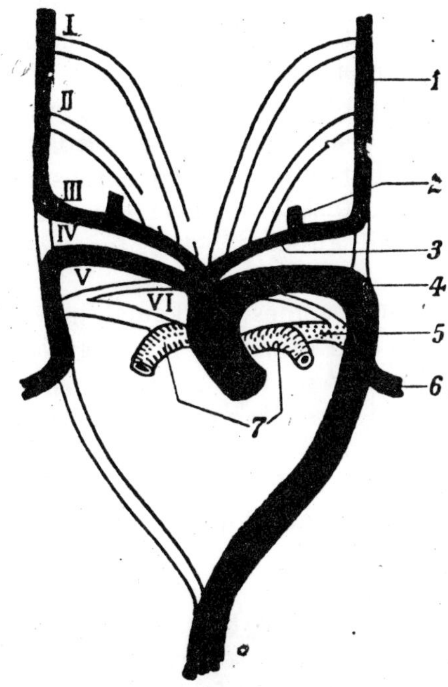

FIG. 59.—SCHEME TO SHOW THE DEVELOPMENT OF THE VESSELS FORMED FROM THE AORTIC ARCHES IN A MAMMAL. (ADAPTED FROM CONGDON.)

1, Internal carotid artery; 2, external carotid artery; 3, common carotid artery; 4, adult aortic arch; 5, ductus arteriosus; 6, subclavian artery; 7, pulmonary artery. The definite arteries are printed in solid black; the transitory portions in outline.

(From "Aids to Embryology.")

it is formed by a thickened rod of ectodermal cells. These cells bud off and wander into the space between ectoderm and endoderm, where they form a sheet of loose **mesodermal** tissue. Thus the typical germinal layers of a triploblastic animal are now formed.

The ectoderm gives rise to the epidermis and its structures, nervous system, sensory epithelium of the sense organs, and the lining of mouth and cloaca.

The **endoderm** gives the lining epithelium of the alimentary canal and its accessory connected glands.

The **mesoderm** produces all connective, muscular, skeletal, and vascular tissues and structures, urinary and reproductive organs.

Just anterior to the primitive streak another indefinite opaque area appears towards the end of the first day. This is a forward extension from the primitive streak, fused, however, to the endoderm. It is the "head process," the forerunner of the notochord.

The ectoderm becomes thickened in front of the primitive streak and forms the **medullary plate,** whose sides are beginning to fold as the **medullary folds.** The mesoderm is spreading outwards.

A semicircular fold—the **head** fold, or blastodermic intucking—appears in front of the medullary plate. This is the state of development at the end of the first twenty-four hours.

II. **The Second Day.**—The folding off of the embryo continues until the anterior end of the embryo is raised up and separated from the underlying yolk. This process of folding continues laterally until about the end of the third day, so that the embryo becomes folded off from the extra embryonic area. At the same time a network of mesodermal cells eventually join to form the bloodvessels within and outside of the embryo. By the end of the second day a blood circulation is established. This consists of—

1. A pair of **vitelline veins,** which bring the nutriment from the yolk via a network of small vessels.
2. A **tubular heart,** formed by the union of the vitelline veins.

3. Anteriorly the heart gives rise to **paired aortæ,** from which radiate vitelline arteries. The flow is forward. There is thus a well-developed yolk-sac circulation. The embryonic veins are only just beginning to develop.

The embryo meanwhile increases in length, while the neural folds rise, bend inwards, and fuse to form the **neural tube.** The anterior of the tube widens to form the brain segments. One pair of swellings is very noticeable—the **optic vesicles,** which are the first traces of eye structure. In the region of the hind brain a pair of ectodermal depressions indicate the position of the ears.

During the latter end of the first day and the second day blocks of mesoderm are cut off by longitudinal and transverse fissures. These blocks, or **mesodermal somites,** begin at about the level of the ear, and develop from before backwards. From them arise the muscles and axial skeleton of the body. The mesoderm adjacent to the somites then splits, so giving a fluid-filled space, the **cœlom.** The somatic layer of mesoderm applies itself to the ectoderm, and they together form the **somatopleure,** or body wall. The inner or splanchnic mesoderm applies itself to the endoderm, and with it forms the **splanchnopleure,** or gut wall. There are usually six or seven pairs of somites at the end of the first day and some fourteen pairs at the end of forty-eight hours. The endoderm in the head region becomes folded off from the general endoderm to form a tubular **fore gut.**

III. **The Third Day.**—Certain obvious external features can now be readily seen:

(*a*) The head is very large, while the typical brain flexures of the higher vertebrates are apparent. These are the flexures of fore brain on hind brain, and of the head as a whole upon the trunk.

(*b*) Owing to the great size and weight of the head it has twisted over to lie upon its left side.

(*c*) The trunk has elongated, and more somites (segments) are present.

(*d*) Four pairs of gill clefts (hyoidean and three branchials) are quite distinct.

(*e*) No traces of limbs are present.

The third day in the development of the chick is the most eventful of the incubation period, as at this time all of the internal organs are initiated.

A. The **alimentary canal** sends out four pairs of pouches to meet corresponding ectodermal ingrowths. The first pouch (hyomandibular) gives rise to part of the Eustachian tube and ear cavity. The second and third (branchials) open to the exterior for a few hours, while the last does not open at all. These pouches or gill clefts correspond to the spiracle and first three branchial clefts of *Scyllium*. Œsophagus, trachea, and lungs are initiated from the straight tubular gut, which is also open to the yolk sac.

The amnion and allantois develop (*vide infra*).

B. The heart has bent to form an S-shaped structure of auricle, ventricle, and a truncus, which gives rise to six pairs of aortic arches. Of these, only three pairs usually are in existence at the same time. They run in the tissue of the branchial arches, join dorsally to supply the head, and pass backward to supply yolk sac and allantois.

C. The retina of the eye is derived from the brain, the lens being formed from an ectodermal ingrowth. The retina develops from the optic vesicle, which grows out, becomes constricted at the base, and invaginated to the outer side to form a cup, into which the developing lens, cut off from the ectoderm, finally fits. The outer part of the cup becomes the pigment layer of the eye and the inner part the retina. The stalk connecting optic vesicle and brain contains the óptic nerve.

The remaining development of the chick may be summarized thus:

IV. **Fourth Day.**—Egg albumen is restricted to a small area and is gradually enclosed by allantois. Flattened conical buds mark the position of the limbs. The permanent kidneys (metanephros) and the ureters develop.

V. **Fifth Day.**—Strong flexion of the embryonic body brings head and tail almost together. The skeleton is laid down as cartilaginous elements.

VI. **Seventh Day.**—Amnion and allantois begin rhythmical movements, which rock the embryo to and fro. The rapid head development is lessened.

VII. **Ninth Day.**—Feathers begin to protrude.

VIII. **Twentieth Day.**—Beak breaks through inner shell membrane, so that chick breathes air. Allantoic circulation ceases, therefore, as the lungs operate.

IX. **Twenty-first Day.**—Chick hatches.

FORMATION OF FŒTAL MEMBRANES

During the development of a reptile, a bird and a mammal there are two structures—**amnion** and **allantois**—which are of extreme importance to the developing embryo and **fœtus** (older stages of development).

1. The Amnion.

This originates as a fold of the somatopleure, which rises up around the body of the embryo. This continuous fold increases in size and curves inwards over the embryo. The crests of the lateral folds meet and eventually fuse along the median line above the embryo. (The head portion of the amniotic fold is initiated first.) The result of the fusion is that the embryo is covered by a double roof of membrane. The inner membrane, formed from the inner walls of the folds, is the **true amnion.** The outer wall—false amnion—is continuous with the outer somatopleure layer of the blastoderm. The amniotic cavity is filled by a watery fluid, so that the embryo floats in a "water jacket," which acts as a "shock absorber."

The yolk is enclosed in a sac formed by the endoderm, but is still attached to the mid gut by a yolk stalk. The yolk sac decreases in size as the food reserve is used by the embryo.

2. The Allantois.

Towards the end of the third day and during the fourth the allantois makes its appearance. It begins as a blind downgrowth of the hind gut (splanchnopleure). During succeeding days this structure forms a bladder-like sac, which extends into the extra-embryonic cœlom. It flattens itself against the somatopleure, which is in close contact with the shell membrane, the albumen having diminished considerably. The mesoderm between the allantois and epiblast becomes highly vascular, and is supplied by the allantoic artery and vein. The allantois, being in close contact with shell membrane and air space, is the respiratory organ of the developing chick until

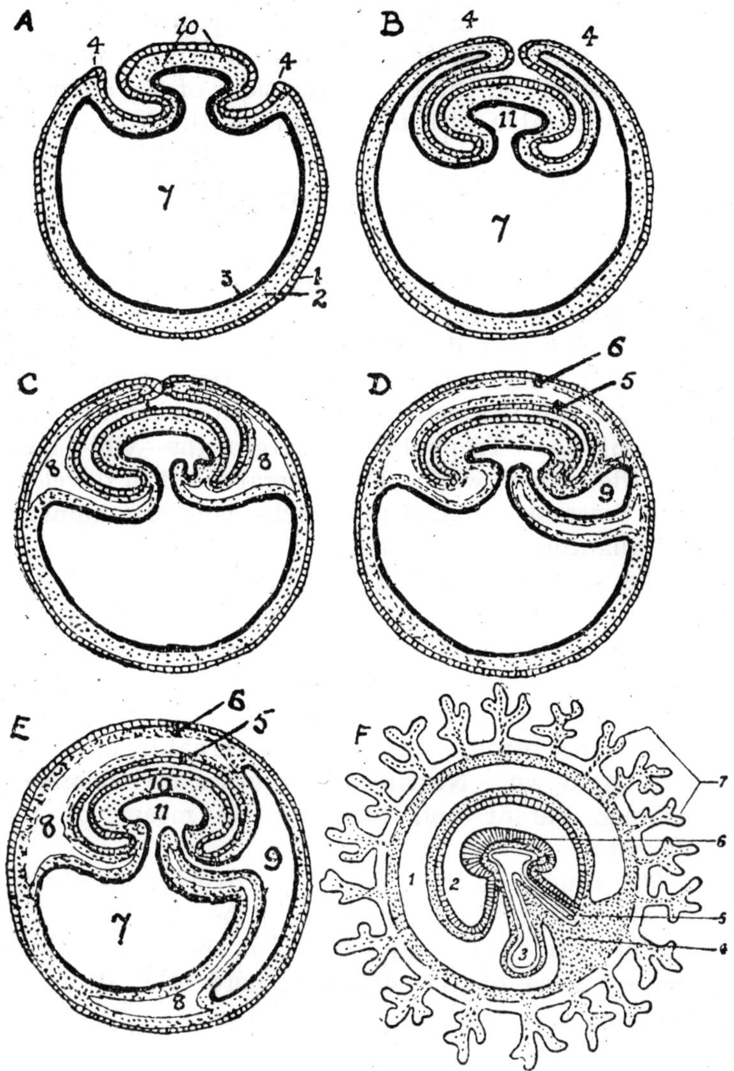

Fig. 60.—A-E, Development of Amnion and Allantois.

1, Ectoderm; 2, mesoderm; 3, endoderm; 4, amniotic folds; 5, amnion; 6, false amnion; 7, yolk sac; 8, cœlom; 9, allantois; 10, embryo; 11, gut.

F, Mammalian Embryo and Membranes.

1, Cœlom; 2, amniotic cavity; 3, yolk sac; 4, placental mesoderm; 5, allantois; 6, embryo; 7, trophoblastic villi.

(F, From "Aids to Embryology.")

the lungs function on the twentieth day. The primary function of the allantois is that of a urinary bladder or the storage of the renal excretions of the embryo. It is comparable with the bladder of the frog.

DEVELOPMENT IN THE MAMMALS

Owing to the retention of the developing embryo within the maternal uterus the ovum does not store much yolk, so that segmentation becomes holoblastic. A solid cell mass is derived from the ovum by cleavage. The outer layer of this mass is the **trophoblast** (ectoderm), as it is the medium by which food is taken into the embryo. Trophoblastic outgrowths—**villi**—bore into the uterine wall. The general trend of development resembles that of the Chick—yolk sac, amnion, and allantois being present.

The yolk sac forms a temporary union with the uterine wall. This is replaced by the allantois, which fuses with the false amnion (subzonal membrane of somatopleure) to form the **placenta.** Outgrowths of the placenta pierce the uterine wall, and are bathed in maternal blood owing to the maternal bloodvessels breaking down. Nutriment and gases are exchanged between parent and offspring by means of the placenta.

The amnion is the "caul" or covering membrane at the birth of a mammal, while the placenta is the "after-birth." The adult navel is the scar marking the entrance of the **umbilical cord**—the stalks of allantois and yolk sac—of the embryo.

CHAPTER XVI

VARIATION—HEREDITY AND MENDELISM —EVOLUTION

VARIATION

"VARIETY is the spice of life," according to one of our saws, but from a biologist's point of view "Variety is the result of life." No two individuals are identical in every part or respect. There are differences, slight or great, between the most "identical" of twins.

In both animals and plants these differences or variations occur. However, a closer study shows that many of the variations of a certain type or species can be arranged to fall symmetrically about a given mean. Thus may be plotted a normal **variability curve,** in which, as the mean type is approached, the number of individuals increase, whether passing down from or up to that mean.

Thus the reader may construct two such variability curves from the following data:

I. VARIABILITY CURVE FOR THE HEIGHT OF ENGLISHMEN

Individuals (*Ordinates*).	*Stature* (*Abscissæ*).
800	69 inches.
700	68 and 70 inches.
600	67 ,, 71 ,,
500	66 ,, 72 ,,
400	65 ,, 73 ,,
300	64 ,, 74 ,,
200	63 ,, 75 ,,
100	62 ,, 76 ,,

II. Variability Curve for Number of Scutes in the Nine Bands of the Armadillo (508 Individuals)

Individuals (*Ordinates*).	*Scutes* (*Abscissæ*).
8	524
11	532
35	540
82	548
94	556
112	564
90	572
46	580
20	588
10	596

Variations may be classed into a number of groups according to different points of view.

1. **From the Inheritance Standpoint.**—The variations may be passed on to the offspring, and are then said to be **germinal** variations (*i.e.*, from the reproductive cells). Germinal variations may be due to a recombination of characters in the germ cells, so giving **combinations.** On the other hand, the variations may be due to some disturbance in the germ cells, and not simply a recombination of characters. Such variations are known as **mutations.**

Variations which are the result of environmental influences affecting only the body of an individual are said to be **somatic** variations. Such variations are non-heritable, and may be termed **modifications.**

2. **From the Effect upon the Organism.**—**Morphological** variations are those of differences in the form, size, and proportion of parts. **Physiological** variations are the differences in performance and quality of parts—*e.g.*, resistance to disease, hardness of bone.

Psychological variations only show as the result of the mental workings of animals.

3. There are two general classes of variations when viewed from a **directional viewpoint:**

(*a*) **Orthogenetic** variations, shown in types related by descent, form a progressive series tending in a definite direction. Many such variations are found in the fossil evidence of evolution.

(*b*) **Fortuitous** variations, on the other hand, are chance differences occurring in all directions.

HEREDITY AND MENDELISM

The old sayings, " Like father like son " and " A chip of the old block," give expression to the same facts which the biologists group together as Heredity. Certain characteristic features, etc., are handed down from parent to offspring, so that " like begets like." Broadly speaking, one does not expect a hen to produce, from its egg, an elephant, because the germ within the egg has inherited the characteristics of a hen. In a similar way the small features of an organism are handed on. Thus blue eyes, brown hair, big feet, etc., may be handed from parent to offspring. Now, the germ cell does not actually possess the individual distinguishing characters of the adult, but rather a certain protoplasmic complex, probably of a chemical nature, which, under suitable conditions, will give rise to an individual with certain structural and functional peculiarities. This point may be illustrated by an electric lighting system wherein certain main switches control a number of lights. The lights are the individual characters which have come into being because the germ cell contains their controlling switches. Thus certain material essentials are inherited. Environment and training, however, can modify hereditary traits in a good or bad direction. Thus, environment and training may accentuate the good or bad inherited characters, although the hereditary material itself still remains practically unchanged. This may be illustrated by a quotation from D. F. Jones:

"The situation is like an exposure on a photographic film. The picture is there. No developer can change its inherent character, but proper development may make it a beautiful picture, while careless handling or the use of wrong solutions may mar or ruin it. But the best developers and the greatest skill cannot make a good picture out of a poor exposure."

Gregor Mendel, Abbot of Brünn, published in 1866 a paper which ranks among the greatest of biological treatises. From his hobby of hybridization experiments with edible pea plants has arisen the important branch of biology known as **Mendelism.**

Mendel experimentally crossed various kinds of pea plants (*Pisum sativum*), keeping particular note of certain definite characters—*e.g.*, seed-colour and form; size and shape of pods; colour of flowers; size of plants, etc. He found that the resulting cross-bred or **hybrid** plants showed **one** of each pair of the contrasted characters of the parent for a particular feature. Thus, when two plants were crossed with a view to observing the behaviour of, say, the stature of the hybrid, a tall plant and a short plant were crossed. Obviously the particular feature under consideration—*i.e.*, stature—could only be one of two kinds, tall or short. The hybrid plant showed the factor for tallness, and was, superficially at least, a tall plant like one of its parents. Hence only one character—tallness—had appeared to the exclusion of shortness. Thus he called tallness a **dominant** character and shortness a **recessive** one. So as the result of a first cross the hybrid, or **first filial generation** (F_1), shows the dominant character of any contrasted pair for the same feature. This may be generally expressed as $D \times R = D$.

Now the hybrid plants, showing only tallness, were self-fertilized, and out of 1,064 plants 787 were tall and 227 were dwarfs, roughly a proportion of 3 : 1. When these **second filial generation** (F_2) plants were allowed to self-fertilize the results were peculiar. The dwarf plants only gave rise to generations of dwarfs, and as such were said to be "pure" for the character of shortness of stature. The tall plants of the F_2 generation, however, gave rise to two kinds. Some produced generations of "pure" tall plants, whilst two-thirds of them gave rise to tall plants and short plants in the proportion of 3 : 1. This could be repeated if this generation were inbred. Hence it is obvious that the dwarf character from the original cross was still in the constitution of the F_1 tall hybrids, although not appearing externally. Therefore, when the germ cells of the F_1 hybrid were being formed, the two characters, tallness and shortness, must separate in order that pure dwarfs may result.

Let us turn back to gametogenesis. When the two germ cells fuse to form the zygote, the tallness and dwarfness are brought in on separate chromosomes—one maternal, the other paternal. Now at meiosis the number of chromosomes is halved and the maternal and paternal chromosomes separate into different germ cells. (N.B.—This does not mean that **all** the maternal chromosomes go into the same gamete and all the paternal ones into the other. As long as the maternal one of each pair arrives in a different gamete from that containing the paternal chromosome, it does not matter what their companion chromosomes are.) Turning back to the example, the tallness and dwarfness will obviously arrive in different gametes in **both male** and **female** gametes.

Hence the gametes of the hybrid F_1 plants will **either** contain tallness **or** shortness, but **not both.** The gametes will therefore be either T or S—*i.e.*, generally D or R. At fertilization several crosses may occur:

1. Either T male×S female=Tall impure.
2. Or T male×T female=Tall pure.
3. Or S male×T female=Tall impure.
4. Or S male×S female=Short pure.

Hence three tall plants and one dwarf arise, one of the former and the latter being pure. This may be summed up in the following table:

TALL PLANT CROSSED WITH A DWARF PLANT, TALLNESS BEING DOMINANT

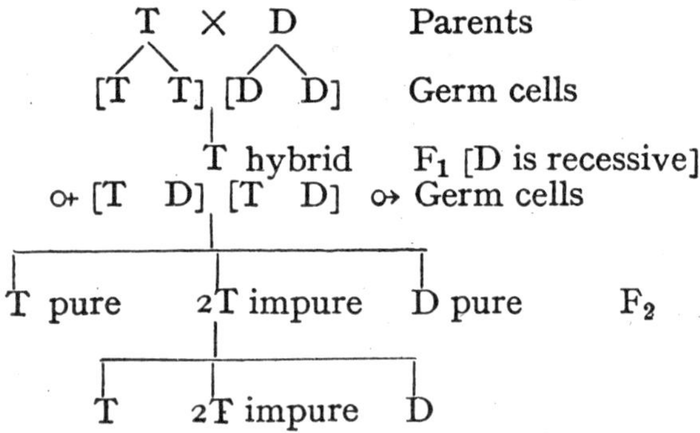

This separation of the factors for unit characters gives the **purity** of **the gametes,** which can contain only one factor of a pair of mutually exclusive or **allelomorphic** characters. In other words, the characters are said to **segregate** during gametogenesis.

When two pairs of alternative characters are considered, then more variation in the recombining of gametes arises. This may be illustrated by taking a cross between two organisms each with a pair of the characters under consideration.

Let AB be the dominant characters of two allelomorphic pairs, the other recessives being represented as *ab*.

AB × *ab* parents

AB (*ab*) F_1

Now the gametes contain only one of each pair, so that both male and female gametes can have the following combinations: AB : A*b* : *a*B : *ab*. In order to show this cross we may tabulate them thus:

		Male Gametes.			
		AB	A*b*	*a*B	*ab*
Female Gametes.	AB	AB AB	AB A*b*	AB *a*B	AB *ab*
	A*b*	AB A*b*	A*b* A*b*	*a*B A*b*	A*b* *ab*
	*a*B	AB *a*B	A*b* *a*B	*a*B *a*B	*a*B *ab*
	ab	AB *ab*	A*b* *ab*	*a*B *ab*	*ab* *ab*

Thus it will be seen that the following individuals may arise from the self-fertilization of the F_1 generation AB (*ab*), remembering always that A and B are dominant over *a* and *b*:

9 AB, of which only one (AB AB) is pure, the others being of various combinations (*e.g.*, AB *a*B : *a*B A*b*).

3 A*b*, a new variation of different kinds (A*b* A*b* : A*b* *ab*).

3 *a*B, a new variation (*a*B *a*B : *a*B *ab*).

1 *ab*, which is a pure recessive for both characters.

The reader may carry this further by working out three pairs of alternative characters—ABC and *abc*.

Mendel's work rests upon two fundamental theses which were new to biology.

1. **Independent Unit Characters.**—An organism, although a unity, is, from the viewpoint of heredity, a collection of a number of independent heritable units unaffected by other characters. Thus tallness, brown eyes, etc., are each unit characters.

2. **Purity of Gametes (or Segregation of Characters).**—A gamete can only contain one of two alternative characters, or, *i.e.*, allelomorphs cannot co-exist in the same gamete. The allelomorphic characters are segregated during gametogenesis. This thesis was purely a theoretical one to Mendel, but it is interesting to notice that modern cytological investigation has confirmed this.

Dominance.—Certain of the determiners of unit characters may dominate during somatic development, so that they are given visible expression in the body. Such characters are **dominant,** whilst those which do not become visible are **recessive.** Dominant and recessive characters are **allelomorphs.**

The work on Mendelian heredity and the interpretation of the facts given in gametogenesis are linked by what is known as the **chromosome hypothesis.** This holds that the behaviour of the Mendelian factors shows a close parallel with the behaviour of the chromosomes in mitosis and meiosis. Thus it may be assumed that the hereditary factors are actually borne by the chromosomes.

EVOLUTION

A considerable number of people hold an erroneous idea regarding the organic processes which are summed up under the term Evolution. To many

Evolution is synonymous with the descent of man from the apes, but this is not so. The evolutionist says that man, ape, and primate have arisen from a common stock in past ages. The doctrine of Evolution is not incompatible with religious beliefs, nor does it imply a state of degradation, but rather it is an ennobling idea. Evolution does not teach that man is the final goal of the evolutionary process. The aim of Evolution is, in general, a perfection of adaptation to the conditions of life as they happen to be at any particular time. So that a type perfectly adapted to one set of conditions may vanish if, consequent on changed environmental conditions, it cannot change to suit new surroundings. Thus a highly specialized creature may give place to a less specialized but plastic type which is capable of adaptation to new environments. Hence Evolution is not only a thing of the past, but of the present and future as well.

Evolution is not a doctrine to be accepted on faith, like a religious creed. Its appeal is to the logical faculties, and as such was not, and should not be, accepted until proved. The **fact** of Evolution is now accepted by practically all biologists, but this fact must be distinguished from the **factors** of Evolution. The latter deals with the causes which have operated in the production of changed types. Many theories have been advanced to explain the way in which Evolution works. But these theories, although probably in some measure true, do not necessarily explain all the factors upon which biologists as yet can only speculate. Charles Darwin established the fact of Evolution only after many years of research. He also explained the factors in his Natural Selection Theory, now known also as Darwinism. But it must be made clear that the latter was only one man's attempt to explain how Evolution occurred, so that

Evolution and Darwinism are not the same by any means.

The evidence for the **fact** of Evolution has been marshalled gradually from all sources of biological knowledge. It is convenient, therefore, to summarize these facts in the groups below.

Evidences of Evolution.

1. **From Palæontology.**—This is the study of the remains of past generations of animals and plants as read in their fossil remains. There are three main classes of fossils:

(*a*) **Actual Remains.**—The organism or parts of it have been enclosed in some preservative, so that their organic nature has remained practically unchanged—*e.g.*, hairy mammoths refrigerated in the Arctic ice, the flesh being still edible by dogs. Hundreds of species of insects have been found preserved perfectly in amber (resin). Shells, bones, teeth, logs, etc., have been beautifully preserved in bogs, etc.

(*b*) **Petrified Fossils.**—Here the organic matter of a dead animal or plant has been replaced, particle by particle, by mineral material. This has been accomplished so completely that the finer microscopical structure of sections of such tissue is practically the same as those from fresh material. Many wonderful examples may be found among fossil plants.

(*c*) **Casts and Impressions.**—The organic material here has eventually rotted away, but has, however, left a cast in the plastic surrounding material. This impression has been filled up by mineral deposits which show the same external shape, etc., as the original organism, just as one might make a plaster cast of an object.

The chances of fossilization are very remote, as the odds are usually against death in or by a suitable medium. Add to this the great uncertainty of finding a good fossil, and it will be seen that the collection of a fossil series is very uncertain. Yet Palæontology has yielded some remarkable fossil series and shed a tremendous amount of light upon evolutionary matters.

In general fossils show that the animal groups (most examples here will be from animals, although the general principles apply equally well to plants) have arisen in a definite geological sequence, the lower animals fossilized in the older rocks, etc. There is a gradual progression from lower to higher types as one proceeds towards the higher (recent) rock strata. The Vertebrate sequence is extremely well shown; the Fishes, Amphibia, Reptiles, Birds, and Mammals in turn have been the dominant or most highly evolved group.

New groups appear towards the end of geological eras, and in the following period become the dominant group, replacing older types of the previous age.

Turning to more specific examples in the geological record, there are very complete evolutionary stories of the development of the horse, camel, and elephant throughout the ages. (Study these in detail elsewhere.)

The horse of today has evolved from a very small forest-dwelling animal. With replacement of the forest by the development of extensive grass-lands, certain structural modifications were made in order that the horse ancestor should be adapted to the new conditions. This has proceeded in two main directions, with a gradual increase in size of the whole body. Firstly, the limbs have elongated and the progress become digitigrade, the middle digit remaining and enlarging, whilst the others have vanished. This made for speed. Secondly, elongation of the neck and increased complexity of the teeth have simplified the grazing problem.

2. **From Geographical Distribution (Ecology).**—The distribution of the organic life of the world forms a patchwork tangle which can only be made clear by the application of the evolutionary idea; that is to say, that the essential factor in all considerations of the relation of types and species must be one of **time.** The new types arise in a given locality and spread outwards, modifying at the periphery of their distribution circle to suit the new environments. There are cosmopolitan groups of animals which have no geographical barriers sufficient to check their migration—*e.g.*, man and his animals and parasites, strong fliers, etc. Restricted groups which are easily barrier-bound are often the remains of formerly successful types, but which survive locally where more favourable conditions exist.

The faunas and floras of continental and oceanic islands can be explained only upon the application of the Evolution idea. The continental island types are of all kinds and of the same type as those of the continent. This is because the island and continent were once one land mass. Upon separation the island types would naturally evolve upon a somewhat separate line, but still the general relationship remains. The fauna and flora of oceanic islands, on the other hand, are like those of the nearest mainland, but are for the most part of the cosmopolitan type, or such as might most readily have blown or drifted there.

The distribution of the Marsupials may be cited as an example. These animals occur in Australasia and America. Those of the latter continent have not evolved so broadly as the Australian types, in which are found the modifications present in the Eutheria—*e.g.*, carnivorous, gnawing, burrowing, etc., Marsupials. Naturally it must be presupposed that the two continents were joined when the Marsupials were the dominant type, and that as Australia became an island continent the Marsupials continued to evolve there, unhindered by the higher Eutherian types. These conclusions of past and present geographical distribution and the existence of now broken land bridges are borne out by the findings of geologists and geographers.

3. **From Classification.**—Since the establishment of modern systematics animals and plants have been grouped according to their similar characters (see introduction to systematic portion). Classification is the systematist's method of showing descent with modification. Thus families are younger than orders, and genera than families. Animals with similar characters are put together, because such similarities imply a common bond.

4. **From Comparative Anatomy (Morphology).**—Here again, when the form of the various parts of animals is studied, many facts support Evolution. The study and comparison of rudimentary and vestigial structures of certain organs with the corresponding well-developed parts of other animals affords considerable support to the Evolution doctrine. The consideration of one or two cases from a large number may suffice here.

Whales, Porpoises, and Seals.—The Whale is a typical Mammal which has returned to the sea. Its mammalian features include, among others, warm blood, hair (in young stages at least), and suckling of young. The change of environment calls for adaptations, so that an erstwhile terrestrial quadruped becomes fish-like in outline, develops a " tail," and a pair of fin-like flippers.

The dissection of the whale's flipper, however, reveals the typical pentadactyle limb of the higher Vertebrates. There is only a slight modification in proportion of parts, etc. This applies to the flippers of Dolphins, Porpoises, and also Seals (Carnivora). The tail of the Whale is a **horizontal** mass of tough tissue without any bony rays for support (*cf.* tail and fins of fishes). The "tail" of the Seal, on the other hand, is made of the hind limbs bound together in a backward-pointing direction, but with the feet free. Hence it is seen that although animals may adapt themselves to a new environment, they cannot alter the ground plan upon which they and the other members of their group have evolved.

In **vestigial structures** are seen the poor remnants of the past which are now useless. Yet in allied types those structures are not vestigial, but may be important in the animal economy.

The vermiform appendix in Man and the Carnivora is useless, whereas in Herbivores (*e.g.*, Lepus) it and the cæcum are large and important.

The third eyelid or nictitating membrane is an important eye-cleaning device in Birds and many other Vertebrates. Yet in Man this structure is vestigial, and remains as the small semilunar piece of tissue (plica semilunaris), situated at the inner corner of the eye. Man is indeed a veritable museum of relics of the past.

That the Snakes evolved from a quadrupedal ancestor is indicated by, among other things, the pair of vestigial pelvic limbs and girdle bones which are embedded in the ventral body wall near the anus in the Python.

5. **From Serology.**—Serology, or the study of the blood in various animals, is the most recent field to yield evolutionary proofs. Ordinary chemical analysis is insufficient to determine the differences between

the blood composition of various animals. More recent work by Dr. Nuttall of Cambridge has evolved the precipitation method of blood testing. This may be illustrated by the following examples:

Freshly drawn human blood is allowed to coagulate and the serum (clear fluid portion) is drawn away. Small quantities of human serum are injected at intervals into the veins of a rabbit. The rabbit's blood forms antibodies to the human blood, which it repels and disintegrates. (This is the basis of the antitoxins of diphtheria, smallpox, etc.) After a number of injections the rabbit is eventually killed, the blood drained away and coagulated. The serum thus obtained is known as "anti-human" serum, and constitutes the basis of the delicate test for human blood in fresh or dry state. If anti-human serum is introduced into a tube of human blood (or stains are soaked in a weak solution of common salt and so a blood solution is obtained which can be used in the same way), a white precipitate is thrown down. This does not happen with blood such as from the pig, horse, etc. Incidentally, the precipitation method of blood testing is being used in legal and criminal proceedings in many countries.

Further research showed that the blood of allied forms reacts to the precipitation test in varying degrees. Thus anti-horse serum gives maximum results with blood from the horse, but also precipitates donkey and ass blood to a less degree and in a longer time.

Thus many thousands of tests have confirmed the evidence of the evolutionary relationship of many animal types. The more distant the bond between two types—*i.e.*, those which must have diverged earlier from a common stock—so does the precipitation become smaller and only after a longer time. Relationship chains have thus been established.

One of the most interesting results of these precipitin tests is obtained from anti-human serum in relation to the monkeys and apes. The Man-like Apes (tailless "monkeys") gave a reaction which closely resembles that of the actual human test. Next in intensity came the Old World Monkeys (*Cercopithecidæ*), followed by less reaction in the New World Monkeys and Marmosets (*Cebidæ* and *Hapalidæ*), and, finally, the Lemurs (the lowest Primates) gave no indication of blood relationship with man at all.

Thus the blood tests have brought very strong confirmation to the Evolution fact, and from a totally unexpected direction.

6. **From Embryology.**—The study of the development of an animal from the egg is termed Embryology. From this science a vast amount of evidence in support of Evolution has been obtained.

It is usually found that the younger—embryonic or larval—stages of animals resemble one another more closely than do the adults; and also the young stages of the higher animals pass through an organization which may have many features in common with an adult of a lower type. In general, of course, most animals arise as a single cell, which by multiplication gives rise to a **blastula,** and then by various methods becomes a two-layered **gastrula.**

The early embryos of a mammal, a bird, and a reptile are very similar, and, moreover, they possess several features which are characteristic of fishes. Practically all the organs of the higher Vertebrates can be seen to develop for a time on lines which are found in the adult structures of the lower Chordates.

The evolution of the blood system, especially in the anterior region, is a good example of this type. All Vertebrates have in their young stages a gill arch circulation similar to that of *Scyllium*, except that the vessels do not break up into capillaries in a gill. This is greatly stressed in the fish-like tadpole of the Amphibia, where gills do occur. In the adults these embryonic arches either disappear or change. The first arch becomes the carotid trunk, the second the adult aortic trunk, the third vanishes, and the fourth is diverted to the lungs.

Again, in all Vertebrates the backbone is preformed as the notochord in the embryonic stages. In fishes intercentral wedges of notochord still remain in the adults. The skull is always preformed in cartilage similar to *Scyllium*, and this chondrocranium, as it is called, is always the forerunner of the bony skull. The heart, kidney, and other organs can be dealt with in a similar manner. The seven-week embryo of Man has a tail which is actually longer than the leg buds.

7. **From Genetics or Experimental Evolution.**—The story of the domestication of animals and the cultivation of plants is in reality a series of experiments in Evolution. Man has in a comparatively short time obtained over 200 breeds of fancy pigeons, etc., from the Rockdove of Gibraltar (*Columba livia*). He has extracted, by judicious crossings, the many breeds of poultry from the Jungle Fowl (*Gallus bankiva*) of India and Malay.

The origin of most of our cultivated plants is known —*e.g.*, cauliflower, cabbage, Brussels sprouts, curly greens from the wild cabbage of the sea-shore.

This illustrates humanly controlled Evolution within a comparatively short time. When the enormous time at Nature's disposal is taken into consideration, it is evident that considerable evolutionary changes have been made possible.

A perusal of the foregoing facts will show that the fact of Evolution is founded on substantial grounds. When, however, the factors or causes of Evolution have to be considered it must be remembered that such hypotheses represent the opinions of various schools of thought, each having in all probability some measure of truth.

The best-known theory of Evolution is that of **Natural Selection,** which was first propounded by Charles Darwin, and is, consequently, often known simply as Darwinism or the Darwinian theory. This theory rests upon certain sets of observed facts, and the inductions from them. Darwin's thirty years of observation gave the three sets of facts—the inductions are obvious.

Fact 1.—That there is a **multiplication** of individuals—increasing in geometrical ratio—by whatever form or forms of reproduction are practised by those individuals.

Induction 1 (partly observed).—It naturally follows that there is not room or food for the offspring of all these individuals, otherwise a state of overcrowding would tend to result. There will be, consequently, a competition between types, particularly among those related to one another in any way—*e.g.*, occupation of same locality; need of same food; need of others for food, and *vice versa*. This induction may be termed the **struggle for existence.**

Fact 2.—That there is always **variation,** to a greater or less extent, in form and function of parts between individuals even of the same generation or brood.

Induction 2.—Success in the struggle for life will go to those types which have any variations giving them advantages over their fellows. Thus those forms with **advantageous variations** will have more chance of **surviving** and reproducing their kind. Some of the variations might well be so disadvantageous as to lead to the quicker extinction of individuals possessing them.

Fact 3.—The successful type would transmit a form or physiology, essentially its own, to its offspring. Hence the **successful variations** would be **continued.**

Induction 3.—The continual handing on of successful variations from parents to offspring might well result in the gradual **change** of type or **species.**

The above facts and inductions constitute the basis of Darwin's theory. Many objections have been made to the theory, but champions of the theory have brought forward other subsidiary theories to bolster up the weak places. Others have opposed the principle of Natural Selection altogether and have brought forward theories to replace that of Darwin. Hence the post-Darwinian theories fall into two classes—those auxiliary to Darwinism, and those directly opposed to it.

Of the anti-selection theories, the best known is that of Lamarck.

The Lamarckian Theory of Evolution.—Lamarck was one of the greatest of French naturalists. His work was for a long time held up to ridicule by contemporary biologists. His doctrine was expressed under the headings of his four laws:

I. That life tends to increase the volume of the body and its parts up to a certain limit.

II. New organs are produced in a body as the result of a new "want" or urge which continues until satisfied.

III. The development of organs and their powers of action are always in proportion to the employment of those organs. Thus constant use brings development and greater perfection, whilst disuse leads to retrogression and atrophy.

IV. That such characters acquired by the organism are passed on to the offspring and so new species might be formed.

Lamarck's doctrine, therefore, held that changed conditions need new physical parts; that change of habits (functions) leads to modification of organs (form). The use of an organ leads to its greater development, while by disuse organs tend to disappear. A physiological balance is maintained, because the stronger things, which prey upon the weaker, reproduce slowly, whilst the weaker increase rapidly. The **advantageous characters** developed by an organism are **transmitted** to the **offspring.**

It is this latter portion of the doctrine which led to Lamarckism being discredited. Many experiments, etc., have been made which disprove the inheritance of acquired characters. However, I would add one note of warning—that, to my mind, experimenters have not allowed sufficient play for the **time** factor.

The Lamarckian Doctrine of Acquired Characters differs from the Darwinian Selection Theory in that the former postulates change by inward striving, as it were, of the organism, whilst the latter states that changes are due to the weeding out of unfavourable chance variations.

Evolution Theory of Hugo De Vries.—De Vries bases his theory on the development of **mutations.** A mutation is what is known also as a discontinuous or saltatory variation, a variation which cannot be placed on a normal variability curve, as can the fluctuating variations. This type of variation is also known as a "sport" or "monster." They are sudden changes in one generation, and they breed true on Mendelian lines.

Thus the Selection and Mutation theories are both of a selective nature. Natural Selection, however, works upon the small continuous variations which we now know as somatic variations due to environmental differences. The essential feature of mutations is that they are germinal in origin, and therefore show as fully formed characters arising from the changed germ. Therefore, De Vries' view gives distinct pure-breeding types at once, if the new inherited characters are not swamped by cross-breeding.

APPENDIX

SELECTED LATIN AND GREEK ROOTS OF TECHNICAL WORDS

abduc, lead from
acro, summit, top
adipo, fat
affer, carrying to
allant, sausage
alve, pit, cavity
amœb, change
amphi, both sides of
ampulla, flask
andr, male
aqua, water
arach, spider
arbor, tree
arc, a bow (curved)
arch, ancient, first
areol, space
arthro, joint
artic, joint
artio, even number
aster, star
atri, hall, vestibule
aur, ear
azyg, unpaired

basi, at the bottom
blast, germ
brachi, arm
brachy, short
branch, gill
bronch, air passage
bucca, mouth cavity

cæc, blind
calypt, covered by hood
cap, capit, head
capill, hair
card, heart
carn, flesh
carp, wrist
cauda, tail
cav, hollow
ceph, cephal, head
cerv, neck
chæt, hair, bristle
chiasm, X-shaped crossing
chondr, cartilage
chrom, colour
chyl, chym, juice, fluid
cili, eyelash
cirr, curl (tentacle)
clav, club
cloaca, sewer (common opening)
clype, shield
cnido, nettle
cœl, hollow
condyl, knuckle
coron, crown
cost, rib
crani, skull
cuti, skin
cyst, case
cyt, cell

dactyl, finger
den (s, t), tooth
dendr, tree, bush
derm, skin
didym, twin
digit, finger (or toe)
diphy (diplo), double
don (t), tooth
dors, back

echin, spiny
ect, outer
effer, carrying away
ejacul, throwing out
elasmo, flat
end, inner
enter, inside
erythr, red

falc (x), sickle
fasc, bundle

fenestr, window
fil, thread
foramen, small opening
fovea, shallow depression

gangli, knot
gaster (tr) stomach
gemin, twins
glen, socket
glia, glue
glom (us, er), ball of yarn
gloss (tti), tongue
gnath, jaw
gon, seed, sperm
gymn, naked
gyn, woman

hæm, blood
helminth, worm
hepar (hepát), liver
hetero, different
holo, entire
hormon, that which excites
hydr, water
hyper, over, above
hypo, lower, beneath

ichthy, fish
ileum, twisted
iliac, flank
incis, cutting in
incu, anvil
inguin, groin
ischia, hip
iter, passage

labi, lips
lacrim, tears
lact, milk
lacuna, space
lagena, flask
lamella, leaf, layer
leuc, white
lingua, tongue
log, discourse
lumen, cavity
lutea, yellow

macro, great, large
macula, spot
malleus, hammer
mamma, breast
mandib, lower jaw

marsupi, pouch
maxill, jaw
medull, marrow
mer (os), part
meso, middle
meta, after
mola, mill
morph, form
myel, marrow
myo, muscle

nar (nas), nose
nect, swimming
nephr, kidney
neur, nerve
nictitat, winking
noto, back
nuch, neck
nucle, little nut

occip, back of head
odont, tooth
œsoph, gullet
oid, like
olfact, smelling
omm, eye
oo (n), egg
opercul, little cover
ophthalm, eye
ops, opt, vision, eye
or- (al, is), mouth
orbi, circle
ortho, straight
oss, ost, bone
ot (i, o), ear
ov (ar, um), egg

palæ, ancient
para, besides
parie, wall
parot, beside the ear
parv, small
pect, breast
ped, foot
pellucid, shining through
pent, five
peri, around
phragm, fence, partition
phyl, tribe
physio, nature
phyto, plant
pil, hair
plant (ar, i), sole of foot

plasm, forming, formed
pleur, side
plex, interwoven
plica, fold
pneu, air
pod, foot
poly, many
proct, anus
proto, first
pseud, false
pter, wing
ptyal, spittle
pulmo, lung
pyl, gate

quadrigemin, quadruplets

rach, spine
radi, foot
ram (i, u), branch
rect, straight
ren, kidney
retic, network
retina, little net
rhiz, root
rostrum, beak, prow

saccul, little sac
sarc, flesh
saur, lizard
scala, ladder, stairway
schizo, cleft, split
sciat, hip
scler, hard
scut, shield
sept, wall
ser (o, u), fluid of the body
serra, saw
set, bristle
sinus, hollow, bay
sipho, tube
soma, body
sphinct, closing
splanch, viscera
stalsis, constriction
stapes, stirrup
stat, standing
stern, breastbone
stom, mouth
strat, layer
striat, furrowed
sulc, furrow
sutur, seam
syn, together

tact, touch
tænia, band, ribbon
tars, ankle
tele, far, end
theca, case
trich, hair
troph, food
tympan, drum

ulna, elbow
umbilic, navel
ungul, hoof, claw
uro, tail (urine)

vagina, sheath
vagus, wandering
vas, vessel
vascul, little vessel
vel, veil
ven, vein
vent, belly
verm, worm
vill, shaggy hair (later velvet)
vitell, yolk
vora, devour

xiphi, sword

zo (a, o), animal
zyg, yoke

INDEX

Figures denote pages; those in Clarendon type denote pages in which illustrations or diagrams appear.

A

Absorption, 202
Acarida (Acarina), 115
Aciculum, 88
Adipose tissue, 213
Adrenal body, 161, 182
Aerobic respiration, 202
Alcyonaria, 65
Alimentary canal
 of *Amphioxus*, 122
 of *Ascaris*, 82
 of *Fasciola*, 71
 of *Lepus*, 175, **176**
 of *Lumbricus*, 91
 of *Nereis*, 88
 of *Periplaneta*, 112
 of *Potamobius*, 102
 of *Rana*, 151, **157**
 of *Scyllium*, 133, **134**
 of *Turbellaria*, 68
Allantois, 246
Allelomorphs, 254, 256
Alveoli, 178
Amino acids, 193
Ammonia, 220
Amnion, 246
Amœba, 120, **121**, 125
Amylopsin, 200
Anaerobic respiration, 202
Anemones, 54, 66
Annulata, 86
Anopheles, 74
Anthomedusa, 64
Anthozoa, 65
Anura, 145
Appendages, of *Periplaneta*, 108
 of *Potamobius*, 101
Arachnida, 99, 115
Araneida, 115
Arcella, 18
Archenteron, 234, 237
Arthropoda, 98
Ascaris, 82
Ascidians, 120
Asexual reproduction, 11
Astacus. *See Potamobius*
Aster, 4, **5**, **9**
Atrium, 122
Aurelia, 65
Aves, 127, 164

B

Bile, 200
Biramous appendage, 99
Bladderworm, 76, 79
Blastoderm, 239
Blastostyle, 61
Blood, 206, 207
Blood platelets, 208
Blood-system. *See* Circulatory system
Bone, 214
Bones, cartilage, 147, 149
 membrane, 147, 149
Branchiostegite, 100

C

Cæcum, 177
Calyptoblastica, 64
Carapace, 100
Carbohydrates, 191
Carnivora, 187
Cartilage, 214
Casein, 200
Cell division, 3
Centrosome, 3

Cephalochordata, 99, 100
Cephalopoda, 117
Cephalothorax, 99, 100
Cercaria, 74
Cestoda, 76
Cetacea, 186
Chætæ, 87
Chætopoda, 86
Chelonia, 163
Chiroptera, 188
Chlorogogenous tissue, 91
Chordata, 119
Chromatin, 3, **5**
Chromomeres, 3, **5**
Chromosomes, 3, **5**
Chyme, 200
Cilia, 29
Ciliata, 29
Circulatory system
of *Amphioxus*, 125
of *Lepus*, 178, **181**
of *Lumbricus*, 94
of *Periplaneta*, 113
of *Potamobius*, 103
of *Rana*, 153, **155**
of *Scyllium*, 135, **136**
Classification, example of, 11
evidence of, 261
Cleavage, 231
Clitellum, 90
Cnidoblast, 57
Cockroach, 108
Cœlenterata, 53
Cœlenteron, 54
Cœlom, 53, 124
Comparative anatomy (Evolution), 261
Conjugation, of *Paramecium*, 33, **34**
of Vorticella, **36**, 37
Connective tissue, 213
Cranial nerves
of *Lepus*, 182
of *Scyllium*, 139, **142**
Craniata, 120, 127
Crocodilia, 164
Crustacea, 98, 99
Culex, 74
Cysticercus, 79
Cytoplasm, 1

D

Darwin, Darwinism, 266
Deamination, 220
Dental formula, 166
Derotremata, 145
de Vries theory, 268
Diastema, 172
Difflugia, 18
Digestion, 198
Digestive system. *See* Alimentary canal
Disaccharides, 191
Distomum hepaticum, 69, **70, 73**
Dogfish, 128
Dominance, 256

E

Ear, structure of, **228**, 229
Ecology (Evolution), 260
Ectoderm, 53
of *Ascaris*, 82
of *Hydra*, 56
Ectoplasm, of *Amœba*, 15
of *Monocystis*, 38
of *Paramecium*, 31
Elasmobranchii, 127
Embryology, 231
of *Amphioxus*, **232**, 233
of Chick, 239, **239, 240, 241**
of *Rana*, 236
and Evolution, 264
Endentata, 186
Endoderm, 53
of *Hydra*, 57
Endophragmal skeleton, 102
Endoplasm, of *Amœba*, 15
of *Euglena*, 23
of *Paramecium*, 32
Energy relationship, **190**
Entamœba, 18

Enterokinase, 201
Enteron, 53
Enzymes, 198, **203**
Epiboly, 237
Epididymis, 184
Epithelial cells, types of, 211
Erepsin, 201
Erythrocytes, 208
Euglena, 22, **25**
Euglypha, 18
Eutheria, 186
Evolution, 256
Excretion, general, 219
of *Amœba*, 16
of *Euglena*, 24
of *Paramecium*, 33
Excretory system
of *Amphioxus*, 126
of *Ascaris*, 83
of *Distomum*, 71
of *Lepus*, 182
of *Lumbricus*, 93
of *Periplaneta*, 113
of *Potamobius*, 105
of *Tænia*, 77
of *Turbellaria*, 68
Eye, structure, of compound, 105
of Vertebrate, **224**, 252
development of, **240**, 245
Fasciola. See Distomum

F

Fallopian tubes, 185
Fats and Oils, 192
Fibrin, 209
Fibrinogen, 209
Fibrous tissue, 213
Fins, of *Scyllium*, 128
Flagellata, 22
Flame cells, 67, 71
Fœtal membranes, 162, 245, **247**
Foods and enzyme action, 203
Foraminifera, 19
Fossils, 258

G

Gametes, 6
purity of, 256
Gametogenesis, 6, **7**
Gastric juice, 199
Gastropoda, 116
Genetics (Evolution), 265
Giant fibres, 93
Gill slits (clefts), 119, 123
Glandular tissue, 213
Globigerina, 21
Glucose, 191
Gonad, 52
Graafian follicles, 185
Green glands, 105
Gymnoblastica, 64
Gymnophiona, 146

H

Hæmocœle, 98, 208
Hæmocyanin, 104, 208
Hæmoglobin, 208
Heart, and main vessels, 241
development of, **240**
Hemichordata, 120
Hepatic cæca, 112, 123
Heredity, 251
Hermaphrodite, 68
Hormones, 201
Hydatid cyst, 81
Hydra, **55**, 56
Hydranths, 61
Hydratuba, 64
Hydroid generation, 54
Hydrozoa, 54

I

Insecta, 107
Insectivora, 188
Interstitial cells, 56
Involuntary muscle, 217

J

Joints, 215

K

Karyokinesis, 3
Kidney structure, of *Lepus*, 182

L

Lacertilia, 163
Lacteals, 202
Lactic acid, 218
Lamarckian theory, 267
Lamellibranchs, 116
Lateral line, 128
Laurer's canal, 73
Leptomedusa, 64
Lepus, 167
Leucocytes, 209
Liver, structure of, 220
Liver fluke, 69
Lobosa, 14
Locomotion, of *Amœba*, 16
of *Euglena*, 23
of *Hydra*, 58
of *Paramecium*, 32
Lumbricus, 90, **93, 96, 97**
Lung book, 115
Lymph, 210
Lymphatic vessels, 202

M

Malaria, 40, **45**, 47
Mammalia, 127, 165
Marsupium, 186
Maturation, of gametes, 6
Medusoid generation, 54
Meiosis, 6, **9**
Mendelism, 251
Mesenteron, 103, 112
Mesoderm, 53
Mesoglœa, 56
Metatheria (Marsupials), 186
Metameres, 86
Metapleural folds, 121
Metazoa, 51
Miracidium, 73
Mitosis, 3, **5**
Mollusca, 116
Monocystis, 38, **39**
Monosaccharides, 191
Monotremata, 185
Mosquito, 43
Mouth parts of cockroach, 108, **110**
Muscular tissue, 215
Mutations, 250
Myctodera, 145
Myocommata, 122
Myomere (myotome), 122
Myoneme, 35
Myriapoda, 99

N

Natural Selection, 266
Nemathelminthes, 66, 81
Nematocyst, 57
Nematoda, 81
Nephridia, 87, 93
Nereis, 87, **89**
Nervous system, 52
of *Amphioxus*, 126
of *Ascaris*, 84
of *Distomum*, 71
of *Lepus*, 181
of *Lumbricus*, 92
of *Periplaneta*, 113
of *Potamobius*, 105
of *Rana*, 159
of *Scyllium*, 138
of *Tænia*, 77
of *Turbellaria*, 68
the sympathetic, 225
Nervous tissue, 221
Neurocœle, 120
Neurone, 221, **221**
Nictitating membrane, 262
Notochord, 119, 124
Nuclear membrane, 3
Nucleus, 2
Nutrition, general, 191
of *Amœba*, 16
of *Euglena*, 24
of *Hydra*, 58
of *Paramecium*, 32

O

Obelia, 61
Oils. *See* Fats
Oligochæta, 90
Ommatidia, 105
Onchosphere, 79

Onychophora, 98
Oogenesis, 6
Ophidia, 163
Oro-nasal groove, 129
Osmoregulation, of *Amœba*, 17
of *Euglena*, 24
of *Paramecium*, 33
Ovaries, of *Amphioxus*, 127
of *Ascaris*, 84
of *Distomum*, 72
of *Lepus*, 184
of *Lumbricus*, 195
of *Periplaneta*, 114
of *Potamobius*, 106
of *Rana*, 162
of *Scyllium*, 143
of *Tænia*, 78
of *Turbellaria*, 69
Oviducts, of *Distomum*, 72
of *Lepus*, 185
of *Lumbricus*, 95
of *Potamobius*, 106
of *Rana*, 162
of *Scyllium*, 143
of *Tænia*, 78
of *Turbellaria*, 69
Ovum, 10

P

Palæontology, 258
Paramecium, 30, **30, 34**
Paramylum, 23
Parapodium, 87
Parthenogenesis, 11
Pectoral girdle and limb, of *Lepus*, 172
of *Rana*, 149, **150**
of *Scyllium*, 128, **132**
Pellicle, 22
Pelvic girdle and limb, of *Lepus*, 174
of *Rana*, 150, **150**
of *Scyllium*, 129, **132**
Pentadactyle limb, 145
Pepsin, 199
Perennibranchiata, 145
Periplaneta, 108, **109, 110, 111**
Peristalsis, 199
Peristomium, 88, 90
Photosynthesis, 190
Physiology and Histology, 189
Pisces, 127
Placenta, 185, 248
Placoid scale, 128
Plasmodium, 40, **45**
Platyhelminthes, 66, 67
Polychæta, 87
Polysaccharides, 192
Polystomella, 20, **20**
Potamobius, **99**, 100, **101, 104**
Primates, 189
Proglottis, 76
Prostomium, 87, 90
Proteins, 193
Protoplasm, 1
Prototheria, 185
Protozoa, 13, 20
conclusion to, 49
Proventriculus, 102
Pseudopodia, 14
Ptyalin, 199

R

Rabbit, 167
Radiolaria, 21
Rana, 146
Receptaculum ovorum, 96
Redia, 74
Reflex arc, **222**, 223
Rennin, 199
Reproduction
in *Amœba*, 17, 18
in *Euglena*, 24
in *Hydra*, 59
in *Paramecium*, 33
in *Vorticella*, 36
Reproductive system
of *Amphioxus*, 126
of *Ascaris*, 84
of *Distomum*, 72

Reproductive system
of *Lepus*, 182, **183, 184**
of *Lumbricus*, 95
of *Nereis*, 88
of *Periplaneta*, 114
of *Potamobius*, 106
of *Rana*, 161
of *Scyllium*, 143
of *Tænia*, 78
of *Turbellaria*, 68
Reptilia, 127, 162
Respiration, general, 202
in *Amœba*, 16
in *Amphioxus*, 122
in *Lepus*, 178
in *Nereis*, 88
in *Periplaneta*, 113
in *Potamobius*, 104
in *Rana*, 152
in *Scyllium*, 133
Rhynchocephalia, 164
Rodentia, 188

S

Saliva, 199
Salivary glands, 112
Sarcodina, 14
Schizogeny, 41
Scolex, 76
Scorpionida, 115
Scyllium, 128
Scyphistoma, 64
Scyphozoa (Scyphomedusa), 64
Secretin, 200, 201
Segmentation, 86, 231
Segregation of characters, 256
Serology, 262
Setæ, 87
Sexual reproduction, 11
Shell glands of *Distomum*, 72
of *Scyllium*, 143
of *Tænia*, 78
Skeleton, 52
of *Amphioxus*, 124
Skeleton of *Lepus*, 170
of *Rana*, 146
of *Scyllium*, 128
Skull, mammalian type, **166**
of *Canis*, **168, 169**
of *Lepus*, 172
of *Rana*, 147, **148, 149**
of *Scyllium*, 130, **131**
Sleeping Sickness, 27
Solenocytes, 126
Soma, 52
Somites, 235
Spermathecæ, 96, 114
Spermatogenesis, 6
Spermatozoön, 10
Spiders, 115
Spiracles, 113, 129
Sporocyst, 74
Sporozoa, 37
Statocyst, 63, 106
Steapsin, 200
Stigmata, 113
Succus entericus, 201
Sweat glands, 220
Sympathetic nervous system, 161, 225
Syncitium, 83
Synkaryon, 35

T

Tænia, 76, **77, 79**
Tapeworm, 76, 80
Teleostei, 127
Telson, 100
Testes of *Ascaris*, 84
of *Distomum*, 72
of *Lepus*, 183
of *Lumbricus*, 95
of *Periplaneta*, 114
of *Potamobius*, 106
of *Rana*, 161
of *Scyllium*, 144
of *Tænia*, 78
of *Turbellaria*, 68
Thrombin, 209
Thrombokinase, 209

Tracheæ, 107
Transport system, 206
Transverse section of *Lumbricus*, 92, 93
Trematoda, 69
Trichocysts, 31
Trophoblast, 248
Trypanosomes, 25, **25**
Trypsin, 201
Tsetse fly, 27
Turbellaria, 67
Typhlosole, 91

U

Undulating membrane, 26, 29
Ungulata, 187
Unit characters, 256
Urea, 220
Ureter, of *Lepus*, 183
 of *Rana*, 161
Urethra, 184
Urinogenital system. *See* Reproductive system
Urochordata, 120
Urodela, 145
Urostyle, 146
Uterus, of *Distomum*, 72
 of *Lepus*, 185
 of *Rana*, 162
 of *Tænia*, 78
 of *Turbellaria*, 69
 masculinus, 184

V

Vacuoles, 3
 of *Amœba*, 15
 of *Euglena*, 24
 of *Paramecium*, 33
Vagina of *Ascaris*, 84
Vagina, of *Lepus*, 185
 of *Tænia*, 78
Variation, 249
Vas deferens, of *Ascaris*, 84
 of *Distomum*, 72
 of *Lumbricus*, 95
 of *Periplaneta*, 114
 of *Potamobius*, 106
 of *Rana*, 161
 of *Scyllium*, 144
 of *Tænia*, 78
 of *Turbellaria*, 68
Vermes, 66
Vertebræ, 119
 of *Lepus*, **171**, **173**
 of *Rana*, 146
 of *Scyllium*, 129
Vertebrata, 119, 120
Vesiculæ seminales, of *Ascaris*, 84
 of *Distomum*, 72
 of *Lumbricus*, 95
 of *Periplaneta*, 114
 of *Rana*, 162
 of *Scyllium*, 144
 of *Turbellaria*, 68
Vestigial structures, 262
Villi, 202
Visceral arches, 130, **131**
Vitamins, 194
Vitelline (yolk) glands
 of *Distomum*, 72
 of *Tænia*, 78
 of *Turbellaria*, 69
 veins, 242
Voluntary muscle, 217
Vorticella, 35, **36**

Z

Zoantharia, 66
Zygote, 10